Communicating Christ Through Story and Song

Orality in Buddhist Contexts

Communicating Christ Through Story and Song

Orality in Buddhist Contexts

Edited by Paul H. De Neui

WILLIAM CAREY
LIBRARY

Communicating Christ Through Story and Song: Orality in Buddhist Contexts

Cover Design: Jon Pon
Copyediting, Typesetting: Paul H. De Neui, Ingrid Johnson, Daniel G. Larson

Published by William Carey Library
1605 E. Elizabeth Street
Pasadena, California 91104
www.missionbooks.org

William Carey Library is a ministry of the
U.S. Center for World Mission
Pasadena, California
www.uscwm.org

Printed in the United States of America

Library of Congress Cataloging-in-Publication Data

Communicating Christ through story and song : orality in Buddhist contexts / Paul H. De Neui, David S. Lim, editors.
p. cm. -- (Communicating Christ in the Buddhist world)
Includes bibliographical references and index.
ISBN 978-0-87808-511-8
1. Missions to Buddhists. 2. Christianity and other religions--Buddhism. 3. Buddhism--Relations--Christianity. I. De Neui, Paul H.
BV2618.C67 2007
266.0088'2943--dc22

2007046639

CONTENTS

INTRODUCTION

It is not without a certain degree of irony that the discussion of orality must be presented in written form. Missioners coming from the so-called literate world have much to learn from the application of principles behind oral communication, however many will not hear these principles until they appear in print. It is for this reason that the Southeast Asian Network (SEANET) proudly presents our fifth volume, *Communicating Christ Through Story and Song: Orality in Buddhist Contexts*. These chapters were originally presented at the SEANET missiological forum held in Chiang Mai, Thailand in January 2007. The conference was attended by over one hundred participants representing sixteen countries. Each of the forum presenters is both practitioner and missiological reflector experienced in the areas in which they write.

This book is divided into two sections. The first section presents the theoretical foundations of orality in Christian communication with biblical and theological emphases. First in this section is Alex Smith's article "Communication and Continuity through Oral Transmission." Smith provides a broad overview of the many historical and missiological applications of various forms of orality. With anecdotes from throughout the Buddhist world Smith illustrates the necessity to explore communication methods other than the printed media in missional activity. David Lim presents a challenge to the entire Christian community in his provocative article, "Biblical Worship Rediscovered: A Theology for Communicating Basic Christianity." A strong advocate for house church multiplication, Lim suggests that the emphasis on large church worship services actually decreases the missional nature of the church. The application of Lim's suggestions are numerous for those engaged in ministry anywhere the church seriously engages with cultural issues but particularly among primarily oral cultures.

Frances S. Adeney's article, "Christian Evangelistic Preaching as Ritual Speech in a Buddhist Context" describes the function of ritual speech in oral cultures with emphasis upon the Buddhist world. How does learning actually occur in oral cultures? Miriam Adeney addresses this question in her article, "Feeding Giraffes, Counting Cows and Missing the Learners: The Challenge of Buddhist Oral Communicators." Adeney's work in the use of story is well documented elsewhere. Here she provides several examples of the power of story illustrating that learning occurs through symbols, action and song. Missiologist Terry Muck reflects historically and strategically upon "Three Reasons Why Christian Witness to Buddhists Has Failed" warning that these areas are some of the most severely abused in oral expressions of the gospel.

The second section of the book presents cases of hope illustrating the application of the principles of orality in various countries throughout the Buddhist world. A. Steven Evans opens this section illustrating how biblical narratives bridge the gap to reach to the deep heart level of worldview including that of the Indian and Tibetan Buddhist world. He closes his article on some suggestions on the selection of appropriate narratives. G.P.V. Somaratna's article, "The Use of Story and Song in Sinhalese Buddhist Funerals" powerfully illustrates the effect of culturally sensitive ritual as a non-literate means of communication from his own Sri Lankan perspective. Dale Jone's article, "Moving Towards Oral Communication of the Gospel: Experiences from Cambodia" describes his own pilgrimage and struggles in this direction. His carefully researched work will assist the reader in understanding the definition of and widespread predominance of primary oral learners not only in the Buddhist world but all around the globe today.

Bruce Hutchinson has provided the readership with the personal account of Barnabas Mam, a Cambodian who has moved through a life of tragedy to a ministry based upon the use of orality reaching out to Khmer Buddhists. His article, "Communicating the Gospel Through Story and Song in Cambodia" gives a first person account of what happens when the gospel is allowed expression in local story and song. John Oswald's work in "Gospel Communication in Tibetan Song" is another illustration of the importance of song in reaching the deepest heart levels of a culture.

We want to thank all those who participated in the organizing of the SEANET forum and conference, particularly Dr. Alex Smith whose continuing efforts have moved SEANET towards broader goals within the Buddhist world. This book would not be possible with the help of all of the SEANET steering committee involved in the planning of the forum in 2007 as well as a number of North Park Theological Seminary students who willingly served as assistants during the entire conference. Special thanks to my students Ingrid Johnson and Daniel G. Larson who helped with data formatting, editing, and indexing to produce the final camera ready copy. We also thank Naomi Bradley and the staff of William Carey Library for making this publication available in the most efficient way possible. Finally, we thank Jon Pon for his artistic cooperation in the design and creation of this volume's cover.

May this volume enable the global Christian community to listen to and learn from those to whom orality is the main form of communication of the gospel as God's song and story goes on.

Paul H. De Neui, Ph.D.
Chicago, Illinois, U.S.A.

CONTRIBUTORS

Adeney, Frances. Ph.D., Sociology of Religion and Social Ethics, Graduate Theological Union, University of California at Berkeley; William A. Benfield Jr. Professor of Evangelism and Global Mission, Louisville Presbyterian Theological Seminary, Louisville, KY, U.S.A.

Adeney, Miriam. Ph.D., Anthropology, Washington State University; Associate Professor of Global and Urban Ministries, Seattle Pacific University, Seattle, WA.

De Neui, Paul H. Ph.D., Intercultural Studies, Fuller Theological Seminary, Visiting Assistant Professor of World Mission, Director of the Center for World Christian Studies, North Park Theological Seminary, Chicago, IL; Missionary, Evangelical Covenant Church, Thailand.

Evans, Steven A. Graduate Studies, East Tennessee State University and Southwestern Baptist Theological Seminary; Research Associate and Communications Specialist, International Center for Ethnographic Studies, Marietta, GA; Research Intern, Centre for Bhutan Studies, Thimphu, Bhutan.

Hutchinson, Bruce. Professional journalist; Missionary, Phnom Penh, Cambodia; Now living in New Zealand.

Jones, Dale. B.A., Cross-Cultural Ministries, North Central University, Minneapolis, MN; Missionary, Mission to Unreached Peoples, Cambodia.

Lim, David S. Ph.D., Theology (NT), Fuller Theological Seminary; Executive Director, China Ministries International-Philippines; President, Asian School for Development, Director of Cross-cultural Studies, Manila, Philippines.

Mam, Barnabas. National Director, Ambassadors for Christ International, Cambodia; Chairman, Bible Society of Cambodia; Senior pastor, Living Hope in Christ Church, Phnom Penh, Cambodia.

Muck, Terry. Ph.D., History of Religions, Northwestern University; Professor of Mission and World Religion, Asbury Theological Seminary. Wilmore, KY, USA.

Oswald, John. Ethnomusicologist and missiological practitioner traveling and working in Asia.

Somaratna, G.P.V. Ph.D., South Asian History, University of London; Senior Research Professor, Colombo Theological Seminary, Colombo, Sri Lanka.

Smith, Alex G. D.Miss., Fuller Theological Seminary; Retired Missionary to Thailand; Minister-at-large, OMF International.

PART I

BIBLICAL AND CULTURAL FOUNDATIONS OF ORALITY IN CHRISTIAN COMMUNICATION

1

COMMUNICATION AND CONTINUITY THROUGH ORAL TRANSMISSION

Alex G. Smith

The Chinese say, “A picture is worth a thousand words.” It is interesting to observe that the front pages of most daily Thai newspapers are filled with pictures with little written commentary. To get the detailed background of the news items behind the pictures one needs to read the text in the pages that follow. This is because the large preponderance of Thai, particularly from rural areas, but also country migrants to the large cities, is often semi-literate or functionally illiterate. So are many urbanites. The pictures tell the story. Compare that with Japan, which is one of the most literate societies in the world. Most of the advertising along the roads of Japan are composed almost exclusively of written letters, with very few pictures. The one notable exception is at restaurants and fast food establishments where the delicacies are displayed both with words and in molded models showing what the dish of edibles one orders will look like.

Oral prevalence among humans has persisted from time immemorial. Later written forms are not to be despised, but do not replace oral ones. They are to reinforce and sustain orality. Despite many libraries full of books, multitudes of magazines on multiple subjects, myriads of daily newspapers, much cyberspace media through emails, text messaging, worldwide websites, personal blogs, and so forth, the reality is that most of the current world’s population of six and a half billion residents, functions primarily in the realm of orality. The peoples of the earth might be classified into four basic groups: 1) totally oral societies, 2) illiterate masses living in the midst of literate groups, 3) semi-literate folks who are often functionally illiterate and 4) fully literate peoples. These are not categories discriminating value, but are stages along a continuum from verbal to written. To a larger or lesser extent, all of these categories have essential dimensions of oral communication. Not all have a written focus. Over a decade ago UNESCO officially estimated that more than one billion people were non-literate, or about one in five then (Søgaard 1993:176). More recent estimates indicate that now four billion are oral learners. Avery Willis of the Southern Baptist's International Mission Board declares, "Seventy percent of the world's people today can't, don't or won't read" (Jewell 2006:56).

Generally, largely literate Western mission workers, who serve across cultures, often are not comfortable working only with oral means. Usually they feel that the best approach to communication is through literate, written forms, including literacy, language reduction to written scripts (often English based), printed translations of oral tradition, and of course, the Bible printed in the local language or dialect. While these approaches may be commendable and worthwhile, the existing oral practices and local forms of communication are often neglected or ignored. This article will attempt to show some of the valuable dimensions of orality that enhance both communication and continuity. The old adage declares, "the pen is mightier than the sword." While there is some truth to that, also note that at times oral means may also be mightier that the pen. Concerted communications to and through mobilized oral masses is potent. For example, oral messages from Ruhollah

Khomeini, which were taped and spread widely among the common folk in Iran, catalyzed and consolidated the revolution, bringing about the downfall of the Shah's regime. Oral approaches can reach everyone in all common societies, while literate means may be limited to the elite, the educated, and those in positions of leadership at many levels.

Anthropological Observations

The media for communication among oral peoples varies greatly in forms, styles, and processes. Common to all is a sense of continuity of values, moral mores, legal codes, and historical import. These provide the fabric for society in social relations, education, law and order and even economic affairs and business. Without written language scripts and published materials, some societies function efficiently and soundly. Within many literate groups are often masses of folk, who operate primarily at the oral rather than literate levels. Then there are those who feel at home in both worlds.

A concise list of four elementary traits each for the categories of communication and continuity through oral transmission might be:

Communication of

1. Truth and Knowledge: general and specialized
2. Social Values: acceptable and unacceptable morals
3. Historical Awareness: tradition and rites or rituals
4. Law and Order: acceptable control for the good of all.

Continuity in

1. Consistency: both positive and negative (e.g. belief that the earth is flat was negative)

2. Constancy: stability and solidarity through oral socialization and education

3. Connectedness: to past heritage and to future aspirations

4. Constraint: boundaries for society, and norms for peaceful functioning

Ancient beginnings: Creation Myths and Stories

It is common knowledge and not surprising that many oral cultures have myths that tell of creation or legends that describe the great flood, often with their own versions passed down verbally for centuries, generation after generation. The Siamese, Thai, Lao and Dai people have a legend of the first couple created on earth. Those forebears are known as Pusangasaa and Yasangasii or Ta-kalaa and Yai-kalii. This first ancestral couple was the progenitors of all peoples (Harris 2006:1; Google Search).

The Tai Dam people in Southeast Asia, known as Lao Song, have similar oral traditions (Short 2007:1). They believe "God created the Tai Dam, when He put a hot poker into a dried gourd." A research worker among this people group passed on the following background on their beliefs concerning creation: "The Tai Dam believe that the earth and the heaven were held close together by a cord. But the sky was so low, so close to earth, that it made everyday activities difficult. Even the upturned horns of the buffalo got entangled in the low hanging sky. To bring an end to this, the Bent-Over Grandfather of the sky and the Bent-Over Grandmother of the earth together cut the cord between sky and earth. This allowed the sky to float well above the earth, so it could be seen far and wide. It also permitted freedom of movement on the earth.

Soon the earth was in turmoil. People were fighting and a drought covered the whole land. The ancestral Grandparents interceded again on behalf of the people. They performed a ceremony that caused rain to fall incessantly upon the earth, completely covering the mountains. No dry land was seen, and all life died.

In the Heavens, four gourds as big as a house were readied and placed on the receding waters. In them were placed 550 clans of Tai, 330 clans of hill people, many varieties of rice, fish, and every kind of bird and animal. Also, there was a book for the Shaman, the astrologers, the fortune tellers, as well as a book of laws, customs, and festivals.

After three months, the water receded and the gourds settled on dry land in Vietnam, Laos, and China. New societies were governed by wiser men, while the police and Shaman established and upheld the customs and laws. They kept the rivers clean and the land was peaceful for all the descendants.

The story ends with this declaration: "It is our distinct language which is the root and fiber of the Tai Dam nation. Our fame like a loud drum, will resound all over the world" (Short 2006:1).

Oral socialization in the family

Household education and early socializations within families are usually accomplished through the telling of fables, nursery rhymes, bedtime stories, poems and choruses. This is true not only for illiterate societies, but also for highly literate ones too. Thus the principles and value of oral transmissions in all cultures and among all people groups may be considered as universals. They provide continuity as well as communication.

Oral transmission is common to all cultures, including sophisticated literate ones. Most oral transmissions in education and social matters occur in the illiterate or semiliterate cultures. In the majority of cultures, both oral and literate, many forms of orality complement communication related to education and assist in the socialization process.

Here are a few examples:

Farming: Folklore related to agriculture, horticulture and animal rearing is passed on from generation to generation by verbal rather than written means. Knowledge of experiences from past generations, lessons gained through crises, and secrets for increased productivity are often communicated orally. Best selections for natural fertilizers, pesticides, and other practical matters are transmitted orally to the sons and grandsons of seasoned farmers and herdsmen. I remember an old recipe my Australian maternal grandfather passed on to the family related to the curing of raw hides.

Domestic protocol and foodstuffs. Secret recipes for special dishes, or unique cooking directions, step by vital step, are frequently only available through oral transmission to the favored few. My grandmother made culinary delicacies depending only on her experienced mind and hands. With a pinch of this, a cup of that, and an occasional sip to taste she modified until the right combination of flavor befitting her practical experience and oral upbringing was perfected. She had no written recipes and could not tell you one if asked. She excelled in the kitchen through her oral knowledge and experience, learned as the eighth child of a pioneer family.

Medical treatments and healing. In both Eastern and Western cultures from North to South across the globe, healers, shamans, medicine men, spirit doctors, mediums and other practitioners have used remedies, often kept secret, which they have received orally from their forebears. During my early days in Thailand I identified no less than fourteen kinds of "doctors" - from herbalist to surgeon, from spirit medium to

> midwife (Smith 1977:87). I know a current Thai principal of a Bible College in Thailand who was pre-selected to be the family spirit doctor. His grandfather was to orient and train him orally for that role and purpose. When he became a Christian, he rejected that responsibility.
>
> **Drugs and medicines**. Much knowledge of Chinese herbal and other medicines are passed on by oral means. Traditions of cures involving dried dead animal and plant material are transmitted orally from generation to generation. I remember some verbal instructions of remedies my parents and grandparents passed on to me, such as a special poultice made out of common household ingredients.
>
> **Religious practices**. Special rituals, rites, magic, mediation with the spirit world and other practices were communicated orally to the chosen—whether priests, medicine men or shamans. While religious practitioners frequently use specialized or sacred languages orally and symbolically, they do not always understand their meanings. Usually they learn or memorize them by rote through specialized training. Some Buddhist monks would be in this category.

Sometimes the old and the new come into tension and conflict. In the 1970s I made follow up visits to patients who had attended the Manoram Christian Hospital in Chainat, Thailand. One case in particular highlights this conflict. The woman had been treated in the hospital for stomach wounds and given medication including antibiotics. When I visited her in her rural home a few days later, I found the local shaman medicine man treating her in the house. To my horror, he had removed the hospital dressings and put certain grasses and herbs on the wounds along with fresh cow dung!

Oral Tools for Communication

Who has not heard someone say, "I remember when..."? This instantly attracts our attention and grabs our interest. The sharing of oral stories accumulated in memory is vital to the process of continuity with the past and often for relevance to the present, as well as for projections into the future.

Memory is the primary tool for oral history, myths, legends, hero feats and stories that focus on values. The moral of the story is often the climax. Over time these recollections may not always be perfectly accurate in details, as often the extemporaneous story tellers embellished their descriptions and colored their presentations. However, the core facts, central beliefs and basic themes are generally true and consistent in their fundamental conceptualization. The consistency and the continuity of oral transmission over the centuries remain amazingly constant and accurate. This is similar to differing scenery, which may change along a river bank, but the primary flow of the stream stays constant and its direction remains the same. Oral peoples rely heavily on memory. That which contributes to the memorization process and recall is likely to be more from hearing sources and certain contextual visual associations, than from written sources or script forms. Let me illustrate:

> Chinese shopkeepers often astutely keep all balances due from customers in their memories most accurately. No computers are needed in many situations of Asia, just memory. Instant recall and recalculation is promptly done orally. Today with modern machines, computers and accounting equipment this is becoming a lost art in modern business and frequently much slower than that by earlier brain power.

> In North African lives one tribe where key women memorize the whole Scripture and recall it in forms of singing ballads for the people to listen to, week after week. The ear is the primary organ utilized in the reception of oral tradition rather than the eye, which is used more in literate cultures.
>
> In 1978 while living in Bangkok I once needed to buy a part for a 1954 Chevrolet automobile. I went to one section of the capital in a tiny lane off New Road, where many auto parts shops were concentrated together. It looked rather chaotic. No stock card system or records for location by numbers was used. However, the local clerks knew just where to find the part needed. Within minutes the correct item was accurately produced, even though it was for a vehicle from a quarter of a century earlier!

Repetition is a second powerful tool in the oral arsenal. Repetition reinforces communication and consolidates its transmission. It thereby provides a platform for reinforcing continuity in culture and in society's values. In all cultures this may occur through artistic and dramatic means or by special oral techniques and forms. Much oral communication in many cultures is presented through indigenous performances of dance, drama, song and music. The re-enactments of myth and folklore, such as the repeated portrayal of the Ramayana in India or the equivalent Ramakien in Southeast Asia, are typical ways of utilizing these potent devices of oral conveyance. Accompanying the oral transmission through regular repetition, these local flavored means of communication reinforce the values and history of continuity in society. Sometime they may seem boring to outsiders, but to insiders they are the spice of life and the essence of connectedness as the transmission of heritage.

A third important tool of oral communication is story telling. "The power of story to move and change us is undeniable. Missionaries and mission agencies have known and utilized the power of the story of Jesus for centuries" (Moreau 2006:1). Good story telling is powerful. Skillfully used, it is of immense educational value, often unconsciously so. Some of the methods of story telling include different styles and means such as poems, ballads, yarns, parables, riddles, limericks, nursery rhymes, heroic historical stories, ditties, heroic songs, and even modern rap. Folklore is often handed down in story form such as old wives' tales, folk medicinal cures, and tales of bygone days. In olden days, story telling was a key means of entertaining and relaxing for families and groups of people, frequently used on the trail around open air campfires at night or around dinner tables near the stove in log cabins and mud huts during cold winters. This is an unknown art and experience among many in the modern age. Television, movies, videos, MTV, DVDs and other media forms have tended to replace the story teller. Gifted bards are still around and should be encouraged. Donald Larson suggests three key roles for cross cultural workers: learner, trader, and story teller. He laments, "The story teller role is perhaps the easiest one to develop, though one often finds missionaries to be sermonizers, theologizers or lecturers, not story tellers" (1978:158, 161-162). More attention needs to be given in missionary training for developing and sharpening skills in story telling. The use of this mode and role might increase effective communication of Christ to the nations, both literate and oral ones.

A fourth way of communicating in oral societies often revolves around visual objects such as crests, symbols or totems. For example in Southeast Alaska, totems of the three main tribes or nations "are tangible references to the people, events, stories, and legends that figure in the oral histories of Northwest Coast Native peoples." Crests symbolized a group's origins and history and defined their identity and lineage. The pole's meaning is known only if one knows the purpose and occasion of its creation and the people and stories associated with it. Traditionally these were "introduced when the pole was raised, and then passed down orally from generation to generation" (Totem Heritage Center). Totem poles "were not worshipped; they were silent storytellers. There was no written language." Of five major symbolic animals, the raven, which had powers capable of changing his form at will, was considered "a symbol of the Creator" (Totem Bight brochure). Careful research, understanding and application of these oral means of communication are crucial to workers in oral societies. One of the tallest totems in Ketchikan's Totem Museum has an interesting figure carved at the bottom of the story pole. It is the form of a bearded Russian Orthodox priest and indicated the conversion of the tribe to Christianity, following their long traditional history.

A fifth tool relates to the arts, particularly song, music, dance, and drama, which are basic avenues for transmitting the message, especially within oral cultures (Smith 2001:45-46). These can be as developed in non-literate societies as they are in literate ones. Memory and repetition play important roles in this. It is intriguing to watch the faces in Thai or Lao audiences when indigenous forms like *lamlao* are being presented alive. In *lamlao* a bard expertly half chants half sings rhymed verses of the lyrics from memory, accompanied by someone playing a Lao bamboo mouth organ called a *khaen*. Similarly old Irish limericks and more recently African-American rap are primarily oral forms, usually memorized, sometimes extemporaneously developed, and often initially transmitted orally rather than by print media. Charles Wesley and

William Booth capitalized on using the tunes of old familiar oral pub songs and transformed them into Christian hymns, which their followers memorized speedily and loved to sing heartily.

Biblical Illustrations

Significantly, in the Bible God "spoke" more than "wrote." Strong's Exhaustive Concordance lists twelve three columned pages for "said" and "spoke", but only one page for "write" and its derivatives. In creation God repeatedly "said" and it was done (Gen. 1:3f). Throughout Genesis God spoke to Adam and Eve (3:9f); to Cain (4:6-10); to Noah (6:13); to Abram (12:1); to Abimelech (20:3); to Rebekah (25:23); to Isaac (26:2); to Jacob (31:3) and so forth. God also spoke directly to Moses (Ex. 3:4f); Joshua (Jos. 3:7); Gideon (Jud. 6:14); Samuel (I Sa. 3:11); David (I Sa. 23:2); Solomon (I Kg. 3:11) and many others. God spoke to the prophets and through them as mouths to the nations. John the Baptist, Jesus and the disciples spoke to individuals, families, and multitudes. Jesus never wrote a book. The Bible is replete with multiple accounts of dialogues between God and men, and amongst humankind themselves. God primarily communicated orally. The Gospel was to be heralded in the entire world and proclaimed by word of mouth everywhere through the believers' witness.

References in Scripture to writing are limited, such as the Ten Commandments, and the writing on the wall (Dan. 5: 5, 25f). The priests of Levi obviously were literate. Later the scribes meticulously copied Scriptures. God told Isaiah to write upon a tablet with a man's pen (8:1). He commanded Jeremiah "to write all the words I have spoken in a book" (30:2), and Ezekiel to write upon a stick (37:16). The Lord ordered Habakkuk to write the vision plainly (2:2). After researching oral reports and interviewing many eyewitnesses, Luke wrote his Gospel in historical order to Theophilus (Lk. 1:3). The first Church Council wrote the decisions clarifying the gospel related to the Gentiles, but their conclusions were passed on orally to the churches (Ac. 15:20, 27). The Apostles Paul, Peter and John wrote various Epistles to the churches. In the Book of Revelation John was ordered to "Write in a book what you see" and send it to the churches (1:11).

The use of oral stories in Scripture was common: Nathan brought conviction to David through his story of one little lamb (II Sam. 12); Samson used riddles (Judges14:12f); and Jesus frequently spoke in parables, a pattern also found in the Old Testament (Mt. 13:34; Eze. 17:2). Who can forget parables like the Good Samaritan, the Prodigal Son, or the rich man and Lazarus?

Many of the prophets came from farming or shepherding backgrounds, and were likely non-literate, though some prophets were quite literate. In communicating to peoples in oral societies, Ezekiel employed dramatic effects such as eating the scroll (3:1-2), acting out the siege of Jerusalem (4:1-17), and demonstrating the city's desolation by cutting off his hair with a sharp sword, weighing it, burning part of it, and scattering the rest (5:1-17). These approaches would be potent among oral societies. The use of certain objects and symbols such as the Pillar of Fire, the Arc of the Covenant, the two tables of stone, Aaron's rod that budded, and the brazen serpent also had a powerful impact among such peoples.

The Passover was a significant earthshaking event for Israel. Continuity of this historic deliverance from Egypt was constantly being communicated in many ways. Primarily, the heads of Jewish families were to rehearse the works, wonders and word of God related to these events at the annual festival of Passover. Ernest

Wright sees repeated reenactment of the Passover as "the confessional recital of the redemptive acts of God" (1952:13). Other festivals building continuity include Purim, remembering Esther's salvation of the Jews from the hands of Haman, the Amalekite. Similarly, Christ's institution of communion is a clear example of continuity through oral tradition. The injunction is to remember the Lord's death till He comes. The experience of communion symbolically ties believers back into the past historical event of His Death, and projects them forward to the future hope of His second appearing and return.

The oral compositions of many Psalms, probably composed during the night watches, were often set to music. They were the grounds for meditation and reflection, not only on God, His character, wonders, works and words, but also on personal responses of His servants in testimony of His protection and provision, confession of failure or repentance, and praise for restoration, sustenance and deliverance. These still speak to the hearts of humans, but especially to those with oral backgrounds.

Much of the early Church was comprised largely of oral or semi-literate peoples including slaves, the poor, the downtrodden and the disenfranchised. Theological examples from the history of the era and in the New Testament text indicate that orality played a significant role in the spread of the Church and in the nurturing of the believers, often living in harsh environments. Creeds such as the Nicene Creed, spiritual hymns, psalms, invocations, prayers and benedictions were committed to memory and repeatedly used (Eph 5:19; I Ti. 3:16; Phl. 2:6-11; I Pe. 1:23-25; Jude 24-25). Public reading of Scripture without comment made God's Word available to the oral masses (Lk. 4:16-21). Paul commanded Timothy to practice this (I Ti. 4:13).

Historical Traditions

The cultures of biblical times included many oral communities. The early transmission of Scripture was by oral means for decades if not centuries. The oral languages used for the Jewish Scriptures in the Old Testament were mostly Aramaic based and /or Hebrew. For the New Testament they were spoken Aramaic and likely Koiné Greek, the common language that Alexander the Great had instituted across his vast Empire from Persia to Europe from the fourth century before Christ.

Similarly, the Buddha used his own common language of Maghadi in the early spread of his teaching. At his death in 486 BC, the first Buddhist Council called upon Ananda to recite from memory the whole teaching of the Buddha. Ananda had accompanied the Buddha for the majority of his preaching and teaching. This was the first time the Buddhist scriptures had been formally recognized, and this was in oral form (Mizuno 1982: 19-20). For centuries the Buddhist Tripitaka was transmitted orally. Later on their sutras were formally recorded into Pali, followed by Sanskrit. The earliest extant Pali scripts date from the first century before Christ (Maquire 2001:37). As time passed, translations were made into other languages - Chinese, Korean, Japanese, Mongolian, Tibetan, the dialects of Southeast Asia and European tongues.

Through oral communication, Buddhism crossed borders and influenced nations. Before they were written down, the early Buddhist scriptures were "transmitted orally ever since the death of Shakyamuni Buddha three hundred years earlier" (Macquire 2001: 37-38). They basically comprised three main categories, which later became part of the three baskets of Tripitaka or Buddhist scriptures:

1. Vinayapitaka: monastic rules and regulations.

2. Suttapitaka: the *dharma* or Buddha's teachings, stories, parables and Jataka.

3. Abhidharmapitaka: advanced philosophical teachings and codifications for monks.

Much of the content of these Tripitakas were based on oral sources. First, the Jatakas were birth stories of the reincarnations of Siddhartha Gautama, the Buddha. At least 550 Jataka of his former birth stories, now in print, were orally passed down during the early centuries. They are tales with a precise literary format and structure (Ryhs Davids 1989:xvii). They are interesting stories meant to keep the audience's attention, while focusing on the concept of rebirth or reincarnation. My analysis of these Jataka Tales identifies the following order in each account:

1. An introductory saying or theme
2. "This the Teacher (the Buddha) told while at..." (a certain location is named).
3. A story of the present, alleged to have happened within the Order (Sangha).
4. A transition ending with "He brought up the past."
5. A second story from the past, similar to the first story, is told by the Bodhisat (Buddha), who relates an account of the person and of himself from their far distant past lives or rebirths. Some of the Buddha's reincarnations are quite fanciful, including Tree-spirit, Sea Deva, and Cloud-horse. Others identify him in rebirths as various animals and different kinds of persons.
6. Each teaching story concludes with "assigning" the chief characters, the teller of which is Buddha himself, identified by the phrase "but .... was just I."

The second category of orality concerns the bulk of the Buddha's teaching through stories, parables, conversations, riddles and instruction. Usually the Buddha does not tell the seekers the solution to their enquiry nor what they must do about it. The story is the instruction and the application awaits their insight and interpretation. Today too many Gospel story tellers give too much of the application to the listeners, contrary to the model of Jesus. One needs to be careful not to over-interpret the story. One of Buddhism's key writers of textbooks for general consumption is Jack Maguire. He took his Buddhist vows in 1996 and has been a professional story teller ever since, specializing in Buddhist tales. He intersperses these tales throughout his well known textbook *Essential Buddhism* (2001:19f). Ravi Zacharias employs dialogue in a similar approach in his small book *The Lotus and the Cross*, where Jesus Talks with Buddha (2001). Christian workers in other cultures would do well to embrace the story model afresh.

Stories are powerful means of teaching precepts and principles. Here are three interesting Buddhist illustrations:

First, continuity through the ancient myth of the Naga (Mucalinda, the snake) is still perpetrated in modern Buddhism. From the beginning of the world, Narayan reclined on the back of the Naga in the milky ocean. During the third week after the Buddha's enlightenment at Bodh Gaya, he sat meditating on the throne of the coiled Naga, who used his multiple heads to form an umbrella over the Buddha, to protect him from the elements. On one occasion the Naga decided to become a monk and disguised himself as a man and was ordained. Later while asleep, the Naga turned back into a snake. Thus discovered, he was brought before the Buddha, who expelled him from the *sangha*, as only men can be monks. The Naga requested him to require all future monks to become the Naga in name first before ordination. The night before ordination they go through a Naga ceremony wearing a white robe. This Naga rite transfers merit to the parents. Consequently, the initial question asked potential monks is, "Are you human?" (Smith 2005:109; Woragamvijya 1987:25, 28).

Second, a typically Buddhist tale from modern Vietnam tells of the quarrelling of two Buddha images in a temple during the flood season. A man at midnight heard them arguing. Peeking in, he saw a fat clay Buddha on the ground angrily holding a sword in his hand, while holding a wild beast at bay under his foot. As he gestured to another wooden image of the Buddha perched high on a pedestal in the center of the pagoda, he reproached him, "You have no power over the flood waters as you float at their will, and you depend on humans to set you back in the pagoda." The wooden Buddha shouted back angrily, "Remember what's in the Sutras. Nothing is of more worth than to remain within the norms of nature. Heaven and earth cause floods and drought. When the waters rise I float; when they recede I am returned to my pedestal. Neither affects my essence. As I floated I pitied your destiny as your body crumbled under the floodwaters, powerless to save yourself. Yet you still persist in making fun of me." The two images were still arguing when the Sakyamuni Buddha interrupted them saying, "Both of you are wrong. When the floods come, you do not know how to make your six wisdoms and your five powers act to force the waters to recede. You only think of preserving your bodies of clay and of wood. So keep on enjoying the offerings of food the people give you. Instead of being ashamed, you make much noise, never thinking of indiscreet ears." Just then the man opened the door and looked inside the temple. The two Buddha images and the

Sakyamuni still stood in their places, clay and wood, as they had always been" (Schultz 1965:212-214).

Third, in the Philippines I was given a Buddhist news publication, editions of which are produced bi-monthly. The uniqueness of *Phi Shan*, this magazine of Buddhist propagation, is not only in its parallel printing in two languages, Chinese and English, but also the relevant colored comic strips of the stories interspersed throughout. In my copy, the Mahayana Buddhist story of Kuan Yin's miracle was described: Long ago, the Flying Sand Dock was a river, which could not be crossed without a boat. Next to the river was Huan In Cave. A boatman would row people across for money. He loved money as his life, so unless he was paid, he refused to row anyone across. One day, two poor monks begged him to row them across to the cave, but as they had no money, he would not do so. The monks sat down on the bank opposite the cave. Soon they saw another monk come to cross the river. The rower again refused. The monk scolded him, "You are very bad! You should row people across, whether or not they have money to pay. You should do compassionate good deeds. Your outlook on money as your life is the seed of hell. You are breaking the causal link (karma) between the people wanting to cross and the Huan In Cave. I am not going to ride in your boat any more. See if I can cross the river." With this rebuke the monk threw a handful of sand into the river and instantly a sand dock emerged. He immediately crossed over to the other side and disappeared. The two poor monks recognized this was a miracle of Kuan Yin Bodhisattva. They quickly knelt and chanted the Kuan Yin mantra. The rower also knelt and cried in repentance, vowing to do good in the future. From then on the Flying Sand Dock had no need of a boat to row people across (2002:3).

Missiological Reflections and Research

Understanding the oral dimensions and mechanisms of any culture is vital. Serious research of the oral elements in any culture is essential and much needed.

Several years ago one of my sons did research for a project under an Indonesian University. His concentration was on the oral traditions of an unreached people group in one of the large islands of that nation. This was strategic since this group's old oral traditions were near to being lost forever as the older generation, who still faintly remembered the traditions, was dying out. The current generation was fairly ignorant of the ancient traditions of their people. This was the result of culture change and partial integration into another dominant culture and language.

My son spoke excellent Indonesian and also learned the local dialect of the people group well. For several years he spent days each week in the villages with the people. Then at night he sat with the elders around the smoky oil lamps, listening to their stories and common talk as they smoked cigarettes. He observed intently, listened carefully, questioned them specifically on their oral history, and made detailed notes of the information. They shared stories of their old legends, including their dominant ship-boat motif, their ancient songs, traditional stories, folklore, cultural heritage, and so on. With the elders' permission, he made tape recordings of their ancient songs, historical roots, religious heritage, moral values, customs, and traditions. He asked them to explain these and the rationale behind the reasons why the tribe or group did certain practices, performed specific ceremonies, celebrated key festivals and conducted unique rites and rituals. All these were parts of their oral culture as they had no written language of their own.

Later he translated their oral history into Indonesian, which most of them understood and read, even though they used their own dialects in the homes and villages. Thus he presented back to them their own oral heritage for posterity and preservation, along with recording of the songs of their own roots (Thisbaseballmitt 1998).

This is an excellent model to follow for those working in oral cultures. While the process first requires the gaining and maintaining of credibility within the group, it also demands focused determination in research methodology, and vital analysis and application following the project. Keys to communicating within oral cultures need to be identified and utilized with forms that readily fit that ethos and background of the people group.

Considerable study on oral communications needs to be done in all cultures, because herein are the links to identity in society, the bridges of communication, the ladders for learning, and the clues for crossing over into the hearts and minds of the people. Here are several suggestions to implement:

1. Research and note local indigenous stories, commonly told to children and/ or shared among adults and families. Study myths, legends, local heroes, and any tales that give insights back into the history of the people group.
2. Find examples and potent illustrations in each culture that can be used to clearly present the key elements of the Gospel. Create and sharpen good parabolic illustrations. Tell them repeatedly.
3. Pool these resources and research findings into a bank of stories for sharing widely with fellow workers. Don't neglect including the local believers for input into the bank and for their use from that bank of data.

4. Spend considerable time pondering, analyzing, applying and propagating key appropriate stories, especially those that relate to family contexts.
5. Make field notes of their use and the responses of the people to them. Record answers to questions about them. Get feedback on the understanding of them. Especially record how the people specifically feel about each story.
6. Carefully collate this feedback and the results of consistent use over time. Make special notes of outcomes and the effects of experiments on case studies.
7. Critically evaluate all of these dimensions, analyze this data, and apply the findings for further experimentation and reflection. Conduct bold tests to advance the use of oral media. .
8. Recycle positive approaches and effective models, teaching other workers, both expatriates and the local folk, how to use them. Gossip the Gospel in story forms and train the indigenous believers to do this also.

Conclusion and Applications

The principles for using orality for communication are appropriate for all cultures: oral, non-literate, semiliterate and highly literate. *First*, in all peoples and cultures family network structures include many generations, giving a strong sense of continuity and connectedness. *Second*, much of the early socialization and domestic education is carried on through oral means in the home and local community. Even where, in some societies as time goes by the emphasis changes more to literate media, the oral bridges to extensive relationships continue to exist in most of the world.

Too often throughout mission history, indigenous churches in oral contexts became dependent on printed Bibles, hymnals, prayer books, training manuals, church constitutions, and in some cases even Roberts Rules of Order! These were usually translated into the local language, which missionaries had reduced to writing. Besides emphasizing literate means such as tracts, books, literacy texts, and Bible translation in oral cultures, it is wise to give serious thought and effort to revitalizing oral forms for communicating Christ. Viggo Søgaard advised, "That means, for the church, resisting the temptation to make literacy a requirement for salvation and spiritual development." He then warns, "Unfortunately, this has not always been the case. When the Bible became "print," people were separated into two classes: those who could read and those who could not read, and as time has gone by, the church has put more and more of its information and learning into print" (1993:176).

Besides doing careful research and utilizing the five primary tools of oral communication (memorization, repetition, story telling, symbols, and music-dramatic arts), intercultural workers in oral societies should be intentional in following the practical applications below:

1. Using the oral bridges for transmitting the Gospel has distinct advantages over literate devices. Focus on telling stories and dramatizing the message with indigenous song and poetry for communication. Preliterate and semi-literate communities should be encouraged to memorize appropriate sections of Scripture and simple worship liturgy "such as the Lord's Prayer, the Ten Commandments, the Twenty-third Psalm, Romans 12:9-16, the Apostles' Creed, and a few hymns" (McGavran 1970:326). Without this, years are lost while literacy and translation are undertaken. Focusing on the use of indigenous oral means of communication in

propagation can raise up believers, plant churches, and mobilize them in outreach using their natural oral tools. Using their heart language and forms immediately advances the Gospel much earlier than waiting for the literacy process to be completed.

2. Western advocates of the Gospel usually major on reaching individuals. A focus on reaching whole families and their extended networks is likely to be more effective. Search for stories of family conversions, illustrations of how families overcame problems and conflicts through God's grace and similar verbal pictures. These will likely be more efficient and better fitting within oral cultures than the individual approach. Renewed attention to these oral aspects for sharing the good news is needed. Worthy literate projects should be not abandoned. They should supplement the natural forms of orality common to the specific people group.

3. Oral mechanisms for transmitting communication and continuity are the primary links, ladders and bridges for learning clues for crossing over in those cultures by means of their myths, legends, stories, parables, wisdom sayings, and local tales. To these might be added appropriate indigenous artistic communications through dance, drama, music, and song. Encourage the local believers to develop drama of key Bible stories, using native artistic devices and indigenous kinesic movements.

4. Meditation is a dominant practice among Buddhists, but is also commanded for Christ's followers. The Church can enhance and facilitate the central practice of meditation among oral societies quite easily. The story method is an effective oral tool for memorization, repetition, and meditation on stories, parables, riddles, biblical Scriptures, memorized creeds, psalms, and oral doctrinal teaching. Applications of lessons to daily life are just as valid for oral as for literate believers. But be careful not to over-

interpret the story. Let well-told stories speak for themselves. The ABC of learning through story telling is **A**pplication through meditation, **B**ridging by associations within culture and **C**ontinuity in precept and practice related to values.

Jesus said that the world's poor are always with us (Mk. 14:7). So are oral societies and the non-literate masses. Jesus did not demand that the poor change their economic situation in order to meet His salvific aspirations. Rather He accommodated Himself to them. So must the twenty-first century church and missions. The deepest experience of love and the broadest measure of passion are recognized in the reaching out to all people everywhere, where they are, as they are. The prophet "sat where they sat" (Eze. 3:15). Let God's ambassadors follow suit, so that they may be able to find effective ways to communicate Christ to the non-literate masses. Only then will the billions of people in oral cultures and communities comprehend the long standing loving-kindness of the eternal Lord of all the earth.

2

BIBLICAL WORSHIP REDISCOVERED: A THEOLOGY FOR COMMUNICATING BASIC CHRISTIANITY

David S. Lim, Ph.D.

There is a major issue in the church's communication of the essence of the Christian faith among the various religions and ideologies throughout history. The main activity and communication tool of Christendom has been the weekly worship service—convened congregations in church buildings, led by professional (usually educated) clergy and often with increasingly elaborate liturgies. What has this communicated to the world, even to generations of church-goers? Perhaps for most of church history, except in its earliest no-building, non-clerical and non-hierarchical state, the church has through its weekly (and in some instances, daily) worship services conveyed the wrong message of Christ and his salvation on a grand scale.

Public worship has been perceived (quite rightly) by most people to be the most essential practice of Christianity. Church-going has been used to measure a Christian's spirituality, not just by the uninformed, but even by the most committed believers. But is this biblically correct and practically effective? Through its weekly worship services, the church may have been teaching the wrong lessons on the essence of biblical spirituality, and communicating the wrong message on the gospel of the Kingdom of God.

There is a more biblical and more theologically proper way to convey Christianity through the church's weekly gatherings, so that its understanding and practice of weekly worship authentically reflects God's nature, truly edifies its participants, and bears appropriate witness to non-believing outsiders. The New Testament churches and today's house church networks communicate Christianity (and the gospel) much more clearly and accurately, including in oral cultures, with hardly any need for weekly large worship services.

This article draws its inspiration and model from the evangelistic and transformational impact of the "insider movements"[1] in history, and particularly the church planting movements (CPM) of the house church networks (HCN) in China. Among the largest as of June 2003 are: China for Christ (Fang Cheng Pai – 12 million members since 1983), China Gospel Fellowship (Tang He – 10 million since 1980), World of Life (Born Again) Movement (5 million since 1980), Li Xin (Anhui – 5 million since 1985), and Yin Shang (Anhui – 5 million since 1984) (Wesley 2003:230). Though their journey into this communication paradigm to their world was divinely forced upon them through persecution, they should serve as a model for those serving in Buddhist contexts, for their church multiplication occurred mainly in rural areas where oral cultures and folk Buddhist practices prevail until today.[2]

---

1 "Insider movements" refer to rapid church planting movements that are almost always indigenous—self-governing, self-supporting, self-propagating, and lately also self-theologizing.

2 Most important sources are the publications of the Chinese Church Research Centre and China Ministries International (both led by Jonathan Chao and now Edwin Lee), Asian Outreach (Paul Kauffman and now David Wang), Open Doors (Brother Andrew), Overseas Missionary Fellowship and Friends of China (David Adeney, Tony Lambert), Target

Indeed, Evangelical[3] churches in most countries (including Buddhist nations) seem to have been experiencing religious revival and church growth, with saturation church-planting and overflow crowds in Sunday worship services, for the past three decades since 1975. Yet there hardly seems to be any major church multiplication and transformational impact in most contexts at all. What has gone wrong? Perhaps the most important factor is their misunderstanding and mishandling of worship. In rediscovering and applying the biblical teaching on public worship, we are resolving perhaps the most crucial communication problem of Christianity.

So much Christian time, resources, and efforts have been focused in making more attractive (or entertaining) worship services which actually hardly develop strong disciples who can help build the kingdom of God. Is it right for us to just seek more innovative ways to improve the present system? Or perhaps we should be looking for a better system by which our worship truly pleases God, builds His church and communicates His gospel more effectively.

Moreover, in terms of worship styles, celebrative "praise and worship" has become the dominant form in Sunday services as well as both big and small Christian gatherings perhaps in most growing churches worldwide. There appears to be a great revival going on. But in almost every context, these worshipping congregations seem not to have transformative impact on their immediate (and related)

Ministries and Christian communications Ltd.). Cf. Aikman 2003; Deng 2005; Oblau 2005; Hattaway 2003; Kreider 2002; Lambert 1999; and Tang 2005.

3 In this paper, "Evangelicals" refer to most Protestants, including those from the Pentecostal and Neo-Pentecostal (or Charismatic or Full Gospel) traditions.

local communities at all. At both the local and national levels,[4] in spite of this revivalist atmosphere and increase of "born again" converts, the moral degeneration and social disintegration of their neighborhood seem to be unaffected, and in some cases worsened!

In short, has the increase and innovation in worship services been spiritual, meaningful, relevant, and helpful? And *will* they be? This article shall show that public worship is indeed beneficial, but its emphasis in today's church (and historical Christendom) may be really detrimental to the growth of the church and all its members. This is because God has revealed to us in the Bible that there is a better way to worship Him: "in Spirit and in truth" (Jn. 4:23-24).

The good (in this case, worship services) has become the enemy of the best. To work for more instances and more innovation in worship may not be the way for God's desired church growth. The main innovation we are pleading for is to go back to the Bible and recover the simple yet deep worship of the early Church that turned the Roman Empire upside down. Though many have drawn anthropological and sociological lessons and explanations from the rapid evangelism and effective discipleship in house churches, this article focuses on the theological reasons.

This article proposes that God requires four important dimensions for true worship that will convey the right message that will result in biblical and effective church growth and Christian spirituality. These four aspects of corporate worship--that it should be spiritual, rational, moral and missional, would lead us not just to innovate parts of the prevalent worship pattern in our churches today, but also to renovate and transform the entire worship paradigm so that

---

[4] Recent high-profile cases include Bosnia, Nigeria, East Africa (Rwanda and Burundi), Zambia, Guatemala, and presently, Northern Uganda, and East Timor.

God's church will grow to full maturity so as to and truly glorify God and accurately communicate His gospel.

Advantages of Public Worship

There are undeniably many advantages to participating in inspiring worship services. Here are five major ones:

1. Affirmation "God is here!" We can experience God's glory and majesty. We are created to praise our Creator just as the stars and galaxies in the universe were created to glorify Him by their brilliance. We reach our full humanity as we gaze heavenward and direct our thanksgiving and celebration to God. Though we may not usually "feel God's presence" in public worship, at least worship services are occasions to be reminded that we should be conscious of God's existence and be thankful for His blessings.

2. Healing/therapy of our spirit. For many, attending worship services have effected transformation in their inner world. The music and lyrics lift their hearts, whether they come with or without the heavy burdens of life. Many experience their darkness being taken away, their wounds and sins being cleansed away and their broken hearts comforted. Whatever the style, form or shape of words and music, congregants invite God to heal them and make them whole again.

3. Proclamation of truth. This may be the main reason why Evangelicals go to church: mainly to hear the preaching of the Word. Believers can be fed and grow in the knowledge of God and His will as they sing the songs and listen to the teaching from the pulpit. What makes worship truly biblical has less to do with the question of whether we liked or disliked a particular order of

service and much more a question of whether the message really magnified the Lord as expounded from His Word.

4. Sense of unity and universality. More than just listening to music and sermons on stereo, tape or VCD, being present in a congregational worship gives us a sense of the unity and universality of the people of God. Seeing a crowd and doing some activities together with them help create a sense of comfort and security that one belongs to a big family of faith.

5. Celebration/festival. Above all, public worship can have an evangelistic appeal, especially if they are city-wide inter-church affairs. They can catch the attention of the community and demonstrate the joy in our humanity and in the love of Christ. We can also celebrate life by encouraging the use of creative arts in exhibition of painting, pottery, cross-stitching, folk dancing, children's games, street plays and carnivals, etc., and including dinners and group discussions in Christian homes (Jones 1985:87).

Practical Theology of Public Worship

The Bible reveals that there are at least four dimensions of public worship that God has clearly told His people to observe in order for them to truly please Him and glorify Him among all peoples, and these are usually contradicted by large worship services.

Biblical Worship is Spiritual

First of all, biblical worship is the spiritual worship of a spiritual God. Because God is spirit, our worship of Him is not tied to, or dependent on, any particular form or place (Jn. 4:23-24).

> In essence, the worship pleasing to God is inward, not outward, the praise of the heart, not the lips, spiritual not ceremonial. It is not the movement of our bodies in elaborate ritual (however graceful and elegant); it is the movement of our spirit towards Him in love and obedience...The contemporary church is far from having grown out of the need for this warning. Colorful ceremonies, rich pageantry and splendid music are neither pleasing to God nor profitable to men, unless they are the vehicles of something else, namely spiritual worship (Stott 1970:166,168).

Where the Holy Spirit is prayerfully allowed to touch our hearts and where the word of truth is received and obeyed, the Spirit and the truth combine to renew and transform us. The Spirit reveals the truth about God (Jn. 16:13) and His will (16:8-11), and he teaches us to pray as we ought (Rom. 8:26f). To worship God "in spirit" also means that it must be Spirit-led and Spirit-driven (Stott 1970:168f).

Yet Sunday worship services have helped keep Christians immature spiritually. They are kept perennially as spiritual babies who are dependent on pastors, church buildings and church programs to feel spiritual or even just to "be in God's presence." Almost all lay-people, even after forty to fifty years in the faith, would still need to be visited or counseled or prayed for/blessed (by pastors usually), still self-centered, and needing to be served instead of being equipped to minister to others (Eph. 4:11-16). A majority would hesitate to lead in public prayers or to do personal evangelism. Instead of spiritual empowerment, they experience spiritual disempowerment. In short, local churches with their weekly worship services normally produce nominal (or baby) Christians, not Spirit-filled disciples.

This has at least five major implications: To be spiritual, our worship services have to become more flexible, less ritualistic, less professionalized, more personalized and more contextualized.

1. Our worship must be more flexible.

Above all, spiritual worship requires flexibility. Worship in the early church must have been very untidy. The Spirit was seen as a spirit of dignity and informality, of restraint and spontaneity, of discipline and freedom. Change did not produce explosive attitudes if a hymn was changed, or a psalm left out or somebody raised their hands! Living worship is open to the Spirit (Jones 1985:39).

New Testament "singing to one another" assumes the constant composition of new hymns and songs (Eph. 5:19f; Co. 3:16; 1 Co. 14:26).[5] Why? To avoid routine and unmindful singing!

Hymnody in public worship has perpetuated weekly hypocrisy as sincere Christians sing words and phrases they don't really mean or intend to carry out.

> "Take my silver and gold,
> Not a mite would I withhold."

Sung with all serious conviction, people don't realize the demanding response inherent in their words. As weak and sinful human beings, it is easy for us to sing words that have lost their meaning, hence the constant need for new compositions.

To maximize flexibility as in the early church, worship may best be done in smaller groups for they offer a better environment, one that is intimate and informal, without losing the sense of dignity and the presence of God. This informality offers freedom in the Spirit which is not available in the formal settings of big services. Such freedom opens up for its members new experiences of God.

---

[5] On New Testament hymnody, cf. Martin 1964: 39-52.

Freedom from set liturgical forms gives opportunities for finding fresh ways of experiencing our love for God and for each other in word, song and action. Where the Lord's supper is celebrated in the setting of a simple meal at the family table, it follows the pattern of the early churches' *agape* love feast, confirming the historic links with the New Testament church (Jones 1985:149f).

Further, spiritual praying can best be developed not in big gatherings where all pray together or are led by one, but in small groups where each is trained to pray publicly with others. Most Christians find leading prayer an embarrassing trial of faith but praying together can draw us to the reality of talking to God with the help and support of others especially when we need to break through negative periods of emptiness which tend to be neglected if not denied in celebrative gatherings. This is not to suggest that praying in small groups is without problems.[6] Praying together can become boring and may need sensitive spiritual direction (:150f).

The ultimate test of Spirit-led worship has much less to do with talking to God and more to do with listening to God. The main objective of worship is to discover what God wants to say to us. Worship has to go beyond the religious posturing and pretences that hide the real truth of our personal lives. Worshiping in small groups can free us from the burden of requests, where we pester God with so much of our self-centered petitions on Him in repetitive routine discourses. Instead, this should provide a variety of models that will encourage the private prayer life of its members, where they learn how to use silence, how to mediate, and how true worship has to do with a total self-offering of all that we have and are, and that in a life of self-surrender we are most ready to listen to God.

---

[6] For suggestions on how to grow in prayer life, cf. Smith 1989: 94-109; Barrett 1986: 45-56.

2. Our worship must be less ritualistic.

Spiritual worship also means that we can depend less and less on human-made customs and traditions even in our practice of faith. Biblically, true spirituality should lead to less religiosity. Spiritual growth uses prayer and the Word to equip us to drop complex and elaborate ritualism, the vestiges of folk religion where most of us start from except perhaps for those who have been secularized, to develop simple religiosity and more loving activity. The immature need sight, feelings, holy objects and rituals,[7] but the mature develop a servant lifestyle that depend on minimal ritualistic worship. Developing more elaborate (and entertaining) worship services is truly detrimental to our spiritual health.

In much of what we call worship, is God really present? Indeed how many of us can actually recall occasions when the majesty of God's glory broke through the ordinary routine of worship to fill us with light and love, when our faith was confirmed and when the Holy Spirit renewed us and some small miracle of transformation took place in our life as a result? Quite seldom, isn't it? In fact, there are better ways to experience such highs regularly.

The main reason why worship services hinder real spirituality is the institutionalism (and subsequent traditionalism and legalism) that depends on human organization and rules. Worship has become ritualized; it has become a performance of a worship style or "order of worship" (liturgy) finding the right words, right songs and right rituals to glorify God. Roman Catholicism emphasizes the altar, Eastern Orthodoxy the liturgy, Protestantism the pulpit, and Pentecostalism/charismaticism the "song and dance." In all these, the focus of Christian weekly gatherings has been on liturgical

---

[7] On the proper use of rituals, see Olavidez 1984: 24-31.

adoration in large assemblies rather than on mutual edification in house meetings (1 Co. 14:26; He.10:24f, Eph. 5:19f; Co. 3:15-17).

Do our Sunday worship experiences usually go beyond habit and custom? Have people's love for God and for neighbor really increased through the corporate worship carried on weekly? Preparing an order of worship can be a very frustrating affair, for it is humanly impossible to fulfill the needs of each member, from the veterans to first timers in public worship. No matter how much discussion and prayer, no order of worship can add much to our personal relationship with God even if we put more innovation in the building we assemble, the crowd we see, the management of liturgy, the preacher, the music, the time, the space for silence, even the ordinances or sacraments of baptism, and the Lord's Supper. There is no form of worship that will meet all expectations, especially the particular needs of each attendee.

In contrast, using the "simple church" system develops constant dependence upon God and His word ("in spirit and in truth") to move in power for the sustenance and expansion of His kingdom. Instead of relying on some holy people to lead in holy rituals in holy buildings, believers are forced to take responsibility to step out and practically work with God, to build up one another (at least weekly) and to reach out to others as a lifestyle, as part of their Christian identity.

3. Our worship must be less clericalized/professionalized.

Furthermore, worship has become professionalized. Only a few specialists appear on stage to lead the rest to perform the right things at the right time in the right way. In contrast, the Bible especially the New Testament views worship as a spiritual exercise done spontaneously by all believers. Note Paul's instruction to "pray without ceasing," 1 Th. 5:17. After all, every believer is a priest or minister (1 Pe. 2:9f; Rev. 1:6; Ex. 19:5f).[8] Our Lord Jesus himself preferred worship, including prayer, fasting and almsgiving, to be done primarily in the privacy of one's home and frowned on public displays of such (Mt. 6:1-8, 16-18). Even performing religious duties may be counterproductive to one's spirituality. Our Lord Jesus taught that the Good Samaritan (businessman) was more spiritual than the priest and the Levite who may have been rushing to serve God in the Temple (Lk. 10:25-35).

Like the world, we always run the danger of putting our own heroes on a pedestal, especially the preachers with unusual communication skills, musicians, artists, and business people. During public worship we often encourage people to give religious leaders honor which properly belong to God alone (Isa. 42:8)

There are occasions in which appropriate appreciation has to be expressed towards those who have served. But to do this often and before big crowds puts our religious leaders in very risky situations. Not just in the pulpit, music ministry, and organizational leadership, but in every sector of church-life—prayer meetings, youth camps, evangelistic rallies, discipleship seminars, and so on.

Most of the superstars in mega-churches or cable television are hardly servant-leaders who live the lifestyle of our Lord Jesus and the apostles. They seem to have forgotten that we follow a Savior who was little more than a pauper during His entire public ministry. They usually brandish various forms of "prosperity gospel" to audiences who run after what their itching ears want to hear (2 Ti. 4:3). They have subtly become addicted to the applause of people. "The temptation is too great to believe the nice things people tell us in the good moments, especially publicly. Such acclaim has a

---

8 On the priesthood of every believer, cf. Snyder 1983: 168-180, 220-234.

narcotic effect on our perception of the reality of our sinful predicament and our daily dependence on the operating grace of God" (MacDonald 1988:205). No wonder many of them have fallen into scandals regarding finances, sex, and luxurious living.

Doing house-church will reduce our chances of ruining more lives with undue visibility and praise. Let the Holy Spirit work through the whole body of Christ, not just the clergy and the clericalized laity.

4. Our worship must be more personalized.

We all need a spirituality or worship lifestyle that is specifically adapted to our personal temperament, vocation, age, social context, and family situation (Smith 1967). We need a tailor-made or custom-built spirituality.

Too often teaching on worship or spirituality has presumed that there is one model of spiritual life that is good for all. An individual discovers that a specific approach to spirituality is particularly beneficial. This is good and right. But the danger is that this individual becomes convinced that all righteous people should adopt that model, and consequently launches a ministry to promote the merits of his or her approach. It is not hard to find a biblical text that supports the emphasis of a proposed model. As a result, many people are helped. They find the approach to be helpful and effective, hence they promote the same pattern. But the reality is that the model cannot and will never fit all people. Many have felt persuaded that the model being taught is good, but find they cannot live with it in peace; they feel guilty when they are not comfortable with the approach, and often lead frustrated spiritual lives (Smith 1989:66-78).

We have to realize that there is no universal or uniform spirituality (or worship style and devotions) that all Christians will have or need to have. Different people will develop different spiritualities and religiosities. This is liberty. It frees each Christian from the unrealistic and unbiblical expectations of others. We will show later how this truth is best taught and propagated through small group meetings rather than big religious gatherings.

5. Our worship must be more contextualized.

One major factor that will determine our difference of worship style is culture. As human beings, we are raised in various cultures and subcultures. And since God allows us to come to Him as we are, we need not adopt another culture to worship Him. Being saved by grace through faith gives us the freedom in Christ to worship Him in our own cultural ways.

The early church provided worship, teaching, exhortation, and encouragement, but the apostles did not prescribe any specific forms by which these functions were to be done.[9] Christians in China and Vietnam have been worshipping with the sound of silence in apartments as well as in caves and shorelines, and with songs of victory in prison cells. The latter are grassroots spirituals composed, taught, and sung by even illiterate rural women (Oblau 2005:423-425).

For instance, when the nomadic Murle people of Sudan became Christians in the 1970s, they met every night around the fire. This was a normal, accepted activity, but now it took on new meaning. No one man was designated as pastor and mandated to teach every night. Instead, the older men shared in a rotation of teaching. Each

---

[9] On the theological basis for contextualized worship, cf. Lim 2003:81-83; and Kraft 2005.

night a different man would share what he was learning from the Bible (which was being translated) and how those insights applied to Murle life. The Murle followed a worship pattern different from ours, but it worked in their situation. Nothing is inherently wrong with most of the patterns that have been developed, but we should be careful to examine them regularly and not assume that our patterns must be reproduced in new fellowships (Parsons 2006:22).[10]

But sadly, worship services have historically highlighted the cultural immaturity of the church by inhibiting some people of some ethnic groups or economic classes, often unwittingly but in several contexts quite explicitly. People approve of the conduct, language, music, clothes, and interests of those groups they want to be identified with. So each church develops a religious sub-culture which would require newcomers some period to adjust. Very few succeed in becoming "seeker-friendly churches," but since most of them become mega-churches, they have turned the Sunday morning from worship services to evangelistic meetings.

If worship is indeed spiritual, we will see (and should welcome) all kinds of worship patterns, from new church-plants that do look like "church" to us to informal meetings in homes or under trees, all becoming vibrant gatherings of believers in Jesus. Church-life of New Testament Christians was much warmer, more open, more human and even more conscious of God's reality in their worship (1 Co. 14). Yet their worship was actually in small groups—in their homes—not in chapels or cathedrals. They assumed that each one

---

10 Unless Murle Christians transition in house church networks, they will soon be plagued by nominalism, like in Europe.

had a contribution to make, bringing their spiritual gifts to share.[11] Where this is practiced, worship does not need professional clergy to run the service.

Anthropologists have discovered that human festivals are universal. Each culture had traditions of feasting, dancing and costuming for days at a time around bonfires and in the streets. These bonded whole communities together, often including elaborate religious ceremonies (Ehrenreich 2006). These festivities and religious systems are not necessarily evil things; they represent the human search for God's moral righteousness and eternal happiness. In fact, they are good places to start. New converts to Christianity should as much as possible continue using the religious forms[12] and structures that they already have so that they can convey to their compatriots that Christianity comes not to destroy but to fulfill what is good in their culture, including their religious practices.

Biblical Worship is Rational

Secondly, biblical worship must be "in truth." True worship is rational worship. To love God with all our heart involves loving Him with all our mind. We must know God before we can worship Him "in truth." This is the worship of God the Father as He has been fully revealed in Jesus Christ (Stott 1970:162-165). The ultimate test that authenticates true worship is the test of truth,

---

11 On why churches need this paradigm shift into building its people in their everyday life, their ordinary witness and ministry and their spiritual growth, cf. Ringma 1994: 51-71.

12 On the Protestant lack of appreciation for the visual arts and iconography of other Christian traditions and other cultures, cf. Dyrness 2002, esp. Chap. V. On the critique of Evangelical lack of sensitivity in cross-cultural communication, cf. Packer 1980: 100-103.

namely: Does our worship confirm the truth concerning God? Does it confirm the message of the gospel and the authority of Jesus Christ? For where the Spirit works, Jesus is glorified (Jn. 16:14).

1. Our worship must be more biblical.

Evangelicals have always claimed that we worship the only true God, the God of the Bible. However in spite of this theological ideal, in actuality we commonly indulge in spiritual idolatry more than in the worship of the God of the universe. Much like early Israel, we often fall into the trap of radically diminishing God's place in our worldview and in our lives, substituting various "gods" from our cultural environment (Loewen 2006:25).

Of course, we do believe in a universal God who should be worshiped by people everywhere. But that's not the whole story. With the rapid secularization of the world, our God has become a specialized God, restricted largely to preparing people for the afterlife. For those who are from religious traditions that view God or gods who dealt with all of life, they feel they are being taught to worship a much smaller God with a narrow specialization in many Evangelical churches. This is like Israel which struggled to grow in her understanding of Yahweh as more than a tribal God but the God of all peoples. Similarly, when Jesus implied that the Messiah was for the Gentiles also, his own people were enraged (Lk. 4:16-30)!

Having a small God leaves us open to idolatry, to elevate a basic concern to ultimacy; something partial is boosted into universality; and something essentially finite is given infinite significance. For some people, groups, or denominations, the specialized God has begotten a son: my church or denomination. When the church is God, it becomes the source of truth: "what the church teaches is believed, and is believed because it is what the church teaches"

(Loewen 2006:27). God is defined as the one in whom the church believes. Instead of being the reenactments of what God has done, is doing, and will do for people, church rituals become celebrations of the deeds of the church or its functionaries. The body of believers bonds into a group which gets its life and identity from the church itself (:27); such is "church-worship."

Then there is Mammon-worship. The God of materialism supplies the motivation. Consumed with the worship of things, goods, belongings, we have turned to technology to provide them for us, and as technology has performed many miracles for us, we worship it also as our God. The God of technology, in turn, rewards some of us with wealth, which makes us comfortable and gives us security, so we worship it too. The God of wealth, in turn, feeds the God of materialism, making it possible for us to acquire goods we crave (Goudzwaard 1984:13; Walsh and Middleton 1953:131-139; Loewen 2006: 27; White 1979).

Another prominent form of idolatry is that of self-worship. Most of the emphasis in Christianity is on becoming happier here, healed here, more blessed here, and more fulfilled here. Worship must excite our spirits, sermons must entertain and enthrall our minds, music must penetrate and propel us, and the counseling must make us feel better about ourselves. While this may be nice and necessary, without heaven in clear view our Christianity fails to have a heavenward compulsion pulling us close to God. It tends to become instead self-serving entertainment or a therapeutic center. A heavenless church seeks to satisfy longings and needs here rather than serving and sacrificing here with a view to satisfaction there.

Without an eternal transcendent God as our compelling force and heaven in clear view, self becomes the center of attention and increasingly the center of our universe (Stowell 1995:58).

With so many forms of idolatry lurking among our churches, we need to be more biblically literate and serious about obedience to all that the Bible teaches about God and His will. It is through constant study and meditation on the Scriptures that we can grow in the renewal of our mind to know the true God and understand his will.[13] Then we shall not only save ourselves from losing our faith in the true God, but also maintain the right concept and practice of Spirit-led worship.

Biblical worship is, after all, about the kingdom of God (*shalom*) or the Lordship of Christ, which covers all of life, and not just one's spiritual salvation. It calls for transformation of lives and nations solely for the glory of God, not of any individual church leader (1 Cor. 1:18-3:23). Instead, most preaching today nurtures believers to remain as spiritual babies who remain self-centered, longing for more material comforts and more earthly blessings. Most fail to grow into spiritual giants who can "deny themselves, take up their crosses" and follow the Son of Man who has no pillow to lay his head. They hardly learn how to follow Jesus with a servant lifestyle, so as to sacrifice their selves and their possessions for the salvation and welfare of others. As our Lord said, "Any of you who does not give up everything he has cannot be my disciple" (Lk. 14:33, cf. vv. 25-34; Mk. 10:42-45).

2. Our worship must be more interactive.

We also have to use the best way for making worship rational by conducting our meetings in a dialogic or discursive style (Atkerson 2005:35-52). In this way, each member is expected to share his or her insights, inquiries and issues with the others present. Every time such a dynamic ensues, each has to use his mental faculties to

---

13 On how to renew our minds, see Smith 1989: 81-93.

understand and analyze what is being narrated and taught. As they encourage and teach one another, each is being trained to lead in the flexible worship lifestyle of biblical Christianity.

The weekly program in these groups must be dialogic and participative, with a free mixture of activities according to the needs and gifts of the participants, as set by the leaders in close consultation with all the members. Activities include prayer, worship, Bible reflection, fellowship, sharing, and collection and stewardship of resources for community service and missions support. Always try to include a simple potluck meal together. Following the 1 Corinthians 14:26 pattern of meeting, all members should come prepared to "disciple (teach, encourage, and confess sins to) one another,"[14] as they participate in building one another in their body-life together.

Biblical Worship is Moral

Third, our Lord Jesus clearly taught that true worship had a horizontal component. In Matthew 5:23-24, he taught that authentic worship is defined more by the horizontal (reconciling with one's neighbors) than by the vertical (offering worship to God) dimensions of our relationships. The first is necessary to the second. To enter simply into the presence of God in worship is not acceptable to Him unless one exercises love and forgiveness towards one's neighbors. Reconciling love for the brethren is the real test of true love for God (1 Jn. 3: 1-18; 4:7-21).[15] This implies that our worship must become more relational and more ethical:

---

14 On how to disciple one another, cf. Atkerson 2005: 57-67; Barrett 19986: 57-66, 87-97; and Martin 1964: 53-76.

15 Cf. Ahn 2001:153; and Martin 1964: 206.

1. Our worship must be more relational.

Public worship should not only express the theological unity of God's people, it must also be a visible demonstration of this fact. The reality and sincerity of our loving relationships determine the spiritual vibrancy and life-transforming effect of true worship. "When a congregation worships closely in love with each other, there is an unmistakable fusing of their life with the love of God" (Jones 1985: 47).

Biblical worship must be in the context of community and fellowship.[16] We need to develop significant personal relationships that offer mutual accountability at every stage of our life cycle to meet the different temptations and trials in each phase of life. These relationships provide balance, encouragement, and preventative maintenance in each one's life journey. We need this so we can maintain the sort of integrity needed for living as witnesses of the kingdom through friendships. These stretch us to grow toward Christ-likeness and to bear witness to Him in the world. This may be a top priority item for middle class churches in Asia, because a new study has shown that the "love quotient" among us is very low (Kirkpatrick 2001).

In the New Testament, "God's temple" is not a building (Ac. 7:48-50; 17:24), but the body of every believer (1 Co. 6:19f). It is not a local congregation, but the whole people of God (3:16f; 1 Pe. 2:4-10). But what is communicated in our worship services? Is church a building or a people? Sadly it is not just the non-Christian world that identifies Christianity with church buildings, even Christians have the same misunderstanding[17] Hence more

---

16 On the concept of fellowship in the NT, see Martin 1979: 34-45.

17 In some instances, I've asked church leaders to change the picture in their weekly church bulletin from their church building to their

resources have been given to construct and maintain church properties than to build people—to help turn dead stones into living stones in the temple of God.

As we gather together for worship, we are to do it in the context of honesty and transparency rooted in self-introspection (Ps. 139:23f). James 5:16 actually mentions the open sharing of sins.[18] This mean taking time to find out what is below the surface and being ready to forgive. To the extent Christians avoid or are prevented from this corporate journey, we will remain shallow in our personhood and imprisoned in our brokenness.

Only in small groups do we open up the possibilities for people to let others help them deal with their inner struggles. The only way to protect one another in a lifestyle of worship and loving service is to stay close enough to each other so that we are transparent to one another, so that we can correct the aberrant behaviors before they get out of control.

Building such intimate friendships takes time. Hence our God is most wise to schedule Christian fellowship (not worship services) as the priority agenda for each Christian's weekly calendar. "Living worship is about people and relationships, it has to do with what we are together" (Jones 1985:40).

2. Our worship must be more ethical.

For most people, "worship" has been redefined from its original biblical meaning. In both the Old and New Testaments "worship"

---

congregational membership, even if they will pose in front of the church building. So far, I've not seen any of them make the change. In fact, one of the churches that used to use a congregational photo has changed now to that of the church building in their church bulletins.

18 Cf. MacDonald 1988: 55-96, which finds a good model in Alcoholics Anonymous.

referred mainly to one's daily walk with God in the way of righteousness, and secondarily to one's public adulation of God's goodness in the festivals of celebration (held only three times per year in the Old Testament: in the feasts of Passover, Pentecost and Tabernacles). To give honor to God, we are to offer sacrifices of praise with our lips and sacrifices of good works with our lives (He. 13:15f; Mt. 5:16), yet the emphasis is definitely on the latter (Rom. 12:1, "offer your bodies as living sacrifices;" (Rom 12:1), and "whether you eat or drink" (I Co. 10:31).

The above deviations have resulted in a more tragic consequence to the Christian's priorities in worshipping God. For most Christians "worship" has been separated and marginalized from daily life. They think they have "worshipped" if they have attended a worship service on Sunday regardless of their lifestyles from Monday to Saturday. Not only has the time been shifted, but the venue has been relocated also: from their homes and workplaces to their church buildings. Even in the Old Testament, the teaching of the Law and partaking of the Passover Meal were done in the homes, not in the Temple (Dt. 6).

Biblical spirituality does not require more religiosity, because God is not glorified through more worship services! In fact, God requires a very simple religion, with no need for more elaborate or more numerous rituals. The Old Testament prophets had to ceaselessly remind Israel that Yahweh did not require more sacrifices (religious offerings and gatherings), but more obedience to the Great Commandment, particularly to love their neighbors as the expression of their love for God. God even says at one point, "I hate your religious festivals and assemblies" (Isa. 1:11-17; Amos 5:21-24; Hos. 6:6; Ps. 24:3-4). His chosen fast is not more religiosity, but more love for neighbors (Isa. 58).

This comes out clearly also in the life and teaching of Jesus in relation to the Sabbath (especially Mt. 12:1-14). In both these Sabbath controversies, Jesus taught that beyond observing religious laws and practices, the practical outworking of life in love and righteousness is what Sabbaths were for.[19] He warned his disciples about hypocritical worship quoting Isaiah 29:13, "These people honor me with their lips, but their hearts are far from me. They worship me in vain; their teachings are but rules taught by men."

New Testament believers and their leaders held all things loosely: their time, their material possessions, their security and even their lives. They had such diversion times in their long walking trips, on shipboards, and in the homes of people where they visited. They saw all things as on loan, ready to be recalled any moment by persecution or by the Lord himself. Indeed, they were ready for the Lord to return any time soon. Thus, "we must repudiate every pretension to religion which is not accompanied by righteousness. The claim to mystical experience without moral obedience is a lie and delusion... It concerns the very nature of God" (1 Jn. 1:5f; 2:4,9). "Religion without righteousness is vain. Faith without works is dead" (Stott 1970:171).

But Christianity has added church work into her corporate lifestyle, accumulating bit by bit more and more religious events and activities for serious living before God. They also accumulate more payrolls, properties, and other forms of assets that increase vulnerability to internal conflicts and decisions that focus more and more inward and less and less outward. Then gradually they become obsessed with these material things, protecting, competing, and even coveting. They become ensnared in debt (financial

---

19 Yeo 1991: 18 shows that in the New Testament, "Sabbath" rest is now a moment-by-moment routine for believers.

captivity), pride (comparison with others), and greed (an undue sense of discontentment for more “blessings”). Thus it becomes more and more difficult to bring the biblical mandate of generosity to give to others in need and in ministry. “Church work” never seems to be finished; personal and family issues are prioritized, and the world is labeled as a dangerous place.

In contrast, through their simple lifestyle and simple worship in house churches, New Testament Christians could constantly check on one another whether each was living a Spirit-filled life. Such weekly quality-control forced each one to see if his or her life was energized by God’s purposes and motivated by God’s love (He. 10:24f). Such is the priority in the worship agenda of the church, house church style.

“The way of service lies in brokenness, in accepting the discipline of the Holy Spirit. The measure of your service is determined by the degree of discipline and brokenness.”[20] The failure to have this practice happen regularly (if possible, weekly) in the body life of the church is the root cause of the failure of so much “worship” to produce ministry among Christians and mission towards non-Christians.

In terms of communication, people (especially believers) should learn sooner or later that Christianity is not bringing a new religion into a community. It is incarnating into and serving people, starting with a general acceptance and appreciation of their culture and religion, and then discipling the first converts to transform the sinful aspects of their culture and to simplify their religion. All societies have too much religiosity already, including modern secular societies where there is too much consumerism or Mammon-worship.

---

20 Watchman Nee, quoted in McDonald 1988: 198.

Jesus came to bring a simple lifestyle, even in terms of religious beliefs and practices. To seek God's forgiveness for sins, people do not need more complex rituals and ceremonies of penance; they can just confess and repent, "turn from their wicked ways". To hear God's word and follow His teachings, they do not need elaborate liturgies to listen to messages from priests and prophets; they just need to read the word for themselves and discuss how to apply it in their daily lives. In fact, they do not need to do any ritual to make themselves worthy to approach God and to share Him with others.

All peoples and cultures must learn that instead of the periodic and seasonal consciousness of God through the uncommon ("holy" rituals and laws), God can and should be known as the living God who in Christ became a "human for others" in the daily routines of common life. They just have to love Him and follow His word in the world and in daily life with the love and desire to draw others into relationship with Him. This focus on being and doing *agape* shows that God's gracious love in Christ is the most important aspect of His character.

Biblical Worship is Missional

In order to motivate and mobilize more Christians to be sent forth to reach the unreached, it's not enough to just preach the supremacy of Christ and arrange more worship of God to produce sacrificed service to advance the Great Commission (Bryant 2006:16f). Has our worship produced more churches driven by the passion to see God's glory realized in all communities and among the nations?

Most worship services hardly mention evangelizing the nations to glorify God throughout the earth, except perhaps in the rare Missions Sunday and Mission events which usually turn out to focus on local evangelism. There is a vague desire to see God's glory among the nations but the songs and messages in these worship events hardly challenge the congregation to go or send from among themselves and their comfort zones people who will bring in more worshippers of the King of Kings so that more Buddhists, Muslims, Hindus, Jews, Communists, atheists and secularized peoples will join in our worship.[21] If some efforts have been exerted to make our worship truly more missional, then the minimal results should prod us to give more focus and innovation in communicating this Great Commission, which calls for self-sacrificial obedience to bring God's love and glory among the nations. May our worship be measured by how many worshippers go (or are sent) rather than how many worshippers come.[22]

We also need to transform the structures that withhold and hinder this kind of spiritual vitality from happening. The local church structure perpetuates the mental and emotional paradigm that encourages and even molds Christians to become dependent on religious props and the appreciation and admiration of one's peers, so that they become absorbed in self-perfection and church maintenance and take no risk to depend on Christ to expand His

---

21 With weekly worship services, why are the majority of Christians in the world still ignorant of the challenge of the unreached, and many who are aware still feel little or no responsibility? Over 28% of the world has no access to the Gospel. Over 39% belong to an ethnic group without viable churches. There are over 4,000 "least evangelized" ethnolinguistic groups and over 6,700 unreached peoples. Nearly two billion (out of 6.4 billion) still need to hear of the "one true God to worship" for the first time. If present trends continue, the unreached will still represent one-fourth of the world's population in 2025!

22 "[Should] not effectiveness be measured best by how many people a congregation *sends* rather than how many people it *seats*?" (Bryant 2006:17). Cf. Ahn 2001, and Snyder 1989:291.

kingdom elsewhere among the unevangelized to seek the lost, to complete the universal body of Christ, to invite all peoples to join in worship and around the Lord's table.

This perpetuates the dichotomy between "sacred" and "secular." The world of the church with its liturgy, doctrine and structures focused on the worship service is not the world where the laity (more than 99% of the church) lives. These two worlds are very different. The "sacred" includes the certainties about God and experiences of grace and blessings, but the "secular" is a world of uncertainties, changes and struggles. These two worlds seldom meet. For these two worlds to interpenetrate, everyday life with its ups and downs should become more the heartbeat of what's highlighted in the life of the church. But the pulpit seldom touches the struggle of faith and life, but features the clichéd certainties from clergymen who are not in close touch with the real world.

"Church is usually a 'sacred' ceremony which the clergy hope will have some relevance for living a life of faith in the real world. It's high time that we register that such hopes are largely unfounded. Much of what happens at church is repetitive and irrelevant. It's driven more by a desire to maintain a church's doctrinal stand, its particular ethos, its programs, or its particular vision than by a concern to make the hopes, aspirations and struggles of its people central" (Ringma 1994:55).

What is called for is to bring "worship" into the neighborhoods and the workplaces in the public square and marketplace in small groups, not by more ritualistic (nor clericalized) "services," led by ordinary believers who will have been equipped and empowered to do so. Can our weekly meetings really produce such discipled witnesses for God's kingdom? Instead of clericalizing the laity, we should be laicizing the clergy!

Conclusion: Biblical Worship is Self-Sacrificial

In summary, in order to gain truly effective church multiplication in terms of both quality and quantity, our worship services should aspire to be (a) more Spirit-filled, meaning we should become more flexible and less ritualistic, as well as less clericalized and more personalized and contextualized, (b) more rational and interactive, (c) more relational and ethical, as well as (d) more missional or mission-oriented.

In light of the above four innovation points for corporate worship (which also avoids producing superficial and static spirituality of nominal Christianity), this article concludes that the proper and ultimate expression of worship is self-sacrificial service. True worship is a constant "offering of our bodies as a living sacrifice" to know and do the will of God (Rom. 12:1-2). Our entire life must become worship—an offering of our whole life, heart and soul unto God. Sadly, the exact opposite has been the effect: worship services have encouraged the wrong type of spirituality, and "worship" is defined as liturgical or ritualistic performance.

To correct this misunderstanding and miscommunication, we must reduce the size and frequency of gatherings for worship services. In terms of size, we should encourage more small group meetings rather than large assemblies. In terms of frequency, small groups must increase while big gatherings must decrease.

1. Our worship must be smaller in size.

Let's beware of the wrong emphasis that prevails in Christendom churches. We may not be worshipping God "in spirit and in truth" at all. We may be worshipping our worship, and worse, even worship of the wrong kind. It's time to put biblical worship back where it rightfully belongs: in every Christian's home. It has already been shown that historically in all major church renewal movements, the recovery of house-churches or cell structures[23] has been essential (Snyder 1989:290f, 302f; Pierson 2004).

Our concept of worship has degenerated into spiritual showmanship usually on stage, something which our Lord Jesus clearly denounced in Mt. 6:1-18, thereby placing non-functioning people (who are not doing actual disciple-making) in positions of authority, while the functioning ones (who are doing actual disciple-making) are busy taking care of the flock, often in their silent ways even shying away from accepting administrative roles that entail a series of committee meetings. Thus, local churches produce spiritually immature (perhaps often quite hypocritical) leaders who hardly contribute to quality or quantitative church growth at all!

2. Our worship must be less often in frequency.

We are not against worship services and prayer rallies but against their frequency. Attending worship services may be good indeed to uplift the soul and spirit of believers, but God in his wisdom did not require a weekly nor a monthly observance of such. God knows the hearts of sinful human beings who have they strong tendency to substitute simple faith (spirituality) with religious rituals, objects, places, and leaders (religiosity). For instance, in terms of places, Christians can easily make a divide between sacred and secular, thereby considering worship halls to be "sanctuaries," more holy than other venues. Such are the beginnings of superstitions and animisms: to regard certain objects, rituals (even prayers), places, times and people as sacred or more holy than others, that can give

---

23 On the differences between house-churches and cell churches, Simson 2001: 130-155; Garrison 2004: 270-272; and Zdero 2004: 127f, 133f.

one greater access to God's power and his blessings (or "luck") and prevent or overcome evil. It's hard to solely live by grace through faith alone.

God required His people in the Old Testament to have corporate worship only three times a year (Deu. 16:16), and expected none in the New Testament. They simply worshipped weekly in their homes! We can also corporately worship occasionally, perhaps three times a year, and meet in small fellowships weekly in Sabbath-like rest "from house to house." To date, we have been spending two or three hours of our weekly schedules in a counter-productive "spiritual activity" which produces "Sunday Christians."

This article, therefore, calls us to focus not on adding more worship gatherings or prayer rallies, but on working for better quality spirituality expressed through obedient and self-sacrificial lifestyles which are worthy of our God and His kingdom. There may be too many worship gatherings in our world already. God will be more glorified in our worship if we work harder in developing better ways to produce Christians who prefer lifestyles of "costly discipleship" over "cheap grace."

Only then shall we have learned the biblical meaning of worship, to properly give honor and glory to God, living our whole lives to please God, instead of attending liturgical services to praise God. Biblical worship is a way of life not a series of religious meetings (Simson 2001:xv). In the Parable of the Good Samaritan, Jesus was most radical in showing that religious people focusing on leading religious services were unspiritual, whereas a religiously unclean person who cared for a neighbor was most spiritual. Jesus' simple religion had only two fixed rituals: baptism for initiates, and "breaking of bread" for members.

What is the church communicating to the world about worship, its most important faith practice, to both believers and non-believers alike? Is worship liturgy or community? Is it found in big worship services or small house fellowships? In religious rituals or loving relationships? With the right paradigm, we will be focusing on loving and caring for one another and for others, to turn all neighborhoods into communities of love and reconciliation. Worship is meeting in intimate fellowships, preferably without large meetings (except perhaps quarterly) which detract from our goal of transforming all neighborhoods and nations into communities of love where people love God with all they have and love their neighbors as Christ loves them, a combination of the Great Commandment and the New Commandment. Then we will have much time to celebrate life with our neighbors and join local festivals and community affairs.

Fortunately, this article is actually no longer that radical today. The house church movement has already become global and growing rapidly in acceptance as a valid expression of the church. In recent years, most church planters, especially those from the West, particularly the United States, are shifting to church planting movements (CPMs) and indigenous movements (IMs), and hence house church worship and mission paradigms. For those concerned for world evangelization, church growth experts and missiologists[25] have caught up with what many mission practitioners are doing, particularly using Chronological Bible Storying as a primary strategy. The latter have even organized themselves as an alliance of international agencies called "International Orality Network," led mainly by Campus Crusade for Christ, Discipling a Whole Nation (DAWN), Faith Comes by Hearing, International Mission Board of

---

[25] E.g., Gibbs 2000: 83-118.

the Southern Baptist Convention, God's Story, Progressive Vision, Scripture in Use, WorldTeach, Wycliffe International, Southwestern Baptist Theological Seminary, Trans World Radio, and Youth With a Mission (YWAM) (ION/LCWE 2004:66-69).

The greatest burden will be upon the Western (actually Christendom)-originated churches in Buddhist lands: can they work towards transforming their weekly Sunday activities to gather in small house-fellowships rather than in large worship services? Instead of spending so much time in creating worship atmospheres in the church and developing whole worship packages for worship services, can they seek to do actual good works to serve their neighbors, including Buddhist religious leaders and actually do them? If only these Christendom-type churches in the Buddhist world would do this, evangelization of entire communities and even their districts and nations would be truly realized soon!

In short, if we just continue to seek innovative ways to tinker with the present church system and its varied worship styles, we will never be able to attain genuine church growth, much less the church's capacity to bring all peoples among the nations to worship our God.[26] What we need to innovate is the whole church system itself, which has not only ritualized, clericalized and institutionalized worship, but also kept Christians and churches from growing to full maturity in Christ. Let us go back to the New Testament where they worshipped by making melodies and discipling one another weekly in participative small groups called house churches. Isn't this the best, if not the only way, to tell Buddhists and the whole world what biblical Christianity truly is?

---

26 Albert Einstein said, "Insanity is doing the same thing over and over and expecting different results."

3

CHRISTIAN EVANGELISTIC PREACHING AS RITUAL SPEECH IN A BUDDHIST CONTEXT

Frances S. Adeney

I remember going to our Plymouth Brethren Gospel Meeting every Sunday evening as a young person. Our family of eight would pile into our station wagon for the forty-five minute drive from Deerfield to Oak Park, Illinois. To break the monotony of making this trip twice every Sunday, we would often sing hymns or hum our orchestra parts along the way. Among us kids we had a trumpet, a trombone, and a flute player in the junior high orchestra, so we made some pretty good harmony.

When we arrived at Grace and Truth Hall, our storefront meeting house located on a quiet tree-lined street, we would solemnly take our seats as we had during worship that morning. For the evening "gospel meeting" though, the chairs were arranged in straight rows rather than in a circle as they were for the morning "breaking of bread" meeting. There was a plain wooden podium at the front of the room.

The arrangement was different, but the faces were the same. The Butlers had kids our ages—Betsy, Spencer, Nancy, and a few little ones. Miss Ross' flaming red hair was tucked into a neat bun beneath her felt hat. Mr. Ross' stern face glowered under his crop of unruly white hair. And Mr. and Mrs. Rhodes looked placid as they took their usual seats.

Usually only one or two of the twenty-five or so people in the room were strangers to me. The traveling preacher, or "laborer" as we called him, was one. Sometimes a missionary to the Bahamas, where the Brethren had an outreach program, was the speaker. Other laborers were itinerant preachers who made their way from meeting to meeting preaching and teaching the message of Jesus in the Brethren way.

The gospel meeting began with a hymn from the "green book," *Grace and Truth Hymns*. The Little Flock hymnals were used only in the morning meeting, a meeting for the members of the group. For this meeting we used a more gospel-oriented hymn book. For the stated purpose of the Sunday evening meeting was to preach the gospel. And without one new face in that small plain room, the laborer would begin to do just that.

During the four years I attended the Oak Park meeting, I can remember only one time when any new people attended. Every week the faithful gathered to hear the gospel preached. To whom I couldn't help wondering? Why did they gather here every Sunday for an outreach meeting when persons from outside the group rarely ever came?

Evangelistic Preaching as Ritual Speech

Today I will examine evangelistic preaching as ritual speech and explore a few of the benefits that accrue to the church and individuals in the performance of this ritual act. We will then examine the process of adapting evangelistic preaching to a Buddhist context.

Few would question the centrality of self-advocacy in the life of Christian churches and the theologies of its adherents. To promote, extend, and propagate Christian beliefs has been a goal of the church since its inception. The term evangelism signifies the activities that Christians engage in to promote and extend Christian beliefs and practices. Other objectives may be met through those activities as well-education, worship, social solidarity, and formation of institutional definition. But announcing the veracity of Christian belief to those outside the religion remains the major stated goal of Christian evangelism.

A ritual act is one that is performed repeatedly, conforms to certain rules, and carries a symbolic meaning that goes beyond the act itself. Breaking apart a loaf of bread, making the sign of a cross over a sick child, intoning certain phrases before baptism, marriage, or burial are ritual acts of the Christian religion. Those acts, repeated in prescribed ways, at specific times and in particular places carry symbolic power. Many of these activities include words as a central component. Ritual speech, unlike everyday conversation, follows specific patterns, forms, and expressions that distinguish it from everyday conversation. When used for religious purposes, those performative speech acts take on a mystical and sacred power.

The evangelistic service is a central Christian ritual of this type. I do not include in this study other activities that Christians and churches designate as evangelism: liturgical evangelism, lifestyle evangelism, friendship evangelism, theater evangelism. I will focus on the regularly occurring public proclamation of Christianity by the institutional churches. That verbal witness to the Christian faith may be presented in church buildings, public locations, or in media presentations on radio, television, and the internet.

I divide my presentation into four parts: First, the location of this act of ritual speech in the social/historical context of the churches in the United States. Second, the authority of language that privileges the evangelistic speaker and forms the basis of ritual speech. Third, the impact of the ritual speech itself on listeners and on society. And finally, the process of contextualizing this form of evangelism for a Buddhist context.

Through exploring the dynamics of this form of evangelism, I will argue that evangelism as ritual speech authoritatively interprets and reinforces central teachings of Christianity and fosters a sense of identity and solidarity among adherents of the religion. At the same time, the public announcement of the "truth" of the religion carves out a social space for this religion to exercise its values, worldview, and practices in the wider society. This reinforcing of the socially-constructed cultural form of religion occurs whether or not the stated goal of the advocacy effort, to announce the beliefs of Christianity in a manner convincing to non-adherents, is reached.

The Context

Looking at Protestantism in the second half of the twentieth century in the United States, one is struck by the fact that, although the "Protestant Empire" had waned at the turn of the century, Protestant leaders still influenced public opinion. During the 1950s, evangelist Billy Graham was welcomed to the White House to advise the president on national issues. By the 1970s Protestant Christian Jerry Falwell was calling people into a "moral majority" which was already under fire. Pat Robertson's bid for the presidency in the 1980s showed a failure of Christian leaders to gain power in national politics. By the early 1990s, no new public Christian figure advising national leaders arose. The situation of Protestantism seemed to be one of decreasing hegemony, pluralism, and competition with other worldviews and values.

Although that trend continued for many liberal Protestant groups, conservative evangelical Christianity increased its visibility on the political front in other ways. Christian-based single-issue protests grew—against abortion, against homosexuality, against sexual promiscuity. Often couched in terms of family values, those positions gained support by many evangelicals. While the mainline churches declined, the evangelical and fundamentalist groups gained numbers and power.

The trends just described influence evangelistic preaching today, not only in the United States but in Asia. That creates a complex context for analyzing the role of evangelism as ritual speech. Many churches from the United States send missionaries to Buddhist societies, taking their various cultural identities with them. Though the focus may differ from one denomination to another, evangelistic meetings form part of the Christian tradition, focusing and reinforcing beliefs of the congregation. How does this happen?

Authority of Language

The authority to outline Christian beliefs and invite others to adopt them is institutionally situated. The church authorizes pastors, priest, and lay evangelists to speak on its behalf. Disagreements among sectors of the church, on belief, practice, and service, or on forms of evangelism do occur, but the authority of language resides in the various institutions that sanction one or another of the various positions.

Apart from the church's institutional support, the public proclamation of the Christian message would become a mere personal matter, a soap-box-in-Trafalgar-Square event. The evangelistic service, sanctioned by the church, is an event of a different order. The speaker, chosen by the church and educated within its institutions, commands respect based on more than his or her personal character and charisma.

Invested with authority by virtue of the institution that sponsors them, public evangelistic proclamation carries a symbolic power. The preacher speaks not on his/her own voice but with the voice of the church. The resulting ritual speech event provides the opportunity for reiterating, expanding or contracting the world of Christian belief.

The effect of this powerful positioning of the ritual speech of evangelism is that the content and dynamism of the message reinforces the objectification of a socially-constructed reality (Berger 1969). The evangelist's message defines truth for the listeners. By virtue of his or her institutional location, the evangelist is given the power to define reality for the hearers (Lebacqz 1986). The religious experience of the community as they interact with the message further contributes to the maintenance and development of the community (Porterfield 1998:175).

While playing a positive role for many hearers, in a religion as diverse as Christianity, that public power of definition also causes dissension and embarrassment. The most vocal proponents of Christian beliefs are often those with narrow and pejorative views. Because of the power of ritual speech to define belief, those narrow theologies appear to represent the Christian religion. Reformulations of religious beliefs occur, even if unwanted, by a majority of adherents.

An antidote to that unwanted reformulation is for the disaffected groups to engage in similar advocacy efforts that clearly define their own views. This trend can be seen in Christian television programming which includes viewpoints from many Christian denominations. Some of those presentations are formatted in ways that are very different from traditional evangelistic presentations. Formatting the material in new ways allows the group to advocate their religious beliefs without violating the ritual setting of the traditional evangelistic service. At the same time, through television programming, they distinguish themselves from groups purporting different views of the Christian message. The form and content of the ritual speech modifies to fit conditions of the context.

Ritual Speech

This brings us to an appraisal of the ritual speech itself. Ritualized acts are characterized by conformity to rules of place time, length, language, and audience (Bourdeiu 1991). In addition to being presented in a particular context by an authorized speaker, ritual speech conforms to a set of institutionalized, although often unwritten, rules. Those rules differ from group to group but rules are active in every presentation. Contemporary evangelistic services in large free-church style Protestant gatherings usually begin with a time of prayerful singing of praise choruses. African American evangelistic messages are couched in the Black preaching style. Baptist services conclude with an altar call. Audience participation varies and may include singing, giving a testimonial, raising of hands, coming forward, verbally encouraging the speaker, reading along in personal Bibles, and taking notes. These affirmations and augmentations of the ritual speech of the speaker reinforce the message and build a sense of inclusion and solidarity among the audience.

The speech of the speaker also conforms to a set of rules that guide the ritual event. Certain Bible passages are frequently used in these presentations. Reasons for adopting the Christian religion are stressed, again differing from group to group. These include seeking God's favor and avoiding future judgment, gaining inner peace or a more fulfilling life, becoming accepted in a religious community, or becoming a better, freer, more powerful, or more wealthy person. The ritual speech of the evangelistic meeting, in each case, is built around three basic premises. First, something is wrong with the world. Next, there is a divinely oriented solution to the problem. And finally, accepting the Christian gospel message will solve, or begin to solve the problem.

Those three issues, addressed by every religion, form the basis of and provide the direction for the ritual speech of Christian evangelistic preaching. The evangelistic speaker is authorized to speak to those issues and does so in a ritualized fashion. Guidelines established by the institutions, along with expectations presented by the context itself, inform the presentation. The ritual speech does not only point to action. It *is* action, a performance of the religious word to inform and influence the people.

Effects of Evangelistic Preaching as Ritual Speech

The effects of the performative speech act of evangelistic proclamation are many. I want to highlight two of the most important ones.

First, the hearers are reinforced in their beliefs and in their identity as faithful Christians. In addition, the air of facticity surrounding the moods and motivations that comprise the basis of the religion are strengthened (Geertz 1973:90f). At St. Stephens African Methodist Episcopal Church in Louisville, Kentucky, congregants who bring visitors to the service are publicly recognized. Central Presbyterian Church in Louisville publicly announces their pro-gay and lesbian stance as part of the good news of the gospel. Southeast Christian Church in Louisville provides shuttle buses from their huge crowded parking lots and sets up information booths and racks of literature that give information and schedules of church activities. At the small Brethren meeting I attended as a child, I usually got my head patted by one of the elders who would say, “How good to see the little lambs here tonight.” In these and other ways, followers of the religion are drawn together and given a sense of the solidity of their beliefs.

Second, evangelistic preaching creates a social space for the religion. Religious organizations, like political parties, are differentiated entities that perform discreet functions in modern societies (Bordieu 1991, Bellah 1970). Recognition of religious pluralism and presentation of various claims for meaning-construction and for allegiance create a competition among religious groups. The evangelistic service, whether or not it is successful in bringing new followers into the religious fold, establishes a position for the religious group in societal life. At the same time, it encourages followers to strengthen their allegiance to the group by demarcating clear and reasonable ideological parameters (Geertz 1973:205). In this way, the religion, while not adhered to by all in the society, establishes itself as a respectable cultural entity. When this does not happen, as in the case of the recent arrest of Bruce Deiuss, an evangelistic preacher at a tent meeting revival in Alabama for preaching too loudly, the identity of the group itself is threatened (CBN News August 29, 2006).

Questions for Evangelistic Preaching in Buddhist Contexts

Appraising Christian evangelism as ritual speech in the context of the United States provides a groundwork for research into evangelistic preaching in Buddhist contexts. I have described evangelistic preaching as socially-sanctioned, authoritative public performances of ritual speech. That ritual speech fosters adherence to Christianity by its followers and helps to establish the religion as a viable part of society and contemporary culture.

In a Buddhist context where Christianity is not the dominant religion, how can Christian evangelistic preaching be adapted to fulfill the goals of reinforcing Christian beliefs in adherents and creating a social space for Christianity? The process of cultural adaptation requires both a study of local religions and a practice of building relationships in the community. An interpretive approach to gaining knowledge of another culture requires a willingness to temporarily let go of one's own convictions, meeting the other on their turf (Adeney 2003:186). Four questions can help us do that as we assess the contextualization of evangelistic preaching.

Situational Appropriateness

First, does the current form of evangelistic preaching fit into the societal milieu? In a Buddhist context, with its focus on harmony, a Christian worship service should not stand out or appear strange. If identified as a "foreign religion," as Christianity has been in Thailand, for instance, people will not be interested in listening to the message of the gospel.

Drs. Nantachai and Ubolwan Mejudhon of Bangkok have developed what they call "meekness evangelism" which first inquires into the needs of a community and then fits the evangelistic proclamation into local community gatherings. In December, 2005, they organized a harvest festival in a village near Roi-et in Northeastern Thailand. Finding that the people of those small villages had discontinued their traditional harvest festival due to lack of funds and transportation, Nantachai's English Teaching

School, located in one of the villages, organized the festival and sent vans to nearby villages to gather the people. A stage was set up, funding was provided for local women to bring food, village teenagers played rock music, and children performed traditional Thai dances. In that very local and very Thai cultural setting, Nantachai preached a Christmas sermon, telling the story of Jesus' birth and death for the salvation of the world.

Any passerby would have recognized this festival as a local Thai gathering. And it was. Everyone was there for this festive occasion. The evangelistic preaching was strong and emphatically Christian. But it was done in a Thai way and blended into the cultural surroundings.

Offensive Elements

What forms of preaching might offend local Buddhists? Christians can evaluate their own evangelistic preaching, identifying possible offensive elements in a particular setting. Many proclamation styles that originated in the West have been directly transplanted into Buddhist settings. Some of those styles cause offense. For example, seeing a street preacher on a busy corner in a Northeast Thai town, I noticed that he was alone and seemed to have no audience at all. He held a megaphone and his voice could be heard even through the car windows when driving past the corner. It struck me as odd that a Thai man would be preaching in this fashion without the presence of other Christians to support him. The use of the megaphone also seemed a jarring disruption to the quiet rhythm of the local market. The Thai emphasis on communal activities as well as the Buddhist injunction to "do no harm" both seemed to be under attack by this aggressive form of evangelistic proclamation.

Later I learned from a worker in Nantachai's church that this was a common form of preaching done by a local church near Roi-et. This direct appropriation of a Western form of street preaching offended Thai sensibilities. So much disturbance had been caused by this form of evangelistic preaching that the government was considering banning all Christian meetings and ministries from the area. That proposal directly threatened the English Language School that the villagers had requested and which was sanctioned by the Thai government.

Forms of ritual speech differ depending on the social power of the group. What might be appropriate for a majority religion may be inappropriate if used by a minority group. For example, on the Indonesian island of Sumba, the figure of the "Angry Man" occupied an important place in traditional society. This leader held power over the life and death of those around him. Ritualized angry outbursts judged the action of those under his control. Undergirding that ritual speech was the power to act on his threats of punishment or death (Kuipers 1998).

After liberation from Dutch rule in 1945, new structures of power came to the island of Sumba. A national language began to replace the native dialect of the angry man. A new government took over his authority to make judgments thereby reducing respect for the angry man's threats. As the institutional context was reorganized around him, the ritual speech of the angry man changed along with it. He adopted a form of ritual speech common to women in his society. In doing so he used his reduced power, exchanging threats of domination which he could no longer fulfill for a message of lament, deploring his loss of status in Sumbanese society.

Christian workers in Buddhist societies as well as local and international leaders need to study the power structures of their society, differentiating among forms of ritual speech that might be used successfully by a religious group. Imitating the ritual practices of the powerful may lead to ridicule or opposition whereas finding a non-offensive form of ritual speech for a minority group could lend power to the message of the gospel for Christians and Buddhists alike.

Cultural Forms

The message of salvation through the death and resurrection of Jesus is a universal message. The church that Paul describes in Galatians spreads throughout the world, equalizing Jew and Greek, bond and free, male and female (Gal. 3:28). The description of the universal church in Ephesians describes God uniting all things in Christ (Eph. 1). But equality among believers and a universal church do not imply sameness. In order to proclaim the gospel in Buddhist societies, even to those that already accept Christianity, must be different cultural idioms, styles, and practices need to be adopted. This realization leads to the next question, "What cultural forms can be appropriated to communicate the gospel in Buddhist contexts?"

The harvest festival near Roi-et shows how the process can be undertaken. Nantachai first formed relationships in the village. After establishing trust, he found out what the people felt that they needed. They wanted to learn English. They wanted to renew their traditional harvest festival. Nantachai's group worked in the village for years before any evangelistic preaching was undertaken. When the gospel was introduced through preaching, that evangelistic preaching molded itself to the cultural forms of village life.

This is just one example. Much can be learned from Buddhist cultures about what forms of preaching might be acceptable and interesting to Buddhists. Mahinda Deegalle writes of preaching as performance in Sri Lanka (Deegalle 2006). She argues that the role of Buddhist preaching has been ignored or underestimated by academia. The Buddhist preaching tradition, called *bana*, has been a crucial and important characteristic of Theravada Buddhism in medieval Sri Lanka and has remained active as a form of making merit until today (Deegalle 2006:5). A more informal tradition of preaching in Theravada Buddhism includes "sermons composed for the occasion and delivered in the local language"(Gomich quoted in Deegalle 2006:5).

Here we see preaching as a form of ritual speech in Buddhism. Can this cultural form be understood by Christians and implemented as a form used for Christian evangelistic preaching? The emphasis in Buddhist preaching on the hope for the laity to attain nirvana (Gombrich quoted in Devalle 2006:5) might be used as an entry point to speak of the hope of salvation through Christ.

Missionary Engagement

If missionaries from the United States, South Korea, or other countries are leading worship in a Buddhist context, their sense of appropriate forms for evangelistic preaching also needs to be considered. Worship in churches planted by missionaries has more often than not reflected the cultural forms of the sending church. Posing the questions of appropriate cultural forms and non-offensiveness to Buddhist cultures will move evangelistic preaching services into local cultural forms.

As this transition takes place, we need to ask if there are certain elements of evangelistic preaching that are necessary to communicating the gospel. Is extending an invitation to repent and receive the good news essential? Are certain forms of address for prayer, for example, praying in Christ's name, crucial to evangelistic preaching? Is a communion service, however occasional, a central practice that should be included in evangelistic services? What is essential to the message and what is relative to the worship forms of sending churches? Can one cultural form be transposed into another without changing the essential story of redemption in Christ? How might this be done in a specific Buddhist context?

We might also inquire into the Western forms of worship that are used in Buddhist settings. Are Christians comfortable with those forms? Have they been accepted and perhaps modified to fit into the local cultural setting? An excess of meaning in ritual expressions may have molded the Western forms of ritual speech into culturally appropriate forms (Gadamer 1975). Missionaries must be wary of criticizing Western forms of evangelistic preaching just because they originated in the United States or Europe for they may already be "owned" by the local church and thus considered appropriate forms of communicating the gospel in that setting. For example, when Indonesians took control of Dutch Reformed churches after World War II, they began to see their worship and preaching forms as Indonesian and no longer considered them Dutch imports (Adeney 2005:18).

Are there cultural forms, on the other hand, that are inappropriate because they are inconsistent or contradictory to the Christian gospel? For example, a church congregation in a village in Java allowed their parking lot to be used by "ladies of the night" during the week. That inconsistency with Christian morality weakened the public witness of this church. A debate about blood libations as part of the eucharistic service in Africa became a major issue for the Episcopal church a number of years ago. Whether or not this local cultural practice could be adopted without losing the centrality of Christ's sacrifice for sin in the churches was the focus of this controversy. Are there cultural forms in Buddhist preaching traditions that would be inappropriate to use in Christian evangelistic preaching? If so, what might they be?

If missionaries are still present in the churches, their sensibilities to the service also need to be taken into consideration. For a worship service to perform the ritual functions described in the first half of this article, participants must be comfortable with most of the elements of the service. I suggest a "75% rule" be applied. Are missionaries comfortable with 75% of the service and uncomfortable with 25%? If so, a cross-cultural adaptation is becoming effective. If, on the other hand, missionaries are 100% satisfied with the service, it is probable that few local cultural forms are becoming incorporated into the worship. But if the missionaries are uncomfortable with more than 25% of the service, it may indicate that Christian orthodoxy is being threatened. This same 75% rule could be applied to local church leaders whose congregations are pushing for more culturally appropriate forms of worship.

Balancing the Four Questions

This leads us to a tricky balancing act in evangelistic preaching as ritual speech in Buddhist contexts. As missionaries learn about Buddhist societies, develop relationships with Buddhists, learn and adapt to their cultural forms, both Buddhist and indigenous, avoid culturally offensive elements in evangelistic preaching, and apply the 75% rule to the evangelistic services, things get complicated. A certain amount of negotiating between local cultural forms and Christian theologies must be done.

That negotiating is best accomplished by congregations and denominations in deliberations that include local laity and clergy, missionaries and sending organizations and denominations. We can be grateful that God's Holy Spirit is active within and among Christians everywhere and can help us with that task.

Although it is true, as several have noted, that the Christian church is unique among human institutions because it exists primarily for non-members, it is still part of its responsibility to serve its own. Evangelistic proclamation as ritual speech occupies a special place as a ritual that can serve both members and non-members alike. We depend on God's activity in our hearts and in our communities to help us find our way to evangelistic preaching that is nurturing, relevant, powerful, and sustaining to the church and at the same time becomes a witness to surrounding Buddhist communities.

4

FEEDING GIRAFFES, COUNTING COWS, AND MISSING TRUE LEARNERS: THE CHALLENGE OF BUDDHIST ORAL COMMUNICATORS

Miriam Adeney

How do Buddhists learn? In many cases, they do not learn by reading. Even in the West, print reading is decreasing. Yet if people do not read the Bible, will they be condemned to second-class citizenship in the kingdom of God? Can they grow to spiritual maturity? Will they ever be able to "rightly divide the Word of truth?" Or will they always stand like children with their noses pressed against the window, gazing at the bright lights inside? Evangelists and disciplers ponder these questions.

We have an obligation to communicate the whole gospel in ways that make sense, and to help bring disciples to maturity. Not just the educated and economically secure deserve our attention, but all who want to follow Jesus wholeheartedly. Jesus told Peter to "feed my sheep," not "feed my giraffes," as John Stott has observed. It is natural to focus on those who are most like us in every country—islands of elite who have books, telephones, computers, or at least literacy. We tell ourselves that these are the leaders. But that is not necessarily so. God grants wisdom at the grassroots. All across the Buddhist world, there are fellowship groups led by faithful believers who will never go to seminary. Some have no access to internet. Many are primarily oral learners. How do we teach them?

What is an oral learner? Not necessarily an illiterate. “Secondary orality” refers to people who can read but would rather not. They prefer other media. Asia is full of young people who watch Anime videos and play computer games. While not the focus of this article, they represent a huge segment of the Buddhist audience and must be the focus of someone’s future research.

The title of this article is based on a proverb attributed to the Buddha: Someone who recites doctrine but does not practice it is like a cowherd counting the cows of others. We want believers to live their faith, not just speak about it. Otherwise we might as well join those hapless cowherds. We can count converts. But if they have not absorbed and understood gospel teaching, they will not be disciples. They will continue grazing in other pastures. To prevent that, we must investigate how to communicate effectively.

Learning Through Memorization and Recitation

When I was a little girl, I would wake up in the morning and shuffle sleepy-eyed down the stairs and into the kitchen. There I would see my Dad sitting at the table, reading the Bible—and memorizing it. The summer that I turned thirteen, it was my task to repaint the interior woodwork upstairs in our house. To redeem the time, as I lugged a paint can from one spot to another, I also lugged along a Bible. That summer I memorized the book of James. Other books followed. Today whatever serenity and smile I have comes because my roots run down into the Word.

Buddhists Recite

Memorizing Scripture is a matter of course in most of the world's religions. For Jews, memorizing Torah was "sweeter than honey, more precious than gold." The Lord Jesus himself learned Scripture as he read it aloud in the synagogue (Klem 1982:63-67). For Muslims, silent reading is not the right way to employ God's Word. Scripture must be absorbed and spoken aloud. Then "the speech of God comes into the storehouse of memory and the currency of our lips" (Cragg 1975:41). For Hindus,

> It is not the dead or entombed manuscript but the correct and clear speaking of the memorized word in the here and now that makes for a living language and scripture. Large numbers of copies of the Living Bible stacked in bookstores or reverently placed on personal bookshelves are not living scripture according to the Hindu. Only when a passage is so well learned that it is with one wherever one goes is the word really known...Books...represent a lower, inferior, second order of language suitable only for the dull (Coward 1988:117-118).

Scripture should be recited aloud. Buddhists believe this too. When one walks past a temple, it is common to hear the chants of monks and schoolboys. "From Ananda's first repeating of all Buddha's teaching right up to the modern-day chanting of the *nembatsu*, the oral text has continued as the dominant force in Buddhist spiritual life," according to Harold Coward in *Sacred Word and Sacred Text: Scripture in World Religions*. "The oral word is experienced as being much more powerful (than the written)" (1988:146-148). Silent reading is too passive.

> When you identify with the chant, it has the function of structuring spiritual space...When I chant, it brings memories of my father, of gatherings with others... The mind opens...like flower buds being opened to receive the sun...Rather then recite the *nembutsu* [the mindfulness of the Buddha] quietly within yourself, say it out loud; bring it out and listen (S.K. Ikuta).
>
> To me the chant is meditative. It induces peace from the hustle and bustle of life. It is very comfortable. It has seeped in...it is part of my consciousness (Unidentified source).
>
> My father taught me scripture. I would repeat after him. After ten years he taught me how to read and what it meant. Later on in the University I studied these texts (Y.Kawamura).

These Jodo Shinshu testimonies collected by Coward underline the centrality of recitation. He comments,

> If Buddhist scripture is not learned in childhood through ritual repetition, if the oral teachings are not nourished and reinforced in adulthood by private and public repetition of the texts, then the psychological foundation will be missing and sermons and study of books may become empty exercises (1988:148).

Group recitation promotes harmony and accuracy as people listen to each other. Priests in their use of words in sermons and teachings may conflict with one another but the chanted texts, memorized and communally repeated, do not change. A major purpose of the three early Buddhist councils was to recite the teachings and check for errors. "Group listening to check for errors is still an accepted method of verification in rural India today" (:148).

Christians Recite

How does this apply to Christian teaching? Consider an example from Pakistan. Over thirty years of ministry, two missionary women have seen 640 Muslims come to Jesus. Most of these converts have continued to be faithful. Memorization of Scripture has played an important role. As soon as a Muslim confesses Jesus, he is required to learn thirty-four specific verses from the gospel of John. If he or she is not literate, he or she has to find some other believer who already knows the verses. The result is that the nonliterates feel empowered. They own the message. Some have become excellent evangelists.

The teenagers in this fellowship, who are literate, receive prizes for memorizing whole books of the Bible—perhaps a radio for Colossians or Philippians, or a bicycle for Ephesians or Galatians. With such motivation, teens immerse themselves in the Bible. Although this ministry has focused on women, today there are eleven pastors who were little boys in this fellowship.

Memorized Scriptures figured prominently in European church history. For example, among the Waldensians, who spread the Bible in the Provencal language at the end of the tenth century, "much of the preaching consisted in reciting long passages of Scripture in the vernacular. Many could not afford an expensive handwritten copy of the Bible, and the ecclesiastical authorities could too easily rob them of such a book, but they could not erase the words which were treasured in the heart" (Nida 1952:83). Memorized Scripture cannot be taken away. Two centuries later,

Wycliffe's "Poor Priests" walked from town to town across England, reading the Bible and reciting extensively from memory.

Western educators devalue memorization. They argue that "rote memory" can be mindless. People in fast-changing societies need problem-solving competencies, not outdated facts. Yet Buddhist-background believers come from a tradition where sacred scriptures are chanted and memorized. They feel honored when they are directed to memorize God's Word. As Marku Tsering observes, "The catechism is a teaching method now out of favor in the West, but it has a long tradition and is much beloved in Tibet" (2005:261).

First passages should be chosen both for content and for sound. The Bible version should be mellifluous. The teacher also should memorize the texts so they can be recited together. In Thailand, veteran discipler Chaiyun Ukosakul suggests several strategies to make memorizing easier. When teaching doctrines, he develops formulaic phrases (1993:244). For example, he encapsulates "the whole history of salvation" in kernel form in four Thai phrases, each of whose second syllable rhymes with the first syllable of the next:

Kum-nerd (the beginning)
Gerd-baap (the origin of human sin)
Prap-tuk (the conquering of the suffering)
Kuk-kao (the kneeling down in prayer)

Rhymes help learners remember. Numbers also can help. Consider the four noble truths, the eight-fold path, or the three jewels in the lotus. At the beginning of his teaching, Ukosakul introduces an overarching framework. All the ideas are hung from this framework. This is important for oral learners, he believes. He also emphasizes a "revisiting strategy," returning to an idea repeatedly in order to reinforce it, rather than presenting it in a block of information just once.

Recently I taught a course on Islam to Brazilians preparing to be missionaries. We discussed a creed based on the names of Jesus which could be memorized and recited in the home, the courtyard, the fellowship group, or the church, "first and foremost worship lifted up to God, and secondly witness or testimony to all those present" (Van der Werff 1989:190-191). Here are a few excerpts:

> I bear witness to the Messiah's names in the Gospel.
>
> The Messiah is the Word of God, eternal with God, of God, as life, light and love incarnated as a human
>
> The Messiah is the Lamb of God who takes away the sin of the world
>
> The Messiah is the Teacher.
>
> The Messiah is Living Water.
>
> The Messiah is Bread from heaven sent from God to all who hunger.
>
> The Messiah is the Light of the world enabling the blind to see.
>
> The Messiah is the Door opening to God's kingdom.
>
> The Messiah is the Good Shepherd.
>
> The Messiah is the Resurrection and the Life who raises Lazarus and is raised by God.
>
> The Messiah is the Way, the Truth, and the Life.

The Messiah is the Vine, his disciples are branches.

The Messiah is king.

Those who believe that Jesus is the Messiah, the Son of God, have life in his name.

By the end of the recitation, several Brazilians were in tears, giving proof of the power of this recitation. Among Buddhists, the word "teacher" or "wise one" might be substituted for "Messiah." When such a creed is spoken, "witness takes the form of a direct recital, an adoring witness, an undebatable praise," allowing the Word and the Spirit to work, rather than our arguments (Van der Werff 1989:189). Evangelism and discipling occur simultaneously.

Learning Through Stories

Once upon a time there was a boy named Suk. When he was ten years old, his whole family was murdered. Because Suk was guarding the rice field at the time, he escaped the massacre. Immediately he fled to the top of a tall tree with creeping vines. Later some sympathetic villagers hid him. But his presence put them in danger. They advised him to try to catch up with a cart which had passed by on the road. Suk chased the cart, finally grasping the wheel frame and hanging on. He begged the driver for help. This merchant had compassion on Suk, and eventually adopted and educated him. When Suk grew up he became a monk, and lived virtuously ever after.

"The Story of Bhikku Suk" is part of a long narrative composed in the late 1800s and widely known throughout Cambodia (Hansen:2003). Today it is part of the standard secondary school curriculum. It teaches Buddhist ethics, Cambodians affirm. Consider the metaphors. Buddhist allusions abound:

*Suk: *sukkha*, “happiness, peace,” opposite of *dukkha*

*Guarding the rice field evokes “guarding” of sensory perceptions and the fruits of *kamma*

*Vines in the tall tree: Thicket of “attachments”

*Refuge: Taking refuge with the householders echoes “taking refuge” in the Buddha’s *dharma.*

*Escape: This word is also used for escape from *dukkha* and from *kamma* and can mean “liberated”

*Cart: This is often a symbol for Buddhism

*Middle of the road: Buddha’s teaching is the “middle path”

*Wheel: Wheel of *dharma* refers to Buddha’s teaching

*Merchant speaks to the boy “in his own language,” just as the Buddha does

*Orphan’s situation parallels that of unenlightened beings

*Merchant liberates him

*When boy is ordained, he brings merit to the merchant and to his dead relatives—grief is transformed to spiritual benefit

According to anthropologist Anne Hansen, the story teaches the listener to ponder “which roads or Paths to follow; and how to define oneself as a Buddhist, a modern person, a Khmer…a moral individual living in the world. Power relationships in this context are morally charged, subject to the workings of karma" (Hansen 2003:831).

This tale often is called "the story of the orphan monk." Images of homelessness and householder are contrasted. The homeless life is a worthy choice. A proverb recommends "leaving behind son and wife, and father and mother, and wealth and grain, and relatives, and sensual pleasures to the limit, one should wander solitary as a rhinoceros horn." Yet, while this may be ideal in theory, it is not realistic from a Cambodian point of view. All beings have to live in relationship with others. Even the hermit in the forest is defined by the others when he deliberately withdraws from them. Even monks have complex social interactions. Suk develops virtuously not by remaining alone and abandoned but by reaching out to build positive relationships, first with the householders who shelter him and next with the merchant who educates him. Suk contrasts with other monks in the narrative who are "mired in the ways of the world," obsessed with material ambitions and occasionally with sexual misconduct and even murder.

Suk's education helps him make moral choices. For the author, Ind, it was not enough to be a monk. Many monks live badly. A monk must be educated in moral thinking. Suk's education builds on the discernment which he exercises from the beginning, choosing wisely and transforming disadvantages into stepping stones to a pure life.

The merchant's story also is instructive. He responds compassionately to the little boy. Although he could have chosen to ignore the boy, he adopts him. This results in "virtuous friendship…the best possible kind of attachment, as it keeps one on the Path" (:830).

Both *dharma* and discernment are lauded in this story. In particular, tensions between detachment and attachment are explored. Some degree of attachment is seen as inevitable. We are fundamentally interconnected. The challenge is to develop virtuous patterns of interaction and to cling to the wheel of the right vehicle.

Why Stories Matter

The story of Suk is part of a long tradition. The Buddha himself frequently told stories. One was about a man who was shot by a poisoned arrow. His friends called for a doctor. But when the physician arrived, the patient was wary. "Who shot the arrow?" he demanded. Even as his condition deteriorated, his questions continued. "What was the shooter's clan? What kind of wood was the arrow made from? What kind of tip held the poison?" The Buddha's application was clear. We can choose to get help, or we can die asking unanswerable questions (Coward 1988:153).

Buddhist missionaries told stories. In the beginning, missionaries from India to China had little success. Then a monk noticed that Chinese loved professional storytellers. Whenever one arrived in the public square, people flocked to hear him. So monks put Buddhist teachings into stories, and trained missionaries to tell them. Buddhism took root all over China (Wang 1986).

Why are stories so effective? They touch us at multiple levels, affecting not only our cognitions but also our senses and emotions. Listening to a story, we are drawn to characters or repulsed by them. We hear sounds, we feel textures, we smell scents.

Stories surprise us. "What will happen next?" we wonder. "How will it end?" And we hang onto the edges of our seats. Stories lead our imaginations from one discovery to another. Because we participate in these discoveries, we remember more.

Even when a story's locale is different from the listener's, often the hearer will identify with the story more than he would with abstract concepts. Because we ourselves live in specific circumstances, we can empathize with concrete story situations. Stories teach by analogy.

Anthropologists employ at least five approaches when analyzing stories as parts of culture systems: content analysis; psychological analysis; metaphor analysis; dramatistic analysis; and ideological analysis (Adeney 1980:1983). What is considered good form varies from culture to culture. Clichés, though disdained in Western literature, are basic to oral art in many countries. In some southeast Asian traditional dramas, stock characterizations and plot elements carry the narrative (Brandon 1967). An actor's speeches are spontaneous to the extent that, given a plot outline shortly before curtain time, he will pull out of his standard oral repertoire the units required such as a love speech or a battle charade. Accompanying musical strains also convey meaning. Each musical motif is associated with some particular action. A knowledgeable listener can follow the plot even when out of visual contact. Such use of formulaic expressions and conventional structures makes it possible to expand or contract a performance, adapting to circumstances.

From a Christian perspective, how should we view stories? The Bible is not primarily doctrines. It is primarily the stories of people who have known God. With David, we experience doubt. With Jeremiah, we experience despair. With Joseph, we experience family rejection. With Abraham, we experience a derailed career. These people are our reference group, our heritage, our roots. And as the book of Hebrews records, when these great men died, they had not yet received fulfillment of all the promises because they were waiting for us. Without us, the story was not complete. We are called to participate in the ongoing story.

Through such stories, God reveals more and more of himself. This is how Christians look at history. Buddhists view history as a circle going round and round. Christians can appreciate the cycle of the seasons, the cycle of human life, the cycles of civilization. But we see something more. History began with God. "In the beginning, God created." History continued as God interacted with people. Jesus validated human history in a special way when, in the words of T.S. Eliot, "the timeless entered time and redeemed it from insignificance"(ref.?). What happened when Jesus entered time colors the way we interpret all stories now. Clearly we see in the story of Jesus that pain is powerful. Sin can win for a time. Yet beyond the cross is the possibility of resurrection. Beyond freedom to fail is grace for renewal.

How to Create Stories

How then can we create effective teaching stories? A good story is both simple and complex. There should be no extra words. Nouns and verbs should predominate. Adverbs and adjectives should be few. Sounds, smells, tastes, textures, and sights should sparkle through the tale. Unnecessary episodes should be eliminated. Each part should build on the previous one or, by contrast, introduce contradiction, conflict, and tension. Anything else should be pruned, until every sentence counts. This is not your grandmother's rambling gossip session. While life is inclusion, art is selection. Yet, in the end, after all that selection, judicious repetition may be employed, following styles appropriate for a given culture.

A good story is also complex. It deals with some ultimate questions. Where did we come from? Why are we here? How can we live in peace and prosperity? Why do we suffer? How can we tap into power? How can we combat evil? Where is justice? Where is the world heading? What is our destiny after death? The more we combine complex multiple levels of meaning and profound questions with simple focus and expression, the greater the story will be.

Missionaries to primal religionists recognize the importance of "chronological Bible storying." Primal religious myths deal with ultimate realities, supernatural powers and supernatural events, both good and evil. Many of these events take place in primordial, sacred time. Key characters may figure in a whole cycle of stories. Myths function to explain, to teach the next generation, to validate behaviors, to integrate a community, to renew power, to allow artistic expression, to enable spiritual transcendence, and to provide for communal catharsis and emotional purging. Myths are serious. In the same vein, Scripture stories should not be seen as mere entertainment to lure people to consider doctrines. Scripture stories are themselves profoundly serious, and should be presented with a degree of awe and reverence.

For such listeners, it is important to place each story in the context of the whole. In his classic book *Communication of the Gospel to Illiterates_*, H.R. Weber says,

> It is fundamentally wrong to treat illiterates as children, and merely to tell them Bible stories. They are much better equipped than many Western intellectuals to see the whole: the complete redemptive history—creation and eschatology; Christ the centre of redemption, and, linked with this centre, the history of Israel and of mission...Every Bible story that is told

> must be set within the framework of the whole history of redemption. Every Biblical figure must be shown as having a part in the great drama of salvation. This is best done when every story is set within the context of liturgy and sacraments. And the whole redemptive drama must be confronted, *expressis verbis*, with the mythological cycle, the mythological frame, thus making apparent to everybody that the Christian faith means revolutionizing all patterns of thought (1957:44).

The Buddhist worldview is different, however. Like the primal religionist it is pragmatic. Unlike the primal religionist, it is ontologically pessimistic. An integrated metanarrative, or a unity to truth, is not necessarily an ideal for Buddhists. The Buddha's simple, unconnected stories have resonated down the centuries. Simple Bible stories may do the same.

Jesus once spoke about a flock of sheep with a 99% success rate. Only one sheep was missing. But the shepherd was not satisfied. He left the ninety-nine safe, and went out in the dark and cold to look for the one. That one mattered. It was not just a temporary psycho-physical event, a drop of water, a candle flame. That one sheep mattered. Christian historian Herbert Butterfield had this in mind when he wrote:

> If a lamb died in May, before it had reproduced itself, or contributed a fleece for the market, still the fact that it frisked and frolicked in the spring is in one sense an end in itself, and in another sense a thing that tends to the glory of God (1957:85).

Everybody's story matters. In the same way, Christians believe, each people's history matters:

> Each generation is …an end in itself, a world of people existing in their own right…Every generation is equidistant from eternity. So the purpose of life is not in the far future, nor, as we so often imagine, around the next corner, but the whole of it is here and now, as fully as ever it will be on this planet…I do not know of any mundane fullness of life which we could pretend to possess and which was not open to the people in the age of Isaiah or Plato, Dante or Shakespeare. Each generation—indeed each individual—exists for the glory of God (Butterfield 1957:89).

God loves stories. We can tell Bible stories. We can springboard from Buddhist stories. We can create new stories.

Learning Through Symbols

A water lily, a candle flame, a drop from the ocean: word pictures like these decorate the *dharma.* We stand on the shore of the ocean of existence, wanting to cross over to Nirvana. We bathe in the *dharma*. We are lamps. We are doers, not just reciters: otherwise we would be like cowherds counting the cows of others.

A metaphor combines two unrelated concepts. This "semantic tension" awakens awareness. Catherine Spurgeon, who produced the classic study on Shakespeare's imagery, argues that metaphors are more significant than topics or themes in text analysis because metaphors usually appear in passages of heightened intensity. For any body of literature, written or oral, we should ask: What are the major symbols? What images do these people mingle? What likenesses do they perceive? What connections are suggested by the conjunction of meanings in each symbol? (Spurgeon 1935).

Metaphors are said to enhance cognitive completeness, expanding meanings which cannot adequately be explained any other way. Compiling and compressing meanings in one symbol packs that image with power. In Bali, Clifford Geertz speaks of the cockfight as a communicative event with five levels of meaning: masculine competition, blood sacrifice, money exchange, status display, and unleashed ids. Combining all these meanings in the single symbolic system of the cockfight underlines its most important theme, "the display of status relationships and the knowledge that they are matters of life and death" (Geertz 1973:447).

Among the Egyptian Bedouin, an anthropologist finds in the lyrics of folk songs a web of connotations that make messages moving and memorable. "Bedouins are sensitive to the graces and evocative power of…metaphors and new images…Even familiar and ordinary images…derive great connotative richness from subliminal intertextual comparisons. Individuals know so many poems that each new one undoubtedly evokes image-traces and feeling-traces from others with shared words, phrases, or themes" (Abu-Lughod 1986:173).

In East Africa, pastor Justin Oforo says, "Important truths must be expressed through symbols. If an idea is stated plainly, we don't take it seriously. If a speaker doesn't care enough to package the idea attractively, we assume it must not be important" (Classroom conversation). But when a speaker draws on the resource bank of a people's own symbols, it shows that the speaker cares.

If this is true elsewhere, it may be preeminently true among Buddhists. Many Buddhist cultures prefer tact to frank confrontations. Symbols solve this problem. In Japan, according to anthropologist Takie Sugiyama Lebra, "only an uncouth person needs a complete frank, verbal message" (1976:47). If you are a person of any refinement, you will find a more indirect way to get your idea across. In Thailand, Chaiyun Ukosakul recommends gracefully "overshadowing" inadequate Buddhist ideas by Christian ideas rather than frontally confronting them. Because of the high value of tolerance in Buddhism, new believers may shy away from direct confrontations, he says (1993:242). As with stories, so with symbols, Christian communicators can use Bible symbols. We can springboard from Buddhist symbols. We can create new symbols. To start, we should immerse ourselves in Bible proverbs and parables, as well as local ones.

Nor should we overlook humor. In some Asian drama genres, there is the tradition of the wise clown. Consider Semar in the *wayang kulit* shadow plays of Indonesia. Although Semar mocks local values, he also serves as a communal therapist, a mediator "standing outside the trees in order to see the forest." The wise clown is the drama's intellectual who integrates discordant elements, rearranging his audience's cognitive configurations (Adeney 1983:409; Peacock 1968:166). Literary clowns are present in Southeast Asian Buddhist countries as well.

In the history of Filipino drama, script writers in successive eras set plays in the foregoing period so as to satirize the current rulers. The Spanish metaphorically were satirized in the first Filipino novel, which was set in Albania (!). The Americans who followed the Spanish were satirized in a Spanish setting. The Japanese who followed the Americans were satirized in an American setting. In the 1980s in Manila's central Rizal Park, I viewed a drama that satirized then-President Marcos. This play was set in a fabled Muslim Filipino kingdom of antiquity. Humorous symbols can be powerful. In our discipling, could we satirize evil habits as tyrants who deserve to be deposed? Satire gives immense pleasure to people at home with the double meanings of symbols.

Yet symbols can be simple. For years, Annette has taught series of Bible stories to Arab women. The women do not read the Bible. They just listen. Every week Annette illustrates her story with a household object—a broom, a loaf of bread, an egg, or a bucket. Later, when a woman who has heard the story sees this symbolic object in her own home, she remembers the story and tells it spontaneously to those around her.

In north Ghana, Christians tell the gospel using rocks. When people there describe their lineage, they place a line of rocks on he ground, one for each ancestor. Christians have added a big rock for God at the head of the line, and more rocks for Bible characters. They have inserted the God rock in the middle of the line to show the Incarnation. These stories are so popular that nowadays some villages keep a pile of rocks at the front gate just in case a storytelling Christian comes along.

Whole stories may be symbolic, like the parables of Jesus. Years ago a famous Thai intellectual, Kukrit Pramoj, wrote a Buddhist reflection on the gospel (1966). He focused on a blind beggar named Simon. Every day Simon shuffled to the market, and sat down at his regular spot. Vendors greeted him. Some slipped him a little food. Buyers stopped to chat. The children of the market blew through like a flock of birds, and some dropped down beside him while they caught their breath. A girl named Ruth befriended him, and they fell in love.

Then Simon heard that Jesus was coming through town, and that Jesus could heal blindness. “Heal me!” he cried. And Jesus did.

What did Simon see? The filth of a poor Asian market. Vendors’ fatigued faces. Children’s malnourished bodies. His beloved, Ruth, who had been so hideously disfigured by a burn that he could not stand to look at her.

Finally Simon saw Jesus crucified. He fell on his knees and cried out, “Oh God, give me back my blindness!”

It is all very well to sit in the West and talk about joy the author commented. It is charming to paste smiley signs on your cars. But if you live in Asia with centuries of floods, fires, tsunamis, earthquakes, drought and dehumanization whether through torture or routine impoverishing corruption, you may need a measure of blindness. You may not be able to clean up the muddy pond. You may simply aim to rise as a water lily and lie clean on the top.

Learning Through Action

The orchestra tunes up. The drummer tries out a riff. The bow slides smoothly over the strings and a haunting melody emerges. Nearby, bamboo poles are tied together, sections lifted, and walls and floor shape a palace for a day. Meanwhile, several boys are taken to the shrine of the village spirit, who must grant permission before the most important Theravada Buddhist rite can begin: the initiation into monkhood (Spiro 1982:238). Customarily the boys will remain monks for three months.

In Myanmar, where the ceremony is most elaborate, the rite has required three days. Time and tight budgets have eroded the ritual, but the ideal remains. A sponsor decides to fund the initiation for a relative or friend. This earns merit for the donor. Invitations are sent to guests. When the day arrives, a fine meal is served to all. The initiates appear dressed like royalty. They sit on the raised platform. In some cases, they ride white horses, shaded by umbrellas, while guests walk in procession. .Village elders lead the way to the local monasteries. Here they bow to the monks, recite Buddhists precepts, and leave offerings.

Over the next two hours back at the temporary palace, a Master of Ceremony alternates sermons, songs (both religious and secular), legends, jokes, and chants with periodic performances by the orchestra. Then it is "time to invite the Buddha to the palace." The initiates bow repeatedly, to their parents, grandparents, relatives, teacher, and kings in general. Rituals are performed with rice, water, cotton thread, a conch shell, and a flower. All spirits—both Buddhist *deva* and Burmese *nat*—are welcomed and offered food and drink. Some clowns perform.

Then the truly Buddhist ritual begins. The initiation commemorates Prince Gautama's abdication of wealth and his simple quest for truth. The boys take off their princely clothes. Their heads and eyebrows are shaved. Each boy dons the orange cloth of a monk, recites precepts, and returns to the palace not as a prince but as a beggar. A monk preaches a brief sermon. The sponsor and his wife pour a water libation, hope that sponsoring this ceremony will gain them nirvana. The monks chant.

The next morning the boys join the local monks in their daily trek throughout the community to receive alms and food. When an initiate comes to his own home, neither he nor his family may indicate that they have any connection.

Action is a powerful teacher. Learning may occur through liturgical reenactments like these, or through drama, dance, object lessons, service projects, or apprenticeships. Whatever the genre, for many Buddhists, "practice is more important than knowledge" (Guruge 1975:45). Pilgrimages, for example, dot the Buddhist world. In Katmandu I have watched with awe as a line of pilgrims circumambulated a great Buddhist center, taking one step forward, then lying flat on their faces on the ground, then pushing themselves up and taking one more step, as they had done for months in order to arrive at this place.

In Indonesia, I have ascended Borobodor, a stone construction as large as a city block. It rises tier after tier up into the sky. On the lower levels, the stone carvings are intricate, elaborate, lyrical, mellifluous retellings of episodes from the life of the Buddha. As one rises higher, the carving becomes sparer, until at the top the decoration is minimal. The pinnacle is said to contain emptiness, the destination we seek as we shuffle off unnecessary desires.

In Japan, a popular pilgrimage on the island of Shikoku follows the steps of the founder of the Shingon school of Buddhism. Pilgrims visit eighty-eight temples. By foot this requires two months, although today most pilgrims travel by bus. On such pilgrimages. the sights, sounds, smells, tastes, cold and heat, and sickness and jokes reinforce whatever is learned so that it sticks in the mind. Reportedly, Buddhist texts say that "he who braves a difficult pilgrimage will gain Nirvana" (100).

How to Teach Through Action

In a reenactment like the Burmese initiation, a church in Illinois set up seven stations of the cross in their sanctuary for Easter. Pastor Skye Jethani observed people moving from one station to another.

> At each one they read a passage of Scripture, and a second reading guided them to use their imaginations to enter the scene with Jesus. Finally a sensory experience gave their minds a tangible symbol. While holding the bag of silver coins, they contemplated what they valued more than Christ. Children lifted a cross that was suspended from the ceiling while considering if they would have helped Jesus carry his

> burden. Newcomers jumped as someone nailed a spike into a beam while Isaiah 53 was read. Some adults were brought to tears as, perhaps for the first time, they traveled with Jesus through suffering…
>
> Our Good Friday this year included no sermon, no worship team, no technology or drama. Still, people lingered for hours to pray, teenagers returned later in the night with their friends, and children begged their parents for the opportunity to stay longer…
>
> Traditionally, discipleship has focused upon two areas—knowledge and skills…While necessary, both these models miss an important aspect of the human spirit. As a result, what captures the imaginations of most Christians is not God's character, story of redemption, or invisible immanence, but rather the values of Madison Avenue…Those filling the pews every Sunday may be full of information about God, and may be trained to obey God, but without an imagination enraptured by God they will be powerless…On Good Friday we helped people enter the biblical narrative with their imaginations (Jethani 2006:77).

Anthropologist Clifford Geertz, author of the essay "Religion as a Cultural System," believed that "some form of ritualized traffic with sacred symbols was the major mechanism by means of which (most people) come not only to encounter a worldview but actually to adopt it, to internalize it" (1966:100). Recognizing the power of ritual, a Christian leader in Thailand recommends contextualized baptism rituals which include parents prominently (Mejudhon 2005), and another in Japan explores the ministry of abortion-resolution rituals (Dominey 2005).

Apprenticeships are also are good ways to learn. Students spend time with teachers, absorbing their lifestyle. Buddhism admires those who model morality and tranquility. A good teachers is a "living Buddha," an "enlightened being" who may serve as "a ferry boat across a worldly ocean" (Ukosakul 1993:254).

There are many stories in the *Pali Sutta Pitaka* that show how the Buddha taught. Often he redirected questions, as Jesus did, so that people would look at their own lives rather than getting distracted by metaphysical abstractions. He taught only what a given learner needed to know. "He carefully tailored his teaching according to his audience's background. He might give a lesson to his followers in detail all at once or in gradual stages. He would first observe the interests and levels of their learning ability. He would then give them his *dharma* at the appropriate level, shallow, middle or deep" (:105).

In general, Buddhists are more like Hebrews than Greeks in their learning style. There is a dialectic between inquiry and life. Knowledge has to be applied. Teaching spiritual disciplines like meditation, prayer, fellowship, and fasting can meet this need.

Even our words should be active, Ukosakul recommends. When talking about stages in Christian growth, for example, he rephrases categories so that verbs are primary. "We can employ functional phrases such as 'Devote Myself Daily' instead of referring to 'Quiet Time'; 'Submit to God' instead of 'Obedient Life'; or 'Guide Me' instead of 'God's Will and Guidance'" (:246). Similarly, when he teaches about God's nature, he begins with what God does in order to show who God is.

Action learning can be simple. We can listen to a Bible text and compose a detailed creative response. For example, we can turn each verse into a prayer. Or we cam create a song that incorporates major words and themes from each verse. In Asia this may be done best in a group. The group should be composed of peers who feel free to disagree with each other. Age and gender may be considerations. To maintain accuracy, at least one person should have access to the actual text.

Some people learn best in the middle of hustle and bustle. When asked what they missed most about Buddhism, some Burmese Christian converts answered, “The noise and crowds of religious celebrations!” Perhaps at times a glorious chaos and confusion should be our teaching context!

The quiet practice of Zen lies at the other extreme. Tending a stone garden, making tea, arranging flowers, or sitting in silence may order the soul to the glory of God—provided the meditation is not just an emptying but also an immersion in God’s Spirit and Word. Christians detach to attach, like branches to a vine.

Learning Through Songs

“Daddy, was it your dad’s preaching that made you decide to be a Christian?” I asked one afternoon. My grandfather was a pastor.

“No,” answered my dad. “I think it was my mother’s singing.”

Why Songs Matter

Songs teach. In his book *Everything You Need to Know for a Cassette Ministry*, Viggo Søgaard says a new believer from Buddhist background can learn twenty new songs a week with no effort if these are recorded onto a cassette (1975:102).

Songs also keep our memories accurate. When Bible teaching is oral, and every speaker can add his own twist to the text, the teaching may get bent out of shape. But rhythm and melody help to stabilize a text. "The fact that messages are sung helps faithful transmissions because the melody acts as a mnemonic device," says Jan Vansina in Oral Traditions as History (1985:16). In his thesis, *A Manual for Cross Cultural Christians with special Emphasis on Papua New Guinea*, Kevin Hovey adds:

> Even more important than the memory-proneness of material set to music is its ability to resist change, an automatic process in the relaying of information in a non-literate situation (Goody and Watt 1968:30). Primrose, quoting Lloyd Binage, claims that musical materials are the only oral communications accurately transmitted over extended periods of time in East Africa (1974:30)…As Tippett has said, "If folklore is best taught in poetic idiom, most probably this would be the best way to teach the Bible" (1978b).

Admittedly, this varies from culture to culture. The Yoruba of West Africa want their singers to shape messages afresh every time they perform, while the Somalis on the other coast demand that certain kinds of poetry be repeated as exactly as possible. In general, however, songs contribute to stabilizing texts. In his thesis on Discipling Nonliterates, Robert Primrose advises: "To make the material memory-prone, it would need to be given appropriate rhythm and music settings. In fact, all material which must be remembered exactly may need musical and rhythmic settings to render them memorable" (1976).

Songs help us party. We have a God-given need to celebrate. In many cultures, drink and drugs seem to be the natural way to party. By contrast, Ephesians 5:18 counsels, "Do not get drunk on wine, which leads to debauchery. Instead, be filled with the Spirit. Speak to one another with psalms, hymns, and spiritual songs. Sing and make music in your heart to the Lord." As a result, there is a singing Church all around the world, following in the steps of Jews who poured out songs of ascent as they walked to Jerusalem.

Songs also help us cry. Buddhist-background believers often suffer for their faith, as well as from normal human troubles. Songs of lament provide us with an outlet for howling our anguish before the Lord.

Finally, songs help us witness. Even when Buddhists do not want to hear preaching or testifying, they often are entranced by songs. A friend who has traveled extensively for the Education Department in Laos has often found herself at family firesides in the evening where there is no electricity. "Would you like to hear a song or two?" she asks. Her Lao Buddhist/Marxist hosts are delighted, as is her official Lao Buddhist/Marxist guide. Songs can be powerful witnesses, if songs appropriate to the context are chosen.

How to Create Songs

In his thesis, *Toward an Indigenous Hymnody*, Eugene Goudeau suggests practical strategies for creating songs. Nurture local composers; facilitate group writing; run contests for hymns on particular subjects; borrow from near cultures; and commission non-Christian musicians (1980). In his article "Developing an Indigenous Hymnody," Delbert Rice distinguishes four song genres among the upland Filipino people where he lives: ceremonial music (*baki*); conversational music (*ba-liw*); recreational music (*dayomti*); and proverbial music (*gomigom*). The local church has chosen to create songs in three of these genres (1971).

Clearly, it is not just a matter of finding a good tune; the roles of songs and singers in the culture must be studied. In some places, singers and actors are assumed to be immoral, given their public, traveling lifestyle. In other cases, certain genres may be sung only by certain genders, ages, or classes. The lyrics in these songs may yield instructive contrasts to leaders' "discourses of power." A study of the songs of Japanese nannies illustrates this (Tamanoi 1991). In some cases, songs may express ideas which have no other outlet. Among the Bedouin of Egypt, anthropologist Laila Abu-Lughod listened to her friends burst into simple folksongs marked by vulnerability and longing. Since everyone's situation was well known, the causes of these feelings were clear. Yet the singers never would talk about their feelings. They seemed unable to give voice to their passions except through song. Abu-Lughod came to believe that songs were necessary to provide balance in the Bedouin worldview (1986).

Like other media, songs are an arena where people can explore difficult dilemmas and integrate complex themes. In "Song of Our Spirits: Possession and Historical Imagination among the Cham in Cambodia," anthropologist Ing-Britt Trankell discusses this (2003). During curing trances, mediums are possessed by spirits from the historical royal court of Champa. The trance songs help the singers and audience work through

> Not only the ancient military defeats of the Cham by the Vietnamese, but also the people's more recent sufferings under the Khmer Rouge... (so that they) come to terms with both ancient and recent experiences of victimization as well as complicity, suffering as well as guilt, and express ethnic consciousness and pride...symbolically reunifying ethnicity and lost national autonomy (2003).

In Christian history, one body of song that approaches this complexity is the corpus of African-American spirituals, which probe the depths and the heights of human and Christian experience. Both the African and the Cham songs integrate art with

Spirit. Anthropologist John Bowen, in a general review article on Southeast Asia, suggests that this tie is likely regardless of genre. Asian art often includes dialogue with gods or spirits (1995:1053). To ignore the spiritual dimension is an artificial Western compartmentalization.

Shiokari and Eucatastrophe

A small train chugs up a mountainside. On board is a Christian. During the journey, a tragedy occurs: the brakes fail. The train begins to slide backward. The Christian passenger chooses to sacrifice his life. He throws himself under the wheels, stops the train, and saves the people.

This is the plot of *Shiokari Pass*, an award-winning novel and movie by the Christian author Ayako Miura. Japanese see this passenger as a Christ-figure. To embrace suffering is noble. Miura herself valiantly spent seven years in a body cast in a tuberculosis sanitarium after World War II. To embrace suffering for others is seen as Christian. It was Japanese theologian, Kazoh Kitamori, who published *The Theology of the Pain of God* in 1946. God in Jesus enters human pain, pouring his love on us. We can channel this love outward. Rather than destroying desire, we can dare to care.

"Eucatastrophe" is the term that J.R.R. Tolkien coined to describe this pain/grace phenomenon. Tolkien was thinking about fiction. Tragedy and comedy are classic ways to handle narrative. The literary power of tragedy is great. Yet because Jesus died and rose, there is such a thing as a happy catastrophe.

Tolkien's *Lord of the Rings* trilogy illustrates this. Reflecting on Tolkien's character Frodo, award-winning novelist Katherine Patterson says,

> A great novel is a kind of conversion experience...The fake characters we read about will evaporate like the morning dew, but the real ones, the true ones, will haunt us for the rest of our days...We Christians have done a lot of preaching about sin—much of it incomprehensible and much of it doing nothing except laying on guilt and despair...But those of us who have followed Frodo on his quest have had a vision of the true darkness. We know that we, like him, would have never gotten up the steep slope of Mount Doom had the faithful Sam not flung us on his back and carried us up, crawling at the last...When we read fiction that is true, we do not say, "There but for the grace of God go I"—rather, "Here I am" (1988:59).

Such great themes of the Christian faith must flow through our teaching. This seems obvious. Yet often it does not happen. There is a gap between those concerned for appropriate methods—like oral media—and those concerned for adequate content. Because artists produce unsystematically, the Church tends to relegate their creations to pre-evangelism, Easter or Christian events, or youth or mission entertainment. Once people are attracted, the Church reverts to sermons, propositional Bible studies, and literacy programs.

Clearly this is not right. Oral learners need oral media. Yet that media must be filled with balanced teaching. So we must develop accountability structures. We must check that our oral creations reflect key doctrines: God (theology), Jesus and salvation (Christology and soteriology), Holy Spirit (pneumatology), human nature and the created universe (anthropology), church (ecclesiology), and completion of God's plan for creation and history (eschatology). When we discover gaps, we must fill them.

Systematic teaching can be woven through stories or songs or rituals. Some years ago there were young Christians in three Muslim-majority people groups in the Philippines. Most were not literate. Because of political violence, few outside Christians could enter the region. I discovered that they composed ballads. So I proposed a plan: sponsor a two-week ballad-writing workshop. Bring together ballad writers and Bible teachers from each of the three groups. Commission them to compose two long sets of ballads in each of the three languages. First, a set of biographical ballads, spanning from Adam to John on the island of Patmos. Second, a series of doctrinal and topical ballads.

Armed with this body of song, a fisherman or a rice farmer or a mother sweeping her courtyard could sing systematically through the major themes of Scripture. They could go through the hours of the day in the company of Moses and Hannah, Daniel and Esther, Paul and Lydia, and Peter and Dorcas, that great cloud of witnesses. They could learn what they believed through song.

To serve oral learners, we ought to pray for the Lord to raise up poets and composers and performers just as specifically as we pray for evangelists and teachers and medics. We ought to bring artists, songwriters, and dramatists to join forces with Bible teachers and curriculum specialists. We ought to sharpen our teaching songs and teaching through constructive criticism, and hold our creative artists to high standards of accountability. In short, we ought to pour our Bible teaching into appropriate media. How else will the peoples praise Him?

5

THREE REASONS WHY CHRISTIAN WITNESS TO BUDDHISTS HAS FAILED

Terry C. Muck

This article is built on a negative premise which I will begin by describing and defending. The premise is this: the Christian mission movement has been a failure when working with cultures that have a dominant Buddhist element to them. For the purposes of this article I will generously define failure as at least a century of mission effort producing less than twenty-five percent of a culture coming to know Jesus Christ as Lord and Savior.

No culture that has a dominant Buddhist element to it has ever been a Christian mission success—that is, more than twenty-five percent of the people in the culture embracing Christianity.

Korea has come the closest. The most recent figures I have seen for South Korea has between twenty-five and thirty percent of the population identifying themselves as Christian. But if you add North Korean figures to it the figure falls below our failure threshold. Other Buddhist countries don't even come close. Consider nine Buddhist countries:

Burma:	Buddhist: 73%	Christian: 8%
Bhutan:	Buddhist: 78%	Christian: 1%
Cambodia:	Buddhist: 86%	Christian: 1%
Japan:	Buddhist: 55%	Christian: 3%
Laos:	Buddhist: 43%	Christian: 3%
Mongolia:	Buddhist: 23%	Christian: 1%
Sri Lanka:	Buddhist: 68%	Christian: 9%
Thailand:	Buddhist: 83%	Christian: 2%
Vietnam:	Buddhist: 49%	Christian: 9%

Add up the figures of these Buddhist countries and we find that the Christian mission movement has produced in the aggregate less than five percent Christian populations, despite almost two centuries of mission efforts.

Lest we might think that this is the norm for Christian mission efforts, let me compare it with the results from two other heavily missionized parts of the world, Oceania and Africa.

The first mission workers went to Africa in the seventeenth century and by 1900, ten million Africans knew Christ, that is, ten percent of the population. By the year 2000 360 million Africans had become Christian, forty-six percent of the population.

The first mission workers went to Oceania, the South Sea Islands in the 1843 (Neill 1964:419). By 1900 an astounding seventy-six percent of the population were Christian (five million people) and by the year 2000 eighty-three percent professed Christ—twenty-five million.

I should say a word about what “failure” means when we talk about Christian missions. In order to make my point I have chosen to define success and failure in terms of the number of people who become Christian. There are other important ways to talk about success and failure when it comes to Christian mission, ways that were I attempting to make almost another point, I would prefer to embrace. Those other ways can be handily summarized in the word "faithfulness." Thousands of Christian mission workers have gone to Buddhist cultures and "succeeded" if by that we mean they were faithful to their calling and proclaimed the gospel.

And even if we use the definition of success that I am choosing for this article, numerical success, there may be many reasons why people have not come to Christ in significant numbers in Buddhist cultures. It may be that political conditions were not right. It may be that it has not been in God's good timing that the gospel would take root in these cultures. If those are the reasons, then there is nothing to do about them but to continue to be faithful.

But I would like to suggest that we consider other ways to present the gospel to Buddhist peoples that may have a better chance of numerical success now. I would like to raise three issues that might make a difference.

Reason #1: Identity—Oversimplifying Who Buddhists Are

The first is the failure to take seriously the dependence classical, textual Buddhism has on being embodied in folk religion forms in Southeast Asian countries especially. The interdependence, actually, between this high religion and the local folk or popular religion in different contexts, creates a worldview that is often oversimplified by outsiders in such a way that the full impact of the gospel story is muted. Typically, Christian witnesses either overemphasize textual or elite Buddhism (what we might call the "religious studies" mission approach) or overemphasize the folk religion aspect (what we might call the "anthropological" mission approach). They reduce Asian Buddhists to one or the other. Or perhaps it is more accurate to say that they reduce their mission approach to one or the other. In some cases this is based on what might be called wishful thinking, based on the success Christian mission workers have had with animist populations in other settings. See above for the statistics, for example, on success with African animists. Perhaps if we treat Asians as if they were Africans, the thinking seems to go, they will become what we want them to be and we will have better success. Needless to say, this does not work.

Most Southeast Asian Buddhists are bicultural in this sense, a cultural complexity often overlooked by Christians attempting to contextualize the gospel in local forms. Actually, this cultural complexity is being even further accentuated with urbanization and globalization. This additional dynamic makes many Southeast Asian Buddhists tri-cultural, by adding modernization to the ancient mix of Buddhism and folk religion. Ways to address this problem include, first of all, a simple recognition of this fact of cultural complexity, and secondly, an understanding of how Buddhism in particular aligns itself with folk religious forms. My point here is that different world religions all have similar needs for being embodied in folk religion forms, but do it in different ways because of the teachings of their high religious tradition.

In short, three factors must be taken into account in addressing the complex religious identities almost any modern culture faces in a globalized world. The first is the issue of identity formation in the world today—how is identity formed today and how might the advocacy of introducing a new Christian religious identity be fitted into that process. Second, what is it about Buddhism itself, particularly the elite textual form of Buddhism, that influences how it combines with folk religions and secular ideologies in today's world? And third, what does one look for in terms of the specific local context in which one is working that will give us clues regarding combining factors?

Identity Formation

Manuel Castells, the guru of world identity scholarship, identifies (in *The Power of Identity*) four identities that all people are either born to or socialized in (2003). The first is *legitimizing identity*, the identity we take on because of to whom we are born and the primary socialization we receive from that birth group. The identity question at this point is not Who am I? but Whose am I? The second is *project identity*, the identity we take on when we come to the age of majority, whatever that might be in the social group, and either are assigned or choose an occupation, or more broadly, a way of being in the world. We quickly become what we do to a large extent. Perhaps the most important identity in the complex societies into which we are born these days is Castells' third identity factor, what he calls *resistance identity*. Resistance identity really is what we are because of what we are not—what we do not want to be. When we meet other people, we form part of our identity by seeing we are not the other person. In the process of deciding what and who "others" are, we also decide what we are not. "Others" includes not just other individuals but other ethnic groups, other cultures, other religions, and other social classes. Identity formation is not just a positive process but a negative, eliminative process as well. The resulting identity each of us assumes we might call a hybrid identity, a combination of legitimizing, project, and resistance identities.

As you can imagine, in most cultures, the number of possible factors contributing to these three identities is growing exponentially. Whereas in the past, young people met a finite number of others, depending on their location and the exposure their parents granted them, today the number is very large indeed. When one factors in "electronic" others, others we meet on film and television, thousands is probably too low a number to determine in terms of resistance factors. And it is not just the sheer numbers of identity influences that matters. The quality of interactions with "others" determines how important those contacts become in determining who we are. It makes a difference whether or not the others abuse us or confuse us or infuse us with positive role models. Each of us chooses, consciously and/or unconsciously, how important various identity forming factors are. Take just one example, the example of religion. I may identify myself as a Buddhist, but one person may consider their Buddhist-ness to be the most important thing in their life, another may consider it incidental.

My colleague at Asbury Theological Seminary, anthropologist Michael Rynkiewich published an article in *Missiology: An International Review*, in which he attempted to identify all the identity creating factors that influenced villagers in Papua New Guinea, the field on which he worked for years (2007). The resulting complexity of what were usually considered to be simple villagers was truly mind-boggling.

Buddhist Combining Factors

Of course, the way people combine their identity-producing factors is a combination of cultural determinism, free choice, and random chance. Perhaps the single most important factor after birth and occupation is the major religion one is socialized into. Religion rises to the top largely because it is one feature of human existence that is explicitly concerned with identity formation. Religious forces want people to identity with their teachings, with their worldview. And religion has an advantage in the project because religion claims ultimacy, that is, it claims that its identity is the very most important one because it has eternal consequences.

Yet not all religions are the same in the way they consider identity formation, particularly when it comes to combining factors with other identity producing influences. It is a well known phenomenon that wherever Buddhism has gone in the world it has shown it self especially adept at forming partnerships with local indigenous religions. The Buddha did not consider indigenous religions a threat under normal circumstances and acknowledged that his followers would continue to practice some of their local traditions in their developing spirituality. It would not be incongruous to the Buddha today that his followers range from being Bon-Buddhists in Tibet, to Shinto-Buddhists in Japan, to Taoist-Confucian-Buddhists in China, to, increasingly, Christian-Buddhists in the West. We might say that Buddhism has a high combining quotient. Two elements of the *buddhadharma* especially make this possible:

The first is the relativity of the doctrinal element of Buddhism. In the Parable of the Raft, the Buddha said that while a raft (the analogue to doctrine) needs to be built and used to cross the river of *samsara* (phenomenal existence), it is no longer necessary once one crosses the river

The second is the teaching of no-self (*anatta*). If the permanence of personal identity is actually a delusion to overcome (by either enlightenment or a better rebirth), then the measure of what is a good and bad personal identity becomes a pragmatic consideration rather than one of eternal importance. The question is whether or not a particular identity produces good karma or bad karma in a particular context.

Together these two factors might mean that in our desire to make Christian identity the primary one in the Buddhists we meet, we probably don't need to be too concerned with residues of Buddhist identity that come along in the process. Since Buddhists consider those to be temporal identifiers anyway, they can fall away or not. Of course at some point Christian teaching demands full commitment. But perhaps not all at once. Aren't we in it for the long haul anyway?

Local Contextual Factors

We cannot decide this all at once. There is no one method that fits all because every local context is unique. So all we can give here is an example. Let's consider a Thai setting. In a short book, *Folk Buddhism in Southeast Asia*, the authors consider how Buddhism has combined with local rice-goddess myths (Bowers 1999). In some cases the myths have remained free of Buddhist influences and exist alongside the more recent Buddhist teachings. In other cases the myths depict a conflict between the rice goddess and the Buddha, probably reflecting a very real social dynamic that occurred in history as Buddhism won its way. And in still other cases the myths have evolved to reflect an integration between indigenous animism and imported Buddhism. Logically those would be the three possibilities to look for in any cultural context, of course, but one might not find them all in each setting.

The important missiological factor as one seeks to express the gospel of Jesus Christ is that since identity producing factors will tend to be more and more universal among people in direct relation to the smaller and smaller size of the demographic unit you choose to work with, people in well defined geographical areas will tend to respond to the gospel in similar ways. But it takes real work to identity the distinctives in each setting. We might call this the work of religiously exegeting local cultures.

Reason #2: Grace—Gospel as Free Gift

The second is a problem with an accurate contextualizing of the central Christian doctrine of grace. If grace is understood as God's free gift of redemption to undeserving sinners, then mission workers telling the story would be wise to understand how specific cultures understand the concept of gift-giving, and whether or not they have an understanding of the concept of "free gift." Marcell Mauss, in his classic study of South Pacific cultures and their understandings of gift giving, claims those cultures have no real concept of free gift, and gift giving is an elaborate system of obligations and formal social requirements (1954). My thesis is that Asian Buddhist cultures have a very different understanding of gift giving (*dana*) that has to do with karma and merit making. This means that if the gospel of grace is presented in the same way to Asian Buddhists as it has been to South Pacific traditional cultures, and other indigenous cultures, it will be heard quite differently. One of the reasons we have been enormously successful in the South Pacific is that the message of free gift is an extraordinary relief to obligation bound traditionalists; but in Asia, freedom from the obligation to give a return gift is considered one of the essential attributes of a well-given (and received) gift. In Asian, and specifically Buddhist cultures, we must talk about the extraordinary concept of grace in a different way than we do in either indigenous, or Western, cultures.

Let me talk about this by first of all stating two theses:

Thesis #1: The message of grace is free gift—that God through Jesus Christ gives us a gift, salvation, that none of us either deserve or can earn. This is an amazing offer. Yet it is a message that no culture on earth can live up to. It is not too much to say that the primary mission task is to bring this message of free gift to all.

Thesis #2: Different cultures fail to live up to free gift in distinctly different ways. All cultures have gift-giving protocols that distinctly color the way they hear the primary message of Christian gift-giving, that is, grace. The savvy missioner will tailor his or her description of Christian grace so that it answers the way a particular culture places roadblocks in the way of the clear articulation of the gospel's free gift.

I am suggesting that one of the reasons we have failed in Buddhist cultures is that we have not yet presented the gospel of grace in a way that connects with the Hindu-Buddhist understanding of gift-giving or *dana*. We have either presented it in a way that we have found works with indigenous cultures in Africa or Oceania, or we have presented it in the Western way, in a way that connects it with market-oriented economies. Since contrast is a good way to learn and explain, let me briefly summarize those three approaches to gift-giving and receiving—the indigenous, the Western, and the Asian—and then suggest that we have figured out how to best offer the concept of free gift to indigenous and Western, but not as well to Asian. Of course, this is an oversimplification, an ideal type paradigm, and specific contexts will be more complex than this three part typology might suggest (see number one above on complex identities). But it may be useful as a starting place, and set the task before us.

Indigenous Gift Giving

Indigenous gift giving is the kind of gift-giving common to most subsistence cultures. As we mentioned above, Marcel Mauss described this kind of gift-giving economy well in his classic work. He noted that in indigenous cultures, a complex set of obligations attend the giving and receiving of gifts, the nature of the gifts to be given, and the rewards for following the protocols and the punishments for not living up to them. Systems such as these, such as potlatch in Northwestern United States Native American groups, *kula* in Trobriand islander groups, and *pilou-pilou* among the Melanesian groups, differ in detail, but one unified in their recognition of obligations (1954).

In such a setting, the most effective presentation of the gospel focuses on grace or free gift as an antidote. For people's who find themselves overwhelmed with obligations they sometimes exhaust all of their resources to meet, the gospel of story is seen as a welcome relief. By accepting the gospel, one is freed, ultimately at least, from those obligations. The contextualizing challenge in such cultures is to then show how grace and free gift can be combined with indigenous gift giving obligations so that cultural practices are not totally abandoned but sanctified or transformed so as to be compatible with Christian free gift.

Western Gift Giving

Western gift giving is the kind common to market oriented cultures such as the United States, Europe, and most urban areas around the world. Quid pro quo market exchanges become the measure of one's success in gift giving in such cultures. My Christmas card list, for example, increases and contracts, based on who is or is not sending me Christmas cards in return. The language of gift used in such gift giving economies often seems like it is the language of free gift, but the language of free gift often disguises an underlying reliance on reciprocity and blessing—sometimes the disguise is remarkably thin.

In such a setting, the most effective presentation of the gospel has more often than not focused on the congruence of market economies with grace economies. It is not hard, for example, to find in Christian bookstores, arguments that capitalism is the preferred exchange system of the Bible and early church. The contextualizing challenge in such a setting is that one worries that we have over-contextualized the gospel into market systems, where important features of grace are being lost or underplayed. Some theologies of sanctification, for example, overplay the obligations for holy living we all live with; others overplay the capacity we might have for earning our salvation—if we offer enough gifts to God in the form of prayer, charity, and holy living, then cannot help but bless us.

Asian Gift Giving

Asian gift giving is most often associated with what economists often call redistribution or managed economies, where caste or class rules dominate everything about cultural exchanges. One gives in such cultures because the rules of one's caste determine what, when, how, and to whom to give. In India, for example, elaborate texts called *dharmasastras* articulate gift giving in some detail, outlining different rules for different groups of people. Some of these *dharmasastras* are devoted solely to *dana* or gift giving protocols. The distinctive thing about such systems is that the obligations of gift giving—and there are many—have little to do with obligations incurred by receivers of gifts but with spiritual progress and merit that accrue to the gift-givers. In fact, the most pure gifts are given by those who expect absolutely nothing in return, and received by those who are holy themselves—and feel no obligation at all to return the gift.

In such a setting, the idea of free gift is already assumed, as an ideal at least. As we usually present it, the gospel of grace tends to come across as a ho-hum, we-already-know-that message. We need to rethink how we talk about grace in Buddhist cultures in a way that will both show its importance and uniqueness. And that uniqueness lies mostly in the nature of the gift itself. The gift of grace is not a gift that brings one merit, that is, it is not a means to an end of spiritual progress of one sort of another. It does not lead to a better rebirth. The gift of grace is an end itself, something that relativizes everything else about family, caste, indeed, life itself.

Reason #3: Meekness—It's The Attitude

The third is an issue most clearly identified by Nantachai and Ubolwon Mejudhon, that effective Christian mission in Thailand (and other South Asian cultures) must be done with a different attitude than has been traditional of Western Christian missionaries. They call the attitude of choice, "meekness." When compared with the more traditional Western mission attitudes of triumph and victory, meekness doesn't appeal to market oriented mission agencies. But the Mejudhons convincingly show that Thai Buddhists are just as repelled by triumphalism as Westerners are repelled by meekness. The Western way is the aggressive way. The Thai way is the meek way.

The mission implications seem clear. In accordance with Paul's admonition to become what ever we can in order to make the gospel appealing to our audiences, meekness seems the order of the day. It doesn't hurt that the Bible and Jesus had some very good things to say about meekness. "Blessed are the meek for they shall inherit the earth," is a pretty clear statement as to its value. Those who have spent any time at all in southeast Asia have probably heard the Mejudhons' thesis (1998). Thus, I will not repeat it; their work is available for you to read.

But I would like to develop it a bit by looking at it from a slightly different angle. Attitude is not something that either simply appears nor something that can be changed at will. Attitude is often dependent on other factors, particularly the way we articulate the issue at hand (that is, cognitive, rational factors) and the way we behave, the actual way we carry out our missions (that is, volitional factors). Actually, historically, there has been quite a bit of disagreement among Western psychologists about where attitudes, that is, emotions and predispositions come from. Some claim that we are either born with or socialized into certain ways of emotionally responding to the world, and that those predispositions are part of our enduring personality package. Others, such as the great American psychologist William James, claim the reverse, that we do actions and appropriate emotions follow. A simple example: if you want to love unlovable people, that is people you find repellant for some reason or another, you cannot simply make yourself love them. James said that the way to do it is to decide to do some actions consistent with loving a person—charity, for example—and that after you do those actions for a while, the appropriate emotion, love, will follow.

Similarly, by rationally constructing mission goals that are consistent with the appropriate culturally emotion, in this case, meekness, and performing mission in that way, the appropriate emotion, meekness, will follow. Let me use an Asian example by citing a traditional Indian Sanskrit text, a satirical play called in

English *Much Ado About Religion*, a play that illustrates a fundamentally different approach to the religious other that is so at odds with the way rationalistically oriented Westerners view issues of religious pluralism. I conclude that this way of looking at the religious other can be seen as at least as congenial with a number of important biblical admonitions, particularly in the Beatitudes and stories of Jesus' mission efforts, than the more market-oriented approach we tend to be using.

I provide a synopsis of the play, written by Bhatta Jayanta and published by New York University Press (2005). This is one of the volumes of the new Clay Sanskrit Library, an ambitious series of translations and annotations of classical Sanskrit literature into English. *Much Ado About Religion* (*Agamadambara*) is a play that satirizes the relationships among competing religions in ninth century India, particularly Hinduism, Buddhism, and Jainism.

It is the story of a young Vedic "seminary" graduate, Sankarshana, who takes on as his life's calling the unmasking of the heterodox sects of Buddhism, Jainism, and the ascetic life in general. In a series of encounters with the leaders of these movements he brilliantly exposes them as frauds and defeats their religious teachings as false. The play ends, though, not with the victory one would expect for Sankarshana, but his humiliation as an arrogant, young know-it-all who does not really understand life, and the Buddhist, Jain, and ascetic leaders are shown to be the real heroes, appreciated for what they do know, not denigrated for what they don't know.

This is a surprise ending for those of us who are Western Modernists. Sankarshana had clearly defeated the others with his Vedic philosophical arguments. He should have won—but didn't. For Jayanta's Hindu readership, however, it was a confirmation of one of the core values of Hindu India. The question was not how does the one relate to the many, but how do the many make room for the one? (As an aside, it is intriguing to see that core value challenged in present day India by the Modernist thesis which has infiltrated right wing Hinduism and continues to threaten the stability of that society.)

How do the many make room for the one? This is not just a sanskritic insight. It was clearly Jesus' concern also. His eye was always on the sparrow, not the flock. Perhaps the most articulate rendition of the teaching was in his Parable of the Lost Sheep:

> What do you think? If a man owns a hundred sheep, and one of them wanders away, will he not leave the ninety-nine on the hills and go to look for the one that wandered off? And if he finds it, I tell you the truth, he is happier about that one sheep than about the ninety-nine that did not wander off. In the same way, your Father in heaven is not willing that any of these little ones should be lost (Mt. 18:12-14).

I remember clearly my Sunday school flannel graph about the parable of the lost sheep. The shepherd is seen leaving the locked gate of the ninety-nine sheep in the fold to go look for the one. The ninety-nine are safe. The text, however, does not support that. The shepherd leaves the ninety-nine exposed on the hillside in as much danger as the one lost. Jesus did not operate according to the prevailing market mentality—protect your majority assets by not risking them for what you do not have. He risked everything for the one lost sheep. Ninety-nine sheep in the fold are not worth more than one in the bush.

Mother Theresa, to use a more modern Christian example, was similarly disposed, not market savvy at all. When told her little House of Charity operation in Calcutta, India was nothing more than a drop of water in a huge ocean of suffering and could never make a dent in India's poverty, she replied, "I don't use mathematics the way most people do. I count the one we help, not the thousands we are not able to help."

Conclusion

Now, what do these three suggestions have to do with the oral nature of the gospel? More, perhaps, than first meets the eye. When the gospel is expressed orally, we are putting it into play, so to speak, in a specific context. A great responsibility rests on the person expressing it. He or she must do his or her very best to shape the speech to match the truth of the gospel. It is no excuse to say that this is difficult because of the thousands of languages, the millions of words, the near infinite number of cultural contexts, the vagaries of how different people in this single expressional moment may hear what is said, and so on. It is difficult, but difficulty is no excuse. The responsibility remains. We must do our very best.

It so happens that the three areas we have identified, identity, gift-giving, and humility are three areas that are most abused through the oral expression of the gospel. Consider Buddhist identity for example. We have suggested that one of the reasons for failure in witness to Buddhists is because we oversimplify the religious character of people who live in Buddhist cultures. Why do we do this? Perhaps it is at least in part because we unconsciously want to make the other person into an image we can handle with relative ease. We want to be done with knowing who they are and what they might say. That allows us the freedom, then to say our piece uninterrupted by subtly and complexity. In the story we mentioned above, this was the Vedic student's error. He defeated the simple, abstracted thought of his opponents, but in so doing overlooked the complex human beings standing before him.

Oral expression, no matter how it looks, is not a monologue. It is a constant back and forth between two or more people, and much more than simple words or ideas come into play. When philosophers of language talk about the performative aspect of truth, they are referring to this broader, multifaceted aspect of oral exchange that measures not just words said, but actions taken and emotions felt. A first step towards allowing and acknowledging this relationship that occurs the minute we open our mouths is to acknowledge the complex nature of this person's identity, the almost unfathomable richness of another human being.

The oral complexity of gift giving, of free gift, of Christian grace, takes a little different form. Here the danger is to talk about grace as if our language and accompanying actions are graceful. It is one thing to believe in grace. It is quite another to live one's life according to it, and it is often in the oral expressions wc use to tell the gospel story that we become the most un-graceful. Again, it may be that our failure here is unconscious, also, as it most often is with misreading identity. And, again, it is no excuse to plead that only God can be perfectly graceful.

How often do we say the words of grace, but mean the words of personal advantage. How often do we say the words of free gift, but play the role of seeking obligation? How often do we give the gift of the gospel with a patronizing gesture and a condescending heart? This, then, is the final treason, to say the right words, but for the wrong reason, to paraphrase T.S. Eliot.

It is only when the extraordinary difficulty of giving full expression to the gospel of grace becomes apparent to us, it is only then we are ready to speak the Word. This, of course, is why humility is such an indispensable part of the mission worker's make-up. Only when we are brought to our knees, pleading for God to give us an honest assessment of ourselves so that we can make neither the mistake of overestimating our gifts nor selling ourselves short—only then are we ready to serve. Only then can we hope to be a small part of what it will take to have Buddhists hear the gospel truly from our lips. And only then can we truly wait upon God's good timing to bring fruit to this part of the vineyard.

May it be so.

PART II

COMMUNICATING CHRIST THORUGH STORY AND SONG IN BUDDHIST CONTEXTS

6

FROM THE BIBLICAL WORLD TO THE BUDDHIST WORLDVIEW: USING BIBLE NARRATIVES TO IMPACT AT THE HEART LEVEL

A. Steven Evans

It boggles the mind, considering how to help one make the leap from the world of Buddhism to the world of Christianity. Buddhism seems so extremely different—distinctly one in the triad of religious thought that weighs the idea of no god against belief that there is a myriad of gods, as Hindus and animists believe; or against the truth that there is only one true God—the Almighty Creator God, who is holy and just and who seeks relationship with his people. “What can be done to convince them?” one may ask. “What arguments can be conveyed? What logic can be employed? What lifestyle can be manifested?”

The answers come when we realize that it isn’t logic or apologetics, nor is it behavioral science, that will convince people of the relevance to their lives of Jesus’ incredible claim, “I am the way, the truth, and the life; no one comes to the Father but through me” (Mt. 14:6 NASB). It is when we help others experience the loving redeeming God who is active throughout history by proclaiming His Word in appropriate and effective ways that they can see that the Gospel is indeed relevant to them and that it is Good News.

But how do we do that? That is the question addressed in this article. Set before us is a process of discovery, looking at a biblically-modeled narrative proclamation of the Word of God, providing a basis for sharing the stories of God's Word in culturally appropriate and worldview sensitive manners to those of the Buddhist world in order to touch them at the heart level. Before proceeding, however, it may be important to clarify what is meant by various terms used throughout this article, such as "world of Buddhism," "world of Christianity," "worldview," "biblical worldview," "culture," and "heart level."

It may be appropriate to start with the term "worldview." The most common understanding of the term by both secular anthropologists and Christian missiologists deals with the question of perceived reality. Therefore, one's worldview is actually one's perceptions of reality, whether true or not, and how one interprets reality. As such, worldview is the "lens" through which one sees the world around him or her and the "map" by which one navigates in or responds to the world. Some mistakenly equate the idea of worldview with that of culture, but culture is only one of many expressions of worldview. Other expressions include beliefs, values, behaviors, etc.

It could be said that every individual has his or her own worldview. This is true. Organized groups of individuals, however, can also have a collective worldview, whether it is that of a family, neighborhood, village, city, district, nation, religion, ethno-linguistic people group, or race, among others.

Simply put, "culture" can be defined as everything that is part of one's everyday life experience. Behind that simple definition, though, are some very complex indicators. Culture explicitly or implicitly reflects the learned behaviors of a society and the artifacts a society uses to symbolize or identify itself. It should be made clear from the beginning that God does not seek to destroy culture; it is His desire to transform it.

The concepts of the "world of Buddhism" and the "world of Christianity" in the context of this article deal less with Buddhist or Christian culture, which varies from place to place, and more with the idea of a Buddhist or Christian worldview. But even this can pose problems, especially when it comes to the idea of a specific Christian worldview. What is a more satisfactory is understanding that "biblical worldview" (not to be mistaken with biblical culture or the culture of the Bible) takes precedence over a "Christian worldview" in that it addresses the issues of reality from a biblical perspective, where a Christian worldview can be construed by some to include the culture of specific groups of Christians in various locations or of various persuasions throughout the world. It should be noted that similar problems can exist among differing perceptions of Buddhism as well.

The very concept of God is a fundamental issue where Christians and Buddhists have differing worldviews. This has nothing to do with culture, whether Christian culture or Buddhist culture, Western culture or Asian culture, Himalayan culture, or urban culture. However, this one unique element of worldview, the concept of God, shapes differing values, beliefs, behaviors, social structures, and even laws, for each community. We will take a closer look at the Buddhist belief system later in this article in an attempt to have a better understanding of Buddhist worldview that is common through Buddhism around the world.

The idea of reaching Buddhists at the "heart level" will also be explored at length later in this article. At this point it may only be necessary to say that many, if not most, cultural anthropologists, cross-cultural communications specialist, and Christian missiologists concur that stories, whether experienced "live" by real life events, or told and retold by a people in community, not only reveal worldview, but influence, shape, and transform it as well. It is not through intellectual assent, nor is it by deductive reasoning, propositional logic, or abstract analysis that leads one to question his or her own perceptions of reality (the realm where concepts of a "higher being" lie). It is through processing truth embedded in "story" in all of its connotations as it touches the very core of one's being (at the "heart level" so to speak) that causes one to either consciously or subconsciously evaluate and even question existing worldview issues and change them when deemed beneficial to the individual. Life transformation takes place.

Bible narratives have the ability and power to reach into the very core of one's life and touch him or her at the worldview or heart level, transforming one God-ward, and instilling experience, understanding, and expression that weren't there before.

> I will open my mouth in a parable; I will utter dark sayings of old, which we have heard and known, And our fathers have told us. We will not conceal them from their children, But tell to the generations to come the praises of the Lord, And His strength and His wondrous work that He has done (Ps. 78:2-4 NASB).

The Bible is God's storybook. In its parts, it consists of multiple stories, each able to stand on its own merit. Combined, the stories present His story, able to speak to all people, in all places and at all times. God loves a story, or so it seems, and He uses the Book to preserve His story, while He uses people to proclaim it. How do we know? His Word says so.

Consider three specific Old Testament stories from the Word of God. The first is of Moses just before his death. The second takes place about 800 years later, during the reign of Josiah, king of Judah. The third is about 400 years after that, when Nehemiah had charge of rebuilding the destroyed city of Jerusalem. These three stories clearly indicate that it is God's purpose for His Word to be preserved in the Book, as well as proclaimed by His people (Deu. 31-32; 2 Kg. 22-23; Neh. 8).

God told Moses that His Word was to be written down, archived, and watched over by the priests against the day when His people would forget all about God and what He had done for them. At that time, the Book of the Law would be His testimony. God then instructed Moses to take a song that God had given him and put it in the mouths and on the lips of God's people, so that it too would be a testimony to God when His people would forsake Him. That song was about the "Rock," and all throughout Scripture, and even to this day, the "Rock" has special significance to God's people.

Eight hundred years later, what God foretold came to pass. During the reconstruction of the Lord's Temple in Jerusalem, the Book was discovered, and as it was read to King Josiah it was a witness for God, a testimony of who He is and what He had done for His people. Josiah was moved to tears at hearing God's Word, but he was convicted and distressed as well, because what he heard also described the judgment and punishment God would inflict upon His rebellious people. God blessed Josiah and his during his lengthy reign as king, he led the people to be a people of righteousness.

Four hundred years later, after Nehemiah engineered the rebuilding of the city of Jerusalem, God's people called for Ezra the priest to stand before them and read from the Book. They listened and heard as they stood in honor of the reading of the Word. The Word of God was translated for the people so that they could understand it, and as they heard it, they worshipped God and wept, because they did understand, and it brought joy to their hearts and initiated revival among them.

God's storybook is a book of His stories with purpose and with power, as another story, about David and Bathsheba, demonstrates. Ultimately, however, Scripture reveals that stories may be God's preferred method of communication, shown in the story of Jesus and the parable of the sower, the seed, and the soils. Both events illustrate that God, indeed, loves a story and uses them for His purposes (2 Sa. 11-12; Mk. 4:1-34).

The story of David and Bathsheba says that King David got in trouble for being in the wrong place at the wrong time. In Jerusalem, while his armies were out fighting a war, David saw a beautiful woman and wanted her, so he ordered her to his palace and he slept with her. The woman, Bathsheba, became pregnant, and David had her husband murdered and took Bathsheba as one of his wives. That angered God and He sent His prophet Nathan to confront David. Nathan told David a story of a rich man who ordered the slaughter of a poor man's pet lamb and fed it to a visitor. David was incensed and said, "That man must die!" "You are the man," Nathan responded. David was convicted of his sins and pleaded with God to forgive him.

Here we see how powerful a story can be as God used one to confront David with his sin. Now let's see how the use of story was

Jesus' preferred method of conveying God's Word to the people around Him.

The Gospels say that Jesus spoke to the crowds using parables or stories. One such story was the parable of the sower, the seed, and the soils. After he told this story, one of his disciples said to Jesus that they didn't understand it. He told them, "You've been given understanding about the Kingdom of God, but to those who can't see it yet, because their eyes are blinded and their ears are blocked, everything comes in stories, making them ready and receptive, nudging them toward insight and understanding." Jesus then explained the story to them, saying that the seed was the word of God. Through the story and its explanation, Jesus conveyed that it was His intention for the Word to be heard, received, understood, responded to, and reproduced.

Jesus then told more stories about the Kingdom of God, and it is at this point that the writer of Mark says that with many stories like these Jesus spoke to the people, sharing the Word with them, presenting His message to them, "but only as much as they were able to hear it and receive it. He was never without a story when he spoke, and when He was alone with His disciples; He went over everything, explaining what the stories meant."

A Matter of the Heart

"The heart does not respond to principles and programs; it seeks not efficiency, but passion," said authors Brent Curtis and John Eldredge in their book *The Sacred Romance*. "Art, poetry, beauty, mystery, ecstasy: These are what rouse the heart. Indeed, they are the language that must be spoken if one wishes to communicate with the heart. It is why Jesus so often taught and related to people by telling stories and asking questions. His desire was not just to engage their intellects but to capture their hearts" (1997:6). They argue that we have lived for so long in a "propositional" approach to Christianity we have nearly lost its true meaning. "Life is not a list of propositions," they said, "it is a series of dramatic scenes. Story is the language of the heart. Our souls speak not in the naked facts of mathematics or the abstract proportions of systematic theology; they speak the images and emotions of story" (1997: 39).

It seems that many of us now approach the Bible with the same scientific-like curiosity as any other interesting object of study, leading us to an inability to read God's Word as a sacred or holy text. "Our archaeological and increasingly literary approaches to the Bible bring us ever new insights into its sources and construction," said Andrew Walker, author of *Telling the Story: Gospel, Mission and Culture*. At the same time, we should be lamenting "the loss of the scriptural mind." He said, "This loss, this failure to see the wood for the trees, is endemic in the modern Church. We no longer know what the gospel means." (1996:12)

"The gospel was originally a storytelling tradition," said Thomas Boomershine, in his book *Story Journey: An Invitation to the Gospel as Storytelling*. "This storytelling character of the gospel is reflected in the history of the word." He explained that the word "gospel" is a shortened form of the old English word *godspell*, which means a good story or tale that has power, and that the definition of the Latin word *evangelium* implies "a tale whose telling had power," while the Greek word *euangelion*, which has the root word *angelion* meaning angel or messenger, denotes "good news." All three incorporate the idea of one whose shares the message, as well as that of the message itself (1988:16). "The Church now tends to think of the gospel as a set of abstract ideas based on the study of the canonical documents but divorced from story," Bommershine said. "The gospel has lost its original character as a living storytelling tradition of messengers who told the good news of the victory of Jesus." He concluded, "telling biblical stories is foreign to contemporary experience. We continue to read Bible stories to children. But the assumption is that once you grow up and learn to think, you will stop telling stories and start telling the truth. Telling the truth means that you will speak conceptual abstractions" (1988:17). The gospel is just not the message of the Good News. It is both the Gospel story and its telling.

"When Jesus opened his mouth and spoke, what came out, more often that not, was a story," said Eugene Peterson, author of *The Message* translation of the Bible. "His stories draw us into a reality where we find ourselves in touch with the very stuff of our humanity. We discover that there is something more to life, something that we didn't quite see or understand before" (1999:7).

> Jesus throws these simple little stories into our ordinary lives and we think, "What is this doing here?" They appear so commonplace, so insignificant. We expect big things from a teacher the stature of Jesus – bold headlines, eternal truths, religious thunder. But these Jesus-stories are so unpretentious. More often than not, one or another of them lodges unnoticed in our consciousness and then, unexpectedly, begins to release insights, create new perspectives, shift the very ground beneath us so that we find ourselves reeling, reaching out for support. When the story is allowed to complete its work, the sole support we find ourselves grabbing onto is God.

> Jesus was once asked by his friends why he told stories. He responded that he told stories "to create

> readiness, to nudge people toward receptive insight." His stories, besides inviting us into a larger world than we presently inhabit, pull us into it as participants. These are not stories that entertain, that let us sit back on a bench watching the action. We become the action. These stories don't just tell us something new. They involve us in what has been sitting right in front of us for years but that we hadn't noticed, hadn't thought important, hadn't considered to be connected to us and our lives.
>
> And then suddenly we do notice. The story wakes us up to what is there, and has always been there. Without leaving the world we work and sleep and play in daily, we find ourselves in a far larger world. We embrace connections and meanings and significance in our lives far beyond what our employers and teachers, parents and children, our friends and neighbors, and all the so-called experts and celebrities have told us for so long (1999:8-9).

Without intellectual assent or intentional behavioral change, the stories enter the heart and affect change. As Peterson said the individual proclaims, "what are these doing here?" but then finds himself embracing the truths embedded within the stories. "All of a sudden we see things and people we had never noticed before. We hear words and sentences that make sense of what we've had intimations of but couldn't quite place" (1999:7).

Missiologist and cultural anthropologist Charles Kraft said, "For solid changes to happen throughout a culture, people must make basic changes in the worldview of that culture. Just as a tree can only grow as the roots allow it to, so a culture and the society that lives by that culture can only function as well as their 'worldview-habits' allow them to" (2002:2.12).

> Jesus knew this. When he wanted to get across important points, He aimed both at worldview and at consistency between belief and behavior. He sought to change both paradigm and practice. Someone asked, "Who is my neighbor?" So He told them a story and then asked, not the expected question, "Who was the neighbor? – a question about their worldview assumptions. Instead, he asked who was being neighborly, a more important question designed to challenge their behavior. He was leading them implicitly to reconsider and, hopefully, change a basic value down deep in their system and explicitly to change their behavior to match the worldview change. He wanted them to move first to, then through a paradigm shift into a practice shift, the practice of being neighborly, not just believing they should treat outcasts as neighbors (2002:2.12).

British theologian N. T. Wright has a similar perspective. "Stories are a basic constituent of human life," he said. "They are, in fact, one key element within the total construction of worldview. Stories thus provide a vital framework for experiencing the world. They also provide a means by which views of the world may be challenged" (1992:38-39).

Wright argues that this is why Jesus so often told stories, particularly parables. Jesus intended them to challenge the existing Jewish worldview and to provide an alternative picture of reality Jesus called "the kingdom of God" or "kingdom of heaven." Wright said that people's stories" come into conflict with each other because worldviews and the stories which characterize them represent the realties of one's life. People are threatened by the intrusion of an opposing worldview or story because it challenges their understanding of reality. Wright said, "The only way of handling the clash between two stories is to tell yet another story" (1992:42).

Understanding Buddhist Worldview

What is written in ink can fade away by a single drop of water;
what is written on the heart will last an eternity.
(Traditional Tibetan proverb)

The heart of Buddhism is expressed in the "Triple Refuge." Every Buddhist recites the Triple Refuge (sometimes called the Three Jewels or the Three Treasures) daily, and one becomes a Buddhist by reciting it three times: "I go to refuge to the Buddha; I go to refuge to the doctrine, I go to refuge to the community." Included in the triple refuge, then, are the place of the Buddha, his teachings, and the role of the Buddhist community.

The teachings of Buddhism are less concerned with theology than they are with human suffering and achieving freedom from that suffering. Summarized in the Four Noble Truths, which are common to all types of Buddhism, are the teachings that: 1) human life inevitably involves suffering; 2) suffering arises from desires; 3) there is a state of being in which there is no suffering; and 4) there is a way to achieve this state of being. The way to achieve it, Buddhism teaches, is through a systematic approach called the Eightfold Path of Liberation. The Eightfold Path offers ways to cast away any demerits, avoid accumulating new demerits, and accumulate merit for a favorable rebirth. The eight factors that comprise the Eightfold Path can be divided into three broad categories dealing with wisdom, ethics, and meditation.

Wisdom includes right understanding and right intention. Right understanding refers to making sense of the world and questioning one's assumptions. Right intention involves the application of right understanding in one's life and constitutes the core of Buddhist morality. Specifically, right intention includes renunciation, benevolence, and nonviolence.

Ethics is concerned with conduct and the rules that underlie appropriate conduct. They ensure that one's conduct is harmful neither to oneself nor to others. It includes right speech, right action, and right livelihood. Right speech focuses on avoiding gossip, lying, slander, and other kinds of idle or hurtful language. Right action involves the avoidance of: 1) violence toward any living thing; 2) stealing; 3) harmful speech; 4) sexual misconduct, and 5) abuse of drugs and alcohol. These are known as the Five Precepts. Right livelihood ensures that one's way of earning a living does not violate any of the Five Precepts.

Meditation includes the final three factors in the Eightfold Path: right effort, right self-possession or mindfulness, and right meditation. These are closely related and basically involve the cultivation of the wholesome and rejection of the unwholesome–continuously striving to reject unwholesome states of mind and to develop the mental quietness that leads to liberation.

It is hard for much of the non-Buddhist world to understand Buddhism's lack of concern for or interest in a personal God. "It is important to note that the Buddha did not actually deny the existence of God," said Timothy Reagan, author of *Non-Western Educational Traditions*. "Rather, the Buddha argued that curiosity about such matters was like a man who, upon being wounded by a poisoned arrow, refused to have it pulled out until he was told the caste and origin of his assailant, his name, his height, the color of his skin, and all the details about the bow and arrow. In the meantime, he died" (2000:145). Buddhist speculations concerning the origin of the universe and any creator it may have are considered immaterial; it may postpone deliverance from suffering by engendering ill-will in oneself and in others.

It is important to understand that there are two schools of thought in the Buddhist world: Theravada Buddhism and Mahayana Buddhism. Theravada Buddhism emphasizes the original Buddhist scriptural tradition and is sometimes called the Southern School, since it is primarily found in the south Asian countries of Sri Lanka, Myanmar, Thailand, Kampuchea, and Laos. Mahayana Buddhism is known as the Northern School, found in Nepal, Tibet, China, Korea, Mongolia, and Japan. Theravada Buddhism is somewhat austere and involves an emphasis not only on the early Buddhist scriptures, but also on the monastic life. Mahayana Buddhism accepts a wider variety of scriptural traditions and gives greater freedom in terms of devotional beliefs and practices than does Theravada Buddhism, which tends to be more uniform.

Some worldview issues evident in the Buddhist belief system deal with refuge, suffering, truth, the concept of "right" (i.e. right speech, right action, right understanding, etc.), nonviolence, meditation, benevolence, morality, liberation, and merit. Underlying questions to ask concerning all worldview issues are, "If this is so, then what does it mean? What is the significance of it? How do I respond to it? How does the Bible respond to it?"

To understand the Buddhist worldview is to understand the Buddhist mind and heart. To understand the Buddhist mind and heart is to be equipped to select appropriate stories from the Word of God to address the complex issues found within Buddhism. In assessing and understanding Buddhism, it is important to look for those bridges, barriers, and gaps that can either help or hinder reception of the Gospel message – the Good News of Jesus Christ.

Two popular Buddhist folktales are *Empty Cup Mind* and *A Monk with Heavy Thoughts. Empty-Cup Mind* illustrates the value and sometime, necessity of changing worldview, that of replacing the old with the new. *A Monk with Heavy Thoughts* takes us from the mind to the heart, emphasizing the necessity of speaking to the heart and not just the mind.

Empty Cup Mind

> A wise old monk once lived in an ancient temple. One day the monk heard an impatient pounding on the temple door. He opened it and greeted a young student, who said, "I have studied with great and wise masters. I consider myself quite accomplished in Buddhist philosophy. However, just in case there is anything more I need to know, I have come to see if you can add to my knowledge." "Very well," said the wise old master. "Come and have tea with me, and we will discuss your studies." The two seated themselves opposite each other, and the old monk prepared tea. When it was ready, the old monk began to pour the tea carefully into the visitor's cup. When the cup was full, the old man continued pouring until the tea spilled over the side of the cup and onto the young man's lap. The startled visitor jumped back and indignantly shouted, "Some wise master you are! You are a fool who does not even know when a cup is full!" The old man calmly replied, "Just like this cup, your mind is so full of ideas that there is no room for any more. Come to me with an empty-cup mind, and then you will learn something" (Yolen 1999:3-4).

A Monk with Heavy Thoughts

> As two Buddhist monks walked along a muddy, rain-drenched road, they came upon a lovely woman attempting to cross a large mud puddle. The elder monk stopped beside the woman, lifted her in his arms, and carried her across the puddle. He set her gently down on the dry ridge of the road as the younger monk discreetly admired her charms. After bowing respectfully to the woman, the two monks continued down the muddy road. The younger monk was sullen and silent as they walked along. They traveled over the hills, down around the valleys, through a town, and under forest trees. At last, after many hours had passed, the younger monk scolded the elder, "You are aware that we monks do not touch women! Why did you carry that girl?" The elder monk slowly turned and smiled. He said, "My dear young brother, you have such heavy thoughts! I left the woman alongside the road hours ago. Why are you still carrying her?" (Forest 1996:39).

These two folktales are not merely stories for the sake of entertainment. They have been told and retold, passed on from generation to generation, because they are both entertaining and instructive. They teach as well as reflect Buddhist worldview. The truth embedded within them is also biblical, Christian truth as well, by the way. These two stories are used here to illustrate the power of the story in Buddhist culture, as well as provide examples of how the use of stories is a culturally appropriate, accepted, and effective communication method for conveying truth within that culture. This has been the case for many, many centuries.

A narrative approach to religion, encouraging Buddhists to draw closer to faith, is not a new notion. For the ancient Buddhist mystic

Drukpa Kunley, born in 1455 AD and fondly called the Divine Madman by the peoples of Bhutan and Tibet, life was not measured by eight hours of sleep per night or three good meals a day on the table. There was more to life than this, he would say. Though some may laugh at some of his stories and be embarrassed by some of his antics, Drupka Kunley fully understood the power of story and song and the emotions they evoked. He knew that people – ordinary, everyday people who worked hard, believed in God, and supported their rulers – needed to laugh, cry, be shocked, and even be outraged sometimes, to give them a broader, better understanding of life and themselves, leaving them content with what they had around them and within them, rather than seeking after things that would never be.

According to Dugu Choegyal Gyamtso in the book *The Divine Madman*, "[Drukpa Kunley's] style, his humour [sic], his earthiness, his compassion, his manner of relating to people, won him a place in the hearts of all the Himalayan peoples…He may not have been the greatest of scholars or metaphysicians, although he left some beautiful literature behind him, but he is a saint closest to the hearts of the common people…For the common people it was Drupka Kunley who brought fire down from heaven, and who touched them closest to the bone" (Dowman 2000:23). The life, stories, and songs of Drupka Kunley touched, stirred and even changed the lives of the common people in a time when they so desperately needed it. He is a successful example of what the storyteller and his tales can do in the Buddhist world.

So it is that Bible narratives, consisting of the foundational stories of our faith reflecting biblical worldview, combined with more Bible stories that tug at the heartstrings and tickle the very core of one's being, causing him or her to reflect on the issues of life that define reality, shape concepts of God, and provide the basis for right and wrong, can be used as catalysts for worldview transformation and life change. They can lay a foundation for understanding the activities of God throughout history and can point the way to Truth incarnate, Jesus Christ himself.

A well known Buddhist proverb says, "A divine prophecy is required if an enlightened priest is to be born" (Thinley 2005:63). That should be encouragement for us to tell the stories of old (the Old Testament) to pave the way for the coming and significance of the new (Jesus). We also want to share the life and teachings of Jesus, as well as the stories of His death and resurrection, in order to provide a clearer picture of the heart, character and plan of God the Father. A glimpse into the life of the disciple in the fellowship of community can also be conveyed through the stories of Acts.

There are several examples in Scripture of a comprehensive chronological narrative approach to sharing the Word of God. "Oh give thanks to the Lord, call upon His name; make known His deeds among the people," Psalm 105:1 says (NASB). The psalmist then recounts the story of Abraham, Isaac, and Jacob and how it was God's intention to establish His people through them and their offspring. He then moves on to Moses and Aaron and the miracles of God performed in the land of Egypt to convince pharaoh to let God's people go. Finally, the psalmist tells of God's people wandering in the wilderness and how God was visibly with them and how He provided for them. Psalm 106 almost begins where 105 leaves off. It starts in Egypt, crosses the Red Sea, and goes into the desert wilderness, citing in detail the activities of God and His people.

In a similar fashion, but in greater detail, Nehemiah 9:5-37 tells how the children of Israel repented, prayed, fasted, and read from the Book of the Law. Then the Levites offered a lengthy "word" to the people, beginning with creation. They then moved to Abraham, Egypt, crossing the Red Sea, God leading the children of Israel as they wandered in the wilderness, the giving of the Ten Commandments, entering into the Promised Land, and going into the times of the prophets and kings.

The book of Acts has several examples of a chronological narrative approach to proclaiming the Word. One shining example is found in Acts 7:2-53. This is Stephen's defense just prior to his death by stoning. Stephen began with the story of Abraham, then alluded to Isaac and Jacob. From there he told the story of Joseph and moved on to Moses. He then told of Joshua, David, and Solomon, and ended with some of the prophets. What Stephen told was so powerful, Scripture says, that "when they heard this, they were cut to the quick" (Ac. 7:54). Stephen then prayed to God and verbally alluded to God, Jesus, and the Holy Spirit. At that point, he was put to death.

Likewise, in Acts 13:16-41, Paul, who was present during Stephen's stoning and had to have heard Stephen's message, proclaimed to his listeners the Word of God starting in Egypt and going on to the land of Canaan. He touched on the judges and prophets (specifically mentioning Samuel), then told a story of the two kings Saul and David. From there he told of the Savior Jesus. At that point, Paul went into depth concerning the life, death, and resurrection of Jesus.

Finally, brief mention must be made of Hebrews 11 and what is commonly called "the roll call of faith." After providing a definition of faith, the author of Hebrews cited example after example of those deeded faithful, beginning with Abel. Following Abel is an exhaustive list of those people of faith: Enoch, Noah,

Abraham, Isaac, Jacob, Sarah, Joseph, Moses, Rahab, Gideon, Barak, Samson, Jephthah, David, and Samuel. Interspersed among all these names are the deeds of both God and man, providing evidence for why they are included in such a significant "roll call."

The Selection of Biblical Narratives

"The profound truths from God are housed in the simple stories of the Bible," said Indian mission leader Sam Abraham. "God wrote the Bible as seventy-five percent narrative or story, fifteen percent poetry, and ten percent exposition. We are to use the whole story as God gave it and then to go back and discover the spiritual truths the story contains" (2006:1).

Abraham likes to share a story that illustrates how "hidden treasures" can be discovered in God's Word:

> Once there was a man who left his village and went to the city to work. In the many years he was in the city, the man earned a lot of money. Finally, he returned to his home whereupon everyone greeted him as a great friend. This newly wealthy man wanted to use some of his money to give gifts to his true friends, so he thought of a plan.
>
> He left his village for a day and then came back. Then he called everyone together who was saying, "I am your friend," and he asked them to come meet him at the other side of the nearby hill. The wealthy man gathered the people who came and then made an announcement. "I've been working on the path that goes to the river. If you follow the path, you will find some treasures. Now go. Find my gifts for you."

So the people left and started walking down the path. A few people stopped and picked up some dirt from the path. They said, "Let's go home and study this dirt for awhile." Others ran down the path toward the river. When they reached the end of the path, they complained, "We know this path well. There is nothing new. We didn't see any treasure."

The rest of the people walked along on the familiar path. As they moved along, they kept talking with each other saying things like, "Look at this old fallen tree our friend moved out of the way to make our walk on the path easier." Other walkers noticed that the thorn bushes had been cut back to make the way safer.

Instead of running down the path to find the gifts, these people began walking even more slowly, so that they could enjoy the results of the hard work that their wealthy friend had done for them. They recognized that the path itself was a gift from their friend.

Suddenly, one walker stopped, and called everyone over to look. "See by the side of the path here, under this bush. There are jars of sweet potatoes." Then another walker called out, "Look over here, back from the path. I found a big box of brand new cooking pots."

Again and again, the slow walkers kept discovering hidden treasures just off to the side of the path. They realized that these gifts had been placed there for them by their rich friend. The wealthy man knew that his true friends would trust him and love his path, and then they would be the ones to discover the gifts he had placed there for them.

> Those who had rushed down the path that had been lovingly prepared by the rich man missed all of the treasures. They did not go slowly so that they could fully appreciate the path, or the path maker. And those who decided to study the dirt on the path are still studying. They still have not yet traveled the path! (2006:4-5).

"Every story in the Bible is a path prepared for us by God," Abraham said. "Those who will walk slowly through the path of a Bible story can discover hidden treasures, gifts of truth from God. We call the truths that God weaves into every Bible story 'treasures.' The treasures are two kinds: spiritual insights and practical applications." God always has a plan for everyone in each story. "From what those characters in the stories learn (or don't learn), we need to discover what God wants us to learn" (2006:5).

Coupled with the fact that stories are an appropriate channel of communication for oral communicators, there are three criteria for selecting stories: 1) the situation of the moment, where carefully selected Bible stories meet a specific crisis, need, or occasion in someone's life; 2) the desire, need, or opportunity to present a selected panorama of Bible stories spanning Old Testament themes, the life of Jesus, and the book of Acts, where a foundational understanding of God's Word is desired; and 3) the necessity for sharing carefully selected stories to answer questions and increase understanding where there appears to be either a conflict or connection with the hearer's culture and/or worldview or there is a desire to know more of biblical themes and application.

Truth from the Biblical stories can be ascertained not by going into "teaching mode" after sharing a story, but by helping the listener personally discover it through the asking of questions:

"What do you discover about God? What do you discover about humankind? What applications can you make to your life?"

In Dharamshala, the Tibetan capital-in-exile and home of the Dali Lama in the Himalayan region of north India, there was a certain Buddhist monk who began to question the philosophies he held. It was his desire to learn more about this Jesus of whom he had heard. He encountered a Christian familiar with the storytelling method of sharing the Bible and heard stories on the life of Jesus. The monk became so intrigued that he is now investigating the entire Bible through hearing and contemplating a narrative panoramic presentation of the Word of God (Abraham, personal conversation).

Likewise, a Buddhist family in the same region of India experienced crisis after the kidnapping of their child on the border of Nepal. Not knowing where to turn or to whom to turn, they heard of a concept of God unfamiliar to them through the showing of a film that presented a panoramic view of the stories of the Bible from Genesis to Revelation. They became intrigued with the idea of a Creator God who had a personal interest in His created beings. They are now seeking to broaden their understanding of God and the Bible by going through the Bible story-by-story. Not only that, but these stories have had such a profound impact on their lives that they themselves are sharing them with colleagues, friends and neighbors (Abraham, personal conversation).

The challenge is before us. We can choose to be more effective in communicating the inherent truths from God's Word simply by sharing the story and helping the listeners discover truth for themselves. At the same time, we can use our knowledge of Buddhist worldview and heart-level issues to be sensitive in our selection of which stories to share or not that can impact them at a personal level and possibly meet specific felt needs in their lives.

7

THE USE OF STORY AND SONG IN SINHALESE BUDDHIST FUNERALS

G.P.V. Somaratna

A funeral brings family and friends together, and encourages them to share their inner feelings. Funerals provide a support system for the bereaved, helping the bereaved to understand that death is final and reinforces the fact that death is a part of life. It encourages the embrace and expression of pain. It reaffirms one's relationship with the person who died. It also offers a time to share memories of the dead, to talk about life and death, and to say good-bye. Since Christianity is a religion of relationships it provides an opportunity to comfort and share the good news with the bereaved neighbors. This study is on the use of story and song in communicating the gospel to the Sri Lankan Buddhists through Sinhalese Buddhist funeral practices particularly the traditional Christian *Pasan pota.*

The Buddhist Concept of Death

According to Buddhist teaching death is the cessation of physical life of an individual existence. It is not the annihilation of the cycle of births and deaths, for though a particular life span ends, the force which hitherto actuated it is not destroyed (Narada 2000:440). Death is an inevitable occurrence that a person faces in *samsara.* Life is regarded as an unceasing series of rising and falling moments, through *samsara*, a series of births and deaths. Death is merely a dramatic ending of a continual process. In the very next instant after death, rebirth takes place. Rebirth is instantaneous (Narada 2000:451). The person receives another life after the death (Wijesekera 1986:96). Death is not caused by a deity, but is a continuation of a mechanical process in another form of life.

Death is regarded as an occasion of major religious significance by the Buddhists in Sri Lanka. It is believed that it marks the moment when the transition begins a new mode of existence within the round of rebirths of the deceased. They believe that all the merits and demerits that the dead person accumulated during the course of this lifetime and previous existence in *samsara* would automatically be activated in order to determine the next birth.

Popular Belief of Death

Popular Sinhalese Buddhist belief is that the spirit of the deceased dwell in a temporary state, known as *preta*, until it finds a suitable place for rebirth. According to Buddhist teaching *preta* does not undergo the process of conception and birth. It appears instantaneously as a full grown being. In Hinduism and Buddhism, a *preta* is a type of evil spirit. It is especially the evil spirit of the dead person. Often those who die due to execution, accident, suicide or with greed and dissatisfaction become *preta* spirits. Therefore people protect themselves by resorting to various ritualistic practices. The person can remain a *preta* till it receives another life. In Buddhist lore *pretas* are evil, flesh-eating spirits or demons of the dead. They are the result of restless souls.

Sadness at Death

When a person dies he falls into the stream of *samsara* and is lost to the loved ones left behind. A person is ordinarily liable to be reborn in one of the thirty-one planes of existence, after his or her death. Even a person who has done good deeds is not definitely certain where he or she will be reborn. One cannot, therefore, be sure where the dead person would be reborn. The options are so numerous that the person is gone like a drop of water fallen into the sea. Therefore the loved ones who are left find it very sorrowful. The Buddha has stated that the death and birth are both sorrowful. Death is a powerful reminder of the Buddhist idea of impermanence.

Funeral Ceremony

Sinhalese Buddhist funeral ceremonies are associated with the above mentioned beliefs regarding death. Funeral rituals provide an opportunity to assist the deceased person as he or she moves on to the new existence. The message of impermanence, and the opportunity to help the departed loved one, find expression in the Buddhist funeral rites of Sinhalese Buddhists.

Transfer of Merit

The *sangha* plays a prominent role in the funeral proceedings, because they act as agents of transfer of merit from the living to the dead. One of the most important part of the funeral rites is the ritual of transferring merit from the living to the dead person through an offering of clothes known as *mataka-vastra*, to the *sangha* assembled in the cemetery prior to the disposal of the body. The proceedings begin with the administration of the Five Precepts to the assembled crowd by one of the monks. This is followed by the recitation of stanzas in Pali showing the impermanent nature of life. Then they invite the deceased to take a share of the merit.

There is also the ritual of pouring water, to transfer merit accumulated by the living relatives and friends to the dead. This ritual is an act of transferring merit to the departed in order that they may find relief from any unhappy realm wherein they might have been born. This ritual goes back to the teachings of the Buddha, when King Bimbisara was harassed by a group of his departed kinsmen, reborn as *pretas*, because the king had neglected the ritual of giving alms in their name to the Buddha. When the king offered alms to transfer merit to the dead ones as requested by the Buddha, the *pretas* became content and stopped being a nuisance any more (Kariyawasam 1995:46). Thereafter the Buddha preached the *Tirokuddha Sutta*, where he explained the concept of Transference of Merit (*pattidana*). According to this teaching these spirits become contented and bless the donors in return after these rites are performed.

Other funeral rituals where the *sangha* are involved would be known as *mataka-bana* (memorial preaching). The usual practice is to conduct a monk to the house of the dead person, generally on the third day or on the seventh day after the funeral. A *bhikku* (ordained Buddhist monk) would be requested to preach a sermon suited to the occasion. The assembled audience would consist of the deceased person's relatives, neighbors and friends. At the end of the sermon, the *bhikku* would lead the relatives in reciting the necessary stanzas to transfer the merit acquired to the deceased. Similarly, three months after the date of death, *sanghika dana* (an almsgiving) in memory of the deceased would be performed. These rituals may be repeated annually if the family is capable of bearing the cost. The purpose of these rituals is to impart merit to the deceased.

The basis of the practice is the belief that if the dead relative has been reborn as a *preta* the living relatives transfer merit to the departed spirits as these spirits are unable to make merit on their own. They are referred to as *paradatta-upajivi* (beings who live on what others give). There are many other duties and customs that the members of the family had to take into account when a death occurred in the family.

Departed Relative's Spirit Can Be Harmful to the Living

Although the Buddhist teaching is that the souls will immediately get another life form, as we see from the other teachings of the Buddha, there is also a belief that the dead person would be in an intermediary state of *preta* (Law 1936:5). For this reason relatives do what they can to ameliorate their own condition. As soon as the body is washed and placed in the hall of the house they light a lamp and place it by the head of the corpse to prevent the return of the spirit of the dead person.

A departed relative in the state of *preta*-hood could be harmful to the living in the family. It is believed that they plague those who do not perform the proper funerary rites for the dead. *Pretas* are considered responsible for accidents, bad crops, calamities, both natural and domestic, disease of livestock, illness, insanity and plagues. They are also said to enter a human body and make them sick until death. Further they believe that the dead person's spirit would possess the living relatives and cause insanity.

These beings are regarded as hungry spirits or *preta*s depicted in the *Bhavacakra* (circular representation of *samsara*) as teardrop shaped with bloated stomachs and necks too thin to pass food. Their attempt to eat is incredibly painful. The family will prepare a tray of food for the departed spirit to consume near a lighted lamp (Wijesekera 1986:98). The tray contains the kind of food that the dead person used to like including liquor, cigarettes, marijuana and other items. When the corpse is transported to the burial place, the feet are placed facing the moving direction in order to prevent the dead person's spirit coming back to his house (Pannatissa 1992:72). They also have a tradition of spreading some sand in front of the coffin on the path of the funeral procession. This also is in order to prevent the spirit returning home, as the sand in the path would get erased when the people walked over it.

To the Buddhist mind the dead body itself is a polluting factor. Therefore the tendency is to avoid it. The funeral houses are believed to be visited by hovering evil spirits. The relatives take every precaution to avoid the revisit of the dead person into the house. The grave site is a place which is far away from the human habitation as the graves are haunted by vicious demons. Mahasona, who is supposed to have taken abode in the cemetery, is regarded as the cause of many illnesses. The devil dancers in the process of their ceremonies go in the night to cemeteries to consult the demons because the graveyard is the abode of demons.

Sangha

Funerals are the only life cycle ceremonies in which the *sangha* is permitted to fully enter and they play a prominent role in the proceedings. The visit of the *sangha* to funerals, however, depends on the economic and social position of the deceased person's family. Today monks visit the grave site if they are invited by the family, although such practices were absent in the period prior to the introduction of Roman Catholic funeral practices.

The teaching of Buddhism is that existence is suffering, whether birth, daily living, old age or dying. This teaching is most evident when death enters a home. Buddhism has more to say about death and the hereafter than any other religion. Today most of the important funeral rites are done by monks. These rituals are performed prior to the cremation or the burial of the body.

As noted earlier, monks play an important part in the transfer of merit, known as *pattidana*, from the living to the dead person. *Pattidana* means sharing merits with the departed relatives of this life, and of the past lives, as well as all living beings. If the departed ones need merit, they can then receive them, enabling them to be transcended to a higher level of existence. This is the result of *pattidana kusala*. The dead person is invited to listen to the sermon by placing a tray of flowers with a lamp in the garden of the house where the sermon is preached (Pannatisssa 1992:76).

The Buddhist Funeral

Buddha did not prescribe any specific rites regarding the disposal of a corpse (Dhammananda 2000:32). The Buddha's body was cremated by his disciples. But cremation has been confined to the upper social classes and the *sangha*. The traditional method among the ordinary Sinhalese was that the dead were placed in jungles for vultures to consume (*Attanagaluvamsa* 1931:49). The Buddhists feared the dead bodies as the abode of demons, therefore they took every measure against the dead person's spirit harming them.

In the period prior to the introduction of Christianity, Buddhist funerals were very simple affairs without any religious or social function. Robert Knox reported, "The better sort burn the dead, but the poorer sort who regard not such matters bury them making a hole in the woods, and carrying the body wrapped up in a mat upon a pole on their shoulders with two or three attending to it, and so laying it in without any ceremony and covering it" (1981) . Robert Percival stated that "their burials are not attended with any particular religious solemnity" (Percival 1975:151). The poor did not receive any visitation from the *sangha* at funerals in this period.

According to other contemporary reports soon after death had occurred, most often on the same day, the dead body was wrapped in mats or clothes, tied to a platform made with sticks and carried by two or three people to the jungle close to the village. The place where they laid the bodies was a considerable distance from human habitation. Those who carried the body went with a drummer. Wild beasts, used to eating corpses, had the tendency to jump on those who carried the bodies therefore the loud drum, known as *mala bere* (funeral drum), was originally used to chase away wild beasts.

Roman Catholic Funerals in the Sixteenth and Seventeenth Centuries

After the arrival of Roman Catholic missionaries in the sixteenth century, burial became common among Buddhists in Sri Lanka. During this period the task of directing Christian funerals was undertaken by officials of the church. The Roman Catholic Church introduced burial of the dead in the churchyard within the city limits in the presence of at least one official religious dignitary.

Preparation for death included deathbed prayers and the last rites, administered by a priest. After death, the body was washed and prepared for burial by the women of the family, and either shrouded or placed in a coffin. The deceased was carried in procession to the church for the funeral. The grave was prepared while the requiem mass took place, and a procession then conveyed the deceased to the cemetery. It was customary to bury the dead, wrapped only in winding sheets. A variety of subsequent memorial practices ensured intercession: prayers and funerary rites were repeated one week, one month and one year after the funeral. The wealthy sometimes arranged for personal anniversary rites and chantry prayers to be conducted in perpetuity, while ordinary parishioners were remembered collectively on the feast of All Souls.

Success of Roman Catholic Mission

Although the observers of church growth have stated that Sinhala Theravada Buddhists are among the most difficult to convert in the world outside the Islamic group of countries, Roman Catholic missionaries in the sixteenth century had remarkable success in converting Sinhalese Buddhists to the Roman Catholic faith. According to estimates Roman Catholics were the majority in the areas which came directly under Portuguese rule (Quere 1995:132). Roman Catholics were found even in the Kandyan kingdom which did not come under Portuguese rule (1551-1658). Roman Catholic culture became so deeply rooted that even Buddhists adopted many of their religious and social practices; funeral rituals are prominently among them.

Roman Catholic funerals in Sri Lanka differ very much from those of Buddhists because of the absence of fear of spirits. The first thing that the church does on the news of a funeral is to place a cross before the body thus eliminating the possibility of the presence of an evil spirit. Roman Catholic fathers introduced the burial of the dead in the consecrated ground near the church in the city centre, something which Buddhists found hard to believe. Roman Catholic fathers and sacristans helped the bereaved to deal with the sad occasion. They went to the houses and chanted prayers and sang hymns. The Roman Catholic sacrament of extreme unction brought comfort to the families of the dying. They carried the dead body in a cortège from the house to the church where they held a worship service and thanked God for the life of the person. Thereafter the body was buried in the church yard. Family members were able to visit the grave and keep it clean when necessary.

Passion Poetry

Sinhala Christians employed the *Pasan pota,* which they used during the period of Lent in the church calendar, to sing at funerals while the body was in the house before it was removed to the burial ground. The church was very much a part of the family in the funeral proceedings. The death of Christ as well as those of the saints were repeatedly narrated on these occasions.

Among the changes that Roman Catholics introduced was the habit of keeping the body in the house for some period of time rather than immediate disposal as was done in earlier Buddhist tradition. For the first time the corpse remained in the house for at least one night. It was during this waiting period that they resorted to the use of *Pasan pota*. The written *Pasan pota* was placed on a pillow on a mat in the hall where the body was laid. People sat around it and started chanting and singing.

The Sinhala word *pasan* is a derivation from the Portuguese *paixao* meaning "passion" (Ariyaratna 1987:109). *Pasan* was a set of songs by Sinhala Christians during the period from the sixteenth to the nineteenth century depicting the passion of Christ. They were traditionally sung during Lent by small groups in homes. These songs, sung interchangeably by two groups, were sung with a tone of lament to show devotion and piety. Some fishermen used to sing these songs by kneeling on the beach during Lent (:113).

Passion Story in Prose

In 1728 Fr. Jacome Gonsalvez (1676-1742) wrote a passion story known as *Dukprapti Sangrahaya* in nine sermons of prose (Pieris 1978:127). These sermon stories were presented as a drama in public (:8) and chanted in homes during the Lenten period.

The church created its most magnificent prayers for Lent and Easter. Lyrics and melodies were written in special forms to present the liturgy in an appealing manner. Fr. Antonio Paixoto, a Franciscan friar at Matara, composed in Sinhala some of the Portuguese passion songs during the period 1617-1636 when he was resident in the parish at Matara. The main actor in the passion drama is Mother Mary. The songs express the pain and sorrow of a mother who witnesses her son's death. A seventeenth century Portuguese writer referring to the significance of story telling and song in converting the Sinhala people in that era stated:

> The friar (Paixoto) is well versed in the Chingala language, preaches to the natives in it and since he realizes how fond they are of music and poetry he composed and put on many plays in their own language on the lives of the Saints, of Christ, Our Lord and of Adam and Eve. He also composed verses on the

> Passion of the Saviour, with which, on account of the lamentations they contained and the melody and tune, he at times had the whole congregation in tears and some of the Gentiles who were present received the faith and were converted (Trindade 1972:128).

These Passion shows were performed inside a large shed which was covered at the bottom with *cadjan* (coconut frond) fences about two meters in height. The figurines were moved by the people covered by the *cadjan* fences so that to the spectators it appeared as if the puppets were moving on the stage. A leader, who had an appealing voice, explained the various scenes in a melodious tone.

Passion songs and chants were not accompanied by musical instruments. Even the church organs were silent when these passion songs were being sung or chanted. These songs were especially suitable for those homes where when the bodies of the dead were being kept over night. The words used by Fr. Gonsalvez communicate the sorrow of the Mother Mary, the disciples, Mary Magdalene and others. It became extremely therapeutic as words of the *pasan* songs expressed the emotions of the bereaved family.

When a bereaving mother says that this is my son who is dead in her lament, there is no one who can comfort her. But the *Pasan pota* did just that as it expressed the deep feelings of Mother Mary in words that move the hearts of the hearer. It had a therapeutic effect on the grieving person and all who attended the funeral.

Funeral Procession

The funeral procession, which took the body from the house to the church, was another addition during this era to Catholic funerals. It was usually held in the morning. The male relatives carried the litter. Ahead of the bier marched the flute players. Then came the litter itself with the corpse. After this came the relatives in irregular procession singing and chanting. Singing and chanting played an important role in Roman Catholic funeral liturgy. The family members walked closest. There was abundant genuine grief. All sorts of male acquaintances of the deceased brought up the rear with serenity and piety. All these activities made an impression on the Buddhist onlookers who used to discard their dead abruptly as soon as they could.

Twentieth Century Funerals

Some of these Roman Catholic funeral practices fell into disuse as a result of the repressive anti-Catholic laws in the Dutch period (1658-1796). As a result Buddhism regained ground in a country without Roman Catholic priests and repressive Dutch laws against Roman Catholicism. A partial revival occurred as a result of the arrival of Oratorian fathers from India who maintained an underground church during this era. In the meantime the Buddhist revival movement took many Roman Catholic and Protestant practices and presented them in Buddhist garb (Obeyesekere 1988:128).

In 1939, Marcelline Jayakody, Catholic parish priest of Duwa, revised and reorganized the Passion play using human actors for all parts except Christ and the Mother Mary. In addition to the traditional *Pasan*, Jayakody composed his own hymns for the play. The famous Duwa Passion play which he staged has became popular among the Sinhala Catholics. The traditional Passion show in each place developed an identity of its own. In Katuwapitiya for instance the Three Hours of Agony of Christ on the cross was presented. In most of the churches' Passion shows three hours of agony of Christ are performed with a combination of statues and human actors. However, the use of the *Pasan pota* during funerals has gradually fallen into disuse.

Buddhist Aspects

Buddhist acquired certain aspects of funeral rituals which were unique to Christian belief. Buddhists who used to remove dead bodies within a short time after death without any ceremony or religious involvement acquired many Catholic practices when they decided to retain the body of the dead in the home overnight. Modern Buddhist funerals are very elaborate. Funerals in contemporary Sinhalese Buddhist Society have become as expensive as weddings. Buddhists have acquired much of Roman Catholic practices introduced since the sixteenth century. One finds quite a lot of western and Christian practices among Sinhalese funeral rituals today. The ritual of turning the pictures of the house towards the wall, asking pardon of the dead person by the relatives before the body is taken from the house, and placing the head of the dead person towards the west are some remnants of Christian traditions. They do not bury their dead on Fridays because they have acquired this tradition from Roman Catholicism.

During the period that the body remains in the house the family does not cook or prepare food. The neighbors and relatives provide food to the family of the deceased. They also do not keep the corpse alone at any time from the moment of death to the internment. During that time the villagers, friends, and relatives take turns staying with the family, as well as providing food and helping with any other needs during the ritual.

Conscious involvement in these needs of the bereaved family allows Christians to share the grief with them so that they may know that Christians love their neighbors. This is perhaps the only time and place where Sinhalese society condones such open and outward expressions of sadness. Christian neighbors can be present with the family members who cry, sob and wail.

Overnight

Adoption of Roman Catholic and other Christian practices meant that the body remained in the house at least one night. Today corpses are kept in the house for a few days so that the members of the family who are scattered in other parts of the world may be able to attend the funeral. Today bodies are embalmed and kept as long as seven days in the house. There was not been a tradition of singing and chanting at funerals until the eighteenth century. In the home of a Buddhist funeral in the eighteenth century they learned from the Roman Catholics the use of *Pasan pota,* to occupy the time, till the burial of the body.

In order to compete with the Roman Catholics they began their own chanting of the story of *Wessantara Jathaka* in Sinhala or the *Satipatthana Sutta* in Pali in this period (Sannasgala 1964: 706). However, these practices too have fallen into disuse in the recent past. Now the practice at Buddhist funerals is to remain in the house in quiet sorrow.

The tradition is that the dead body must not kept alone in the house. Therefore help is needed as the grieving family finds it hard to rest for any period of time. There is no religious ritual or Buddhist substitute to use up the extra time available during the home internment. Nowadays this time is used in something as innocent as a carom game or as serious as gambling.

Because of the recent disuse of *Pasan pota* and other chants used in funeral houses by the Catholics and because there is no such tradition among the Protestants, this kind of negative behaviour has crept into Christian funerals as well. Christian leaders have to be aware of the serious repercussions this has upon Christian witness. Why not revive the use of song and chants on the occasion of funerals?

Funeral Orations

Orations are a very significant element in Buddhist funerals before the burial of the body in cities as well as in villages. A Buddhist monk starts the ritual by preaching on the message of impermanence. He also would speak a few words about the dead person before chanting a stanza and wishing the person to be born in a world of gods and ultimately attain *nirvana.*

After the end of the oration the monks who attended the funeral would leave the burial ground giving the opportunity to the family to continue with funeral orations. These orations are used to talk about the excellent qualities of the character of the dead person as there is a taboo against mentioning the failures of the deceased. When a person who is invited to speak is not familiar with the dead person, invariably he will talk of the member of the dead person's family who is known to him. Then he would say that such relatives would indicate the pious nature of the deceased. These orations are made in order to comfort the members of the family, of their loss. However, Buddhism is unable to offer hope beyond emphasizing the karmic rewards.

Funeral orations in the Buddhist setting can be long. The chief organizer of the funeral assigns speeches with the concurrence of family members. If a Christian pastor is a friend of the family he would usually be given an opportunity to say a few comforting words. Many pastors have made use of this occasion to say some thing on the Christian view of death on such occasions. For many who are gathered at the graveyard this may be the first time that they hear of a Christian view of death.

Emphasis in the sermon should be on the hope of the Christians, the death and resurrection of Christ. The language should be sympathetic, no reference to Buddhism or Christianity should be made. It should not be a syncretistic message, which most traditional Christian leaders make today, as they would not be useful to generate hope or a challenge to the audience. The Christian orator should take every precaution to prevent any kind of derogatory remarks on the Buddhist way of living.

Christian Orations

Funerals help us search for meaning in the life and death of the person who died as well as in our own life and impending death. When someone we love dies, we naturally question the meaning of life and death. Why did this person die? What happens after death? These are some of the questions which will emerge. Buddhism offers the concept of karma to answer this. However, there will be people who are not satisfied with this answer. During the funeral oration Christians can offer the answer and hope experienced in Christian faith. This does not mean one would find definitive answers but it may give an opportunity to think things through.

At traditional Buddhist funerals, the eulogy attempts to highlight the major events in the life of the deceased and the characteristics that he or she most prominently displayed. It is an opportunity for Christian neighbors to remember the person who died. If the pastor knew the person it is the time to tell what he thinks about the moments he shared with the one who died. The funeral invites us to focus on our past relationship with that person and to share those memories with others. This is helpful to mourners, for it tends to prompt more intimate, individualized memories. The sharing of memories at the funeral affirms the worth we have placed on the person who died. While doing this it is essential to show the Christian identity of the orator.

Contemporary Buddhist Funerals

Funerals have become social events in Sri Lanka today. Friends and relatives make it a point to come to the funeral house to pay respect to the dead as well as to please the living. These visitors may come from work places where a member of the family is employed. Visitors to Buddhist funerals would be Christian, Muslim and Hindu neighbors and friends. A Christian neighbor and friend can be a participant in many of the traditional activities in a funeral house. Since people consider it honorable to keep the body in the house till it is taken to the cemetery there are many activities where the friends and neighbors can get involved.

One of the most important actions necessary as soon as a death occurs is to help the family in the grieving process. If the Christian has some time to spare it would be valuable to be with the family at this period. It would be a great comfort to them. The traditional Buddhists would welcome such help. There is no need of verbal communicating of the Gospel in this situation, but being with them and showing Christian love would be appreciated.

Next is the requirement of food to the members of the bereaved family. Tradition is that no food will be prepared in the funeral house. It is the duty of the relatives and neighbors to provide food to the family in this period. The Christian could take part in this tradition and provide the food and speak comforting words to the family. Some part of these comforting words should come from the Christian background. This is the time that the Christian can casually narrate stories.

Participation at a Funeral

When we care about someone who died or his family members, we attend the funeral if it is possible. Physical presence is the most important show of support for the living. We show that they are not alone in their grief by attending the funeral. It is an occasion when the members of the family of the deceased would try to cope with the sorrow of a loss of one of their loved ones.

While the funeral in a Christian home is not intended for evangelism, the behavior of Christians at a funeral make an impression on the minds of the visitors who normally would not have an opportunity to witness the Christian attitude to death. There would be people for whom this would be the first time experience of a Christian funeral.

Funerals let us physically demonstrate our caring by offering our support. Words are inadequate so we silently demonstrate our support. We have an opportunity to embrace, to touch, and to comfort the bereaved at funerals. This physical show of support is one of the most important healing aspects of Christian concern for the bereaved neighbor. The fact that the Christian is free of fear of evil forces at funerals and other taboos entertained by Buddhist could be utilized to strengthen the bereaved.

Banners

Funerals are a way in which we as individuals and as a community convey our beliefs and values about life and death. The very fact of a funeral demonstrates that death is important to us. For the living to go on living as fully and as healthily as possible an understanding of death would be useful.

Today there is a practice of displaying banners expressing the sorrow of various social groups that are connected to the family of the bereaved. There are funeral societies, trade unions, and various other groups which would come with their banners to display their sorrow on this occasion. These banners remain during the period the corpse is in the residence. They are displayed in prominent places. Some Christian churches have used this practice to display such comforting words as, "I am the resurrection and the life. He who believes in me will live, even though he dies" (John 11:25). These could easily be done in Christian funeral houses. Churches can have their neutral banners indicating the name of the church or the society to display their sympathy in Buddhist funerals as well.

Songs

Research demonstrates the value of music for helping people deal with pain and stress. Most therapists can tell us stories about how music helps people manage grief and pain. No one can tell us how music therapy works, but there is overwhelming evidence that it does. People who are in sorrow may be able to sing songs which generate hope and comfort. They not only remember the music; they may even hum a tune or play a part of it when they are alone.

Traditionally there is a discouragement of music in Sinhala Buddhist worship. When the lay people observe the eight precepts on Buddhist festival days they promise, among other things, not to engage in dancing, singing, music and watching drama. Ordained Theravada monks are strictly prohibited singing and dancing in their 227 precepts. Therefore there is no room for songs and music in Buddhist funerals. The Buddhist funerals ceremonies are spent mostly wailing, weeping and speaking well of the dead.

Songs at the Home of the Deceased

In Christian funerals the members of the family may ask that people sing the hymns and choruses that the dead person liked. This will help them to talk about their loss and to process their grief. Meaningful songs point the audience to the hope which Jesus offers through his death and resurrection.

Non-Christians who attend Christian funerals will notice the attitudes that the Christian show in their bereavement. Hope in Christ and his victory over death can be expressed on these occasions by chanting the holy word. The non Christian visitor would be able to listen to the songs and chants and also find a calm and hopeful atmosphere in the Christian funeral.

Traditional Christians have continued to use hymns and songs in the home at funerals, during funeral processions, and at the graveyard as a part of their ritual. However, newer Christian churches headed by converts from Buddhism lack of this kind of traditional singing during funerals. Since most of the membership of these new churches come from a Buddhist background the leadership should make a conscious attempt to introduce meaningful therapeutic singing suitable to funeral occasions.

Songs in the Funeral Service

A funeral is regarded as a solemn and serious occasion. On such occasions the musical instruments selected in the Sinhalese Buddhist environment are very important. Some new churches have taken guitars to funerals to accompany hymn singing. There has been a tendency to object to such usage. The Salvation Army uses the accordion and the drum for funeral processions. However, while the body is in the house the music should be confined to non-instrumental singing only in order not to confuse a Buddhist visitor.

Songs should be meaningful and clear in expression. Translated English choruses lack accurate meaning. Tunes selected should suit the solemn occasion. Christian leaders have the responsibility to compose meaningful hymns which can be used on these occasions.

Christian Burial Societies

In the Middle Ages, members of the labouring classes who could not afford the cost of a funeral formed burial societies and contributed regular dues to a common fund. Such societies have become popular in Sri Lankan work places and villages. The church could organize such societies not only to help Christians but also to assist the poor. This is one way of receiving acceptance in an otherwise hostile Buddhist environment. Under such circumstances Christian leaders would be able to take part in the funeral proceedings and to be with the grieving family to comfort them.

Conclusion

Most of the successful, attractive, and therapeutic practices regarding funeral ceremonies of the past have been abandoned by the Church today. The church has not yet offered an adequate alternative to the ancient traditions of story telling and song as done in the *Pasan pota*. The modern translations of American choruses and hymns have failed to achieve the soothing and comforting effects of the traditional Christian music. It is true that funeral services undertaken in many Christian denominations offer hope to the members of the family regarding their deceased loved one. But they have failed in dealing with the grief in the family. There is a serious need to lift up the morale of the bereaved family. Therefore there is a solemn need of songs and hymns of the nature of *Pasan pota.* Till such time that the Protestant and Evangelical churches create their own songs and chants it may be advisable to revive the use of the ancient *Pasan pota*. The Buddhist who lacks the fellowship of God and the personal involvement of a saviour could have this personal aspect of life and death communicated in a touching way through song and story.

8

MOVING TOWARDS ORAL COMMUNICATION OF THE GOSPEL: EXPERIENCES FROM CAMBODIA

Dale Jones

For years I have committed myself to communicating the gospel clearly and effectively and discipling men and women to be followers of Jesus. I have always found great satisfaction when my students would come to fully understand a Biblical truth as if a light went on in their hearts, and to see that truth bring a change of mindset and behavior. What a joy it is to see people freed from the darkness of sin and ignorance and their lives changed forever by the power of communicating God's truth! I have come to share the Apostle Paul's heart as expressed in his letter to the Saints in Rome, "I am not ashamed of the gospel, because it is the power of God for the salvation of everyone who believes" (Rom. 1:16). Clearly, the communication of the gospel is power—to save and to transform.

As a Westerner, for years I believed that the clearest and most effective way to communicate the gospel was through literature. I focused on laying out the truths of Scripture systematically in tracts for evangelism or in books for discipleship, carefully selecting each word and phrase to carry just the right meaning or connotation. For my first six years as a missionary in Cambodia, I committed myself to translating evangelism and discipleship materials into Khmer, the Cambodian language, with the intent of producing a complete set of tracts, booklets, study guides and workbooks that would bring a person from knowing absolutely nothing about God or the gospel, through the stages of coming to faith in Christ, becoming a disciple of Jesus, and finally, to be trained in ministry. I hired a team of proficient translators and worked in partnership with other missionaries to ensure that the quality of our work was top-notch. I was convinced that once the machine was built – this curriculum for making disciples – the gospel would go forth and Cambodia would be transformed.

The materials we produced were truly of high quality. We used great liberty in contextualizing, adapting, and modifying the text in light of Khmer culture to ensure good understanding. Our translators and editors worked hard to make certain that the best possible vocabulary was employed. As we finished one book after another we were excited to use them, anticipating great fruit for our labors. I decided to test our books on a group of believers I was discipling, made up of Khmer adults who had all studied in high school.

How extremely disappointed I was! Our workbooks included simple questions for the student to answer, but time after time I was perplexed by their lack of understanding. The translators and I were shocked at the inability of the students to answer even some of the most basic questions! Over and over I felt as if I were bashing my head against a wall trying to help them understand the material.

In the course of time, I have all but abandoned using any of the materials we had so meticulously produced. Through the experience of many years of ministry in Cambodia, I have come to realize that the most effective teaching or preaching times were when I used absolutely no books at all! Sharing stories and illustrations, music and drama seemed to be more fruitful than engaging in a more academic pursuit of Scripture. I have learned, through the School of Hard Knocks, something that many other missiologists have more recently begun to explore and develop – communication methods for oral learners.

If we are to effectively communicate the gospel to the lost in this world, I am convinced that it is absolutely vital that we change our methods of communication from academic, book-focused, deductive, analytical/Western methods to oral, story-based, inductive, experiential and reproducible means of communication.

The Apostle Paul stated, "I have become all things to all people so that by all possible means I might save some. I do all this for the sake of the gospel that I may share in its blessings." (1 Co. 9:22b–23). For far too long, many Christian ministers have not fully contextualized the gospel by becoming all things to all people. Although this lack of contextualization can be seen in many ways, it has been particularly evidenced throughout history by the focus of many gospel workers on literacy as a precursor to evangelism or church planting. Moreover, the focus of discipleship or ministerial training has traditionally been limited to the literate or "educated." It is time for us to become like our Lord Jesus or like Paul and engage in "incarnational ministry," becoming like those to whom we have been sent. We must be willing to lay down our bias for literates and our beloved methods of education and begin investing in the untapped potential of those whom are primary oral learners.

In this article I will discuss three main considerations that are foundational to beginning to move towards communicating the gospel using oral methods. Please note that throughout this article in order to avoid awkwardness, I will use the phrase "communicating the gospel," implying not just evangelism, but also discipleship and leadership training. The three main considerations

I will discuss are the need for oral communication, the validity of oral communication and issues related to preparing oral communication approaches. I am not intending to offer extensive or exhaustive research on these three considerations. Whole books have already been written on literacy and oral communication. I would rather like to briefly highlight each of these to pique your interest in what I believe is on the cutting edge of missiology today, and to challenge you to consider developing oral communication approaches.

The Need for Oral Communication

Before we can discuss this subject any further, it is necessary to define the terminology. Among the most misunderstood terms regarding this discussion is the word "literate." At what point is someone considered literate? What are the various levels of literacy? In answering these questions, I would like to offer the following definitions supplied by James B. Slack in his unpublished document on "Chronological Bible Storying," as quoted by the International Orality Network:

> "Illiterates" cannot read or write. They have never "seen" a word. In fact, the word for illiteracy in the Indonesian language is *buta huruf*, meaning "blind to letters." For oral communicators, words do not exist as letters, but as sounds related to images of events and to situations that they are seeing or experiencing.
>
> "Functional Illiterates" have been to school but do not continue to read and write regularly after dropping out of school. Within two years [of leaving school], even those who have gone to school for eight years often can read only simple sentences and can no longer

> receive, recall or reproduce concepts, ideas, precepts and principles through literate means. They prefer to get their information orally. Their functional level of illiteracy (as opposed to published data) determines how they learn, how they develop their values and beliefs, and how they pass along their culture, including their religious beliefs and practices.
>
> "Semi-literates" function in a gray transitional area between oral communication and literacy. Even though these individuals have normally gone to school up to 10 years and are classified in every country of the world as literates, they learn primarily by means of narrative presentations.
>
> "Literate" learners understand and handle information such as ideas, precepts, concepts, and principles by literate means. They tend to rely on printed material as an aid to recall. (International Orality Network 2005:22-23)

To bring clarity, one more definition is required for this discussion, "Primary Oral Learners" (POLs) or simply "Oral Learners":

> By "oral learners" we mean those people who learn best and whose lives are most likely to be transformed when instruction comes in oral forms. Many groups transmit their beliefs, heritage, values and other important information by means of stories, proverbs, poetry, chants, music, dances ceremonies and rites of passage. The spoken, sung, or chanted word associated with these activities often consists of ornate and elaborate ways to communicate. (International Orality Network 2005:4)

Based on the definitions of the terms above, the vast majority of the world's population would be considered Primary Oral Learners, or POLs. This is also true in many developed nations where post-modern culture has taken control and electronic media have become the primary source for entertainment, news and information. It has been wrongly assumed that to be able to read and write equals "literate." We must understand that one who is able to read and write is not necessarily literate, and may only be functionally illiterate or semi-literate.

In many nations, reported literacy rates do not reflect reality because the standards for determining the rate of literacy normally include people who are only functionally illiterate and semi-literate. Even in the United States, the figures are deceiving. The National Adult Literacy Survey (NALS) administered by the U.S. Department of Education in the early 1990s reported some shocking results. The NALS study showed that only four to six percent of U.S. adults were totally literate and forty-six to fifty-three percent were identified as unable to function adequately in a highly literate society or process lengthy written information adequately (International Orality Network 2005:20-21).

Unfortunately, many missionaries who have researched the statistics on literacy but misunderstand the various levels thereof, have mistakenly developed evangelism and discipleship approaches based on the assumption that a significant percentage of people are fully literate and therefore capable of understanding their message delivered using literature. Applying the definitions of literacy above to Cambodia's current situation, for example, an extremely small percentage of the population could be considered fully literate. Official estimates of literacy in Cambodia vary, but recently it has been determined that adult literacy is at thirty-seven percent.

(Rosenbloom 2004:3) Included in that group would be semi-literate and most functional illiterates as well. Based on that figure, and my own observations, I estimate that the rate of fully literate people (i.e. not including semi-literates) at not more than twenty percent and probably closer to ten percent, meaning as many as eighty to ninety percent or more of the population are POLs. Other nations in Southeast Asia or beyond are certainly not much different.

Awareness of the literacy rate as it relates to learning styles is crucial in forming strategies for communication, preaching and teaching. With such a strong majority of people preferring or requiring oral methods of communication in order to learn, should we not develop new–or utilize old– oral approaches to meet such an overwhelming need? At the heart of the matter are communication styles and formats. I have observed that to communicate effectively with oral learners, the style of communication needs to match their learning preference. Stories and narrative styles are best understood by illiterates and functional illiterates. In fact, I have found that POLs find it very difficult to understand presentations containing outlines, lists, steps, and principles.

There may be some educators who feel that they are considering this need and have attempted to introduce the subject in their institutions of higher learning by encouraging students to adapt their communication styles to be less formal. Yet, the student will most often reflect and follow the academic and Western-teaching style of his teacher by sermonizing using lists, principles, outlines and expository preaching and teaching techniques. To give but a cursory mention of oral communication methods (i.e. storytelling, parables, repeating, memorization, learning by example, drama and music, etc.) will not produce any lasting effect on the student or his effectiveness in communication. Sadly, many educators in

Cambodia who have been exposed to the need for focusing on specific approaches for oral learners have apparently done little to nothing to change their methods or at best, have only added "orality" as a course of study to their existing curriculum or training program.

If we are going to truly impact the unbelieving, illiterate masses, then our entire approach towards them, from beginning to end, must be reformed. The methods of teaching and communication styles themselves must be revamped, starting with those who are teaching in Bible schools and seminaries.

What am I suggesting? I am not calling for a complete dismantling of institutions of higher learning or eliminating entire courses of study. I am convinced, though, that significant changes are needed at every level, from grass-roots to tree-tops, from the evangelism and discipleship efforts in the most remote villages to the educating of educators in the capital city. There needs to be a groundswell of determination to become all things to all people, for the literate minority to adapt by contextualizing their message and themselves to the context of the illiterate majority. God gave us "His-Story" of redemption in a straight-forward way; likewise, we must strive to share the gospel message in the same manner, as a story. Additionally, we must change our attitudes towards POLs, to no longer look down on them, to no longer think of them as inferior or incapable, to no longer overlook them for training to become ministers or teachers. The POL majority will not be reached by continuing to use our Western styles of communicating. We must find ways to adapt.

One major barrier to being able to make a shift to using oral communication methods is the belief that illiterate people are both ignorant and unintelligent. This common Western mindset has done much damage to the cause of Christ throughout the centuries. Illiteracy may keep people ignorant for lack of opportunities to explore a world that is much larger than theirs for sure, but it is not evidence of lacking in intelligence. I remember being impressed by a waiter in Cambodia who was able to remember meal orders for twelve people without writing a single thing down. Showing my prejudice, I insisted that he write the order down so as not to mess it up and he informed me that he couldn't read. I was skeptical whether we would all receive what we had ordered, but to my amazement, he hadn't forgotten anything. I remember thinking how much better his memory was than mine, how if I go to the market and need more than three things and don't make a written list, I'm sure to forget something.

Since illiteracy is not necessarily a sign of lack of intelligence, how then do POLs and literates differ? The difference is in how they learn. POLs learn through stories or narratives, parables and drama, music and poetry – that is, through oral methods of communication. They can often memorize voluminous amounts of material and recite what they know. Unfortunately, their gifts are largely overlooked and ignored as many of them have had no other choice but to sit week after week through sermons and teachings with points, keys, principles, outlines and neat acrostics that may be nonsensical to them. What would happen if we would focus on pouring the stories of the gospel, parables and scripture songs into their hearts instead?

I do not want to imply, though, that adapting is an easy task. For many years I have tried to utilize oral communication methods and have had only limited success. As a highly literate person it has been a challenge to begin to think and communicate like a POL. I have found it extremely challenging to disassociate myself from writing and simply memorize and tell stories, without slipping into simultaneous exposition or explanation. Moreover, I have also found it quite difficult to get enough of a handle on Khmer storytelling styles to feel comfortable integrating them into Biblical narratives. Even with a commitment and focus on oral communication approaches, I have felt as if I were swimming upstream, against the current.

The Validity of Oral Communication

Another major barrier to using oral communication methods such as storytelling, drama, and music is the mindset that these methods are fine for children, the uneducated or special events but they are not valid for teaching theology or deeper Biblical truth. Traditionally we have been conditioned to think that in the process of growing in Christ we begin with stories, parables and songs and when we are more mature we move on to more "adult" forms of learning like deductive word studies, outlines and systematic theology, as if oral learning styles are like the "milk" of the Word and more academic or literate styles are the "meat"(1 Pe. 2:2-3).

Is this pervading belief in deductive reasoning and text analysis using higher criticism necessary to understand the deeper things of God? No! The Apostle Paul, who is commonly regarded as the Great Theologian, the champion for the gospel to the Gentiles (all of us!), did not come to understand this mystery of God's grace for all nations through some deep analysis or higher criticism of Scripture, but received these truths as directly revealed by God. In Ephesians, Paul confirms:

> That is, the mystery made known to me by revelation,
> as I have already written briefly. In reading this, then,

> you will be able to understand my insight into the mystery of Christ, which was not made known to men in other generations as it has now been revealed by the Spirit to God's holy apostles and prophets. This mystery is that through the gospel the Gentiles are heirs together with Israel, members together of one body, and sharers together in the promise in Christ Jesus. (Eph. 3:3-6).

My point here is that understanding Biblical truth requires revelation and is not dependent upon a particular style of learning. We need to understand the mysteries of God and deep spiritual truths for sure, but the need for depth does not disqualify the primary oral learner from grasping these truths through oral means of communication.

Let us consider Jesus as an example. Obviously because of Jesus' divine nature he was, as a man, capable of so much more than we. But according to Phil. 2:6-7, we understand that Jesus' divine attributes were limited while in his incarnational state as a human. For instance, clearly, Jesus' divine attribute of omnipresence was abandoned in his incarnation; for, as a human he was limited to occupying only one place at one time. His omnipotence and omniscience were also abandoned. Therefore Jesus was born, matured, and needed to learn just as we do and in that way experienced life as a human just like us. Based on the definitions of levels of literacy provided above, it would be safe to assume that Jesus was semi-literate at best (he would not have had access to books or other forms of literature on a daily basis to be considered fully literate) and therefore he was likely to have been a primary oral learner! Jesus' educated contemporaries recognized this, for concerning Jesus they remarked, "How did this man get such learning without having studied?" Jesus answered, "My teaching is not my own. It comes from him who sent me" (Jn. 7:15-16). Jesus' lack of formal education did not keep him from becoming the greatest teacher of all time! It was obvious from this passage that Jesus was educated by the Holy Spirit and Jesus taught what he had been given by God.

And, what methods of teaching did Jesus employ? Although not all of Jesus' teaching was illustrative, we must conclude from the following verse that the vast majority of Jesus' teachings to the crowds were in the form of parables. "Jesus spoke all these things to the crowd in parables; he did not say anything to them without using a parable" (Mt. 13:34). Jesus told his disciples that the crowds were not granted understanding of the mysteries of the kingdom of heaven, but the disciples were granted understanding. Did his teaching style change for the disciples since God was going to grant them understanding? No, they heard the same parables taught, but with an additional commentary in order to bring them understanding. Jesus taught his disciples using the teaching style with which they were most comfortable–oral, narrative or illustrative communication.

It is interesting that Jesus' selection of disciples, who would later be sent to represent him and the kingdom of God, were also uneducated. Jesus did not choose the wisest, most educated men to follow him and take up his cause. He put the fate of the entire church and Christian faith in the hands of a motley crew of fishermen and societal misfits. How many of those men were literate do you suppose? Matthew was likely the only one of "the twelve" who was literate while the others were either completely illiterate or functionally illiterate at best. In Acts 4:13, we read that when the rulers, elders and scribes of Jerusalem put Peter and John on trial for healing and teaching in the temple and had listened to their defense, they were amazed at their confidence since they were uneducated and untrained men. The disciples' lack of literacy notwithstanding, they were powerful men of God with deep spiritual understanding!

If Jesus chose, trained and commissioned a group of POLs who would later give godly and effective apostolic leadership to the church world-wide, then why is it that we have so completely overlooked this group? Have we allowed our prejudice against the uneducated or illiterate to dissuade us from considering them for leadership, even for apostolic leadership of the church? I submit that we have in fact allowed our cultural bias and love for book knowledge as well as intellectual elitism to dominate our values for leadership training. Never once in Scripture are we instructed to apply standards of literacy as qualifications for church leadership! And yet, for many, this has become the most important standard.

I am not intending to give the impression that literacy has no value or that we should disregard the literate or abandon our masters or doctoral programs. Obviously I can read and write as well! It is absolutely essential that we train those who are literate for church leadership as well. However, my intent here is to draw attention to the tragic practice of considering the training of illiterate people invalid.

Issues Related to Preparing Oral Communication Approaches

As we are convinced of the need for developing oral communication approaches to reach POLs and are able to accept that the Bible does in fact validate such an endeavor, two of the most challenging barriers to a proliferation of the gospel and advancement of the kingdom of God among oral cultures have been broken–the unawareness of the great need and the lack of confidence in oral communication approaches. One would hope that then we are ready to begin the process of thinking through the issues related to developing various oral approaches, preparing tools for oral communication, and developing a philosophy of orality that will guide us through the process and keeping us consistent and on track.

First of all, let us consider what the goal should be. If we are working to produce tools or methodologies to communicate the gospel to oral learners, that is to evangelize, disciple and train them as leaders, we must assume that they will have only limited access to the Bible on a daily basis or none at all. Yes, it is possible in most areas to do as Paul exhorted Timothy, "until I come, devote yourself to the public reading of Scripture," (1 Ti. 4:13), as long as there is someone in the area that can read. The public reading of Scripture can be a true source for building knowledge, but it falls far short of communicating directly to the heart of the oral learner! Primary oral learners have a more difficult time assimilating a story read to them than a story that is told. And, if they do not comprehend the story, they certainly will not be able to carry that story with them and retell it.

Oral Bible

What POLs really need is an Oral Bible. I'm not sure who coined the term, but it has been floating around missiological circles for a few years now. An Oral Bible is exactly what it sounds like, a Bible that is carried around in the hearts of people and shared orally with others. As David said, "I have hidden your word in my heart that I might not sin against you." (Ps. 119:11) An Oral Bible is a compilation of stories, songs, poems, etc. that are listened to and memorized by oral learners. It is the Bible written on the hearts of believers and is available for immediate recall and retelling, reciting or singing with others as opportunities are presented.

Clearly it would not be practical to expect everyone to memorize the entire Bible in its current form. Yet, Lena Wan, a missionary from Singapore serving in Cambodia recently commented, "Christians in China memorize entire books [of the Bible] . . . This is what keeps them alive in the prison. They quote whole books while in the cell, especially when in solitary confinement" (Wan 2006). Despite this amazing feat, and despite the fact that POLs are much more adept at memorization than literates, the Bible is much too voluminous to expect every disciple to commit it to memory in its entirety. To facilitate the treasuring of God's Word in the hearts of believers, we must find ways to shape the Bible into an oral form. This is no easy task, particularly as one decides on the content of an Oral Bible—what to include and what not. The stories, teachings, psalms, proverbs, etc. that are included may even vary based on the local context and practicality. Also, decisions about what portions of Scripture are more foundational for evangelism and which ones are more appropriate for discipleship or leadership training need to be made.

Vocabulary

Before specifically dealing with the choices to be made regarding content, it would be beneficial to first consider the issue of vocabulary. In Cambodia, as in many nations, this has become a contentious issue dividing the church into camps, not unlike the ongoing debate in the United States between those loyal to the King James Version and those who have decided to use one of the modern translations of the Bible. Much of the debate in Cambodia centers on the use of correct vocabulary. The Khmer language has both a common vernacular and a high language for royalty. One camp is committed to using the royal language on the premise that they are doing so to honor God. They believe that if one used the common language in reference to God it would be demeaning and dishonoring to him. The other group desires to use the common language, having been convinced that it best reflects the language in which the New Testament was written–common Greek. Many people do not lean heavily one way or the other but fall somewhere in between the two extremes. I personally share the convictions of those promoting the use of common language, primarily because I am committed to using whatever language best communicates the message, and for those who are POLs, their lack of education and exposure to the royal language will be a hindrance to understanding the message of the gospel.

In addition, let us consider the question, "What is language?" Language is but a social tool that God has given us to communicate with each other and in itself is neither sacred nor secular. What could possibly make a word "good" or "bad" outside of a word carrying certain moral implications? To choose language that is understandable and easily recalled and retold is much more effective among oral learners and, let's be honest, among literates as well. It is reasonable for us to make plain the message of the gospel so as to reach as many people as possible.

Reproducibility

One significant benefit of using understandable language is it lends to our message becoming reproducible. This is a critical factor in developing a truly effective oral approach! To fail to achieve a reproducible quality in our approach is to fall short in entrusting the gospel to POLs whom we desire to train to become leaders, pastors, cvangelists and missionaries, for if those we are training cannot do exactly as we have demonstrated to them, then the gospel message will remain in the hands of the educated literate and beyond the reach of the masses.

When developing oral approaches one must always ask, "Is this reproducible?" that is, can a completely illiterate person replicate all that I am saying and doing? To what degree am I still relying on the crutch of literate methods in my attempt to communicate the gospel with POLs? In communication, the crutch of the literate becomes the barrier of the oral learner. It is crucial that we analyze our methods and identify any remnants of a more academic mentality that threatens to undermine the process.

Two main issues are at stake when considering the issue of reproducibility. The first is whether our message is understood. Obviously, in order for the listener to be able to relay the message to others, it is essential to first understand its meaning. The second issue is not so obvious and success in achieving it is much more illusive: Does the listener feel comfortable relaying the message to others by retelling the stories, singing the songs or reciting the poems that have been used to communicate the message to him? Being comfortable in relaying the message is at the core of the reproducibility issue and requires significant work on the part of the one developing the oral approach, even trial and error, to achieve communication that multiplies from one to another.

At this juncture it is reasonable to address the issues of using pictures or visual aids with various forms of oral communication. Many quickly assume that for illiterates pictures are necessary or beneficial to assist in communicating the message. My experience is that pictures are not necessary and can even bring confusion or may distract from the telling of a story, even when its use is intended to be complimentary. Although some have developed visual aids to assist the oral communicator in remembering important points to a story or the sequence of stories, caution should be exercised in employing these aids. The saying that a picture is worth a thousand words may be true, but it is certain that any given picture does not communicate the same one thousand words to everyone! How can we be sure that our pictures or visual aids are communicating the right message? It becomes a matter of interpreting the message in the pictures. Moreover, when it comes to evangelizing, oral communication approaches that are devoid of visual aids or pictures are preferred as the communicator who is armed with nothing but what he carries along with him in his heart is never hindered from sharing just because he doesn't have these devices. The gospel can be sown broadly without restriction at any opportunity that presents itself.

Chronological Bible Storying

There are a number of specific approaches which have been proven successful in oral communication of the gospel. By far, the most important of all oral communication approaches is Bible Storying or Chronological Bible Storying. In essence, it is communicating the story of redemption through telling Bible stories systematically and/or chronologically in order to lay a foundation for understanding the gospel. While studying for a degree in Cross-Cultural Ministries, I learned the importance of focusing on communicating the gospel as a story, since approximately seventy percent of the Bible is narrative (Falley 1987). I am convinced that the gospel is best understood through the telling of those stories, for POLs as well as literates.

There are a growing number of people who have developed or have begun to develop a Chronological-Bible-Storying approach to reach POLs and a quick search on the internet would reveal the extent of this trend. However, there are a range of differences between the story sets that people have developed as well as differences in the stories themselves. There are a number of factors related to developing stories or story sets that are necessary to consider ensuring that what we have developed actually becomes an Oral Bible for the POLs with whom we are working.

Contextualization Versus Faithfulness to the Biblical Text

It has always been my desire and commitment to make the gospel relevant to the culture in which I am ministering. Equally important is the faithful communication of Biblical truth. At times these two commitments have seemed to conflict with each other, forcing me to wade through some murky waters to find a solution. Commitment to the meaning of the Biblical text is of the highest priority and to convey any other meaning, whether by commission or omission, is unacceptable. It is necessary to condense stories to some degree and/or to modify the way that stories are told so as to facilitate the telling of the story or make it more usable within a particular context.

Sadly, condensing or changing stories has been taken to an extreme by some. I have read some stories that have been rewritten for oral story telling that were so condensed that they no longer seemed like the same stories. So much was left out that if we were to read the story in its original form in the Bible we would certainly feel that what was given orally was inferior. If we are intending to develop an Oral Bible, then it is important to instill confidence in people that what they have heard orally is not second-rate, simplified, changed or watered-down. We need to ensure that the Oral Bible they've received is as much the Word of God as what has been written! Unfortunately, such a haphazard handling of Scripture has done much to damage the cause of oral communication methods and has brought undue criticism.

Conversely, to simply retell memorized Bible stories word for word from Scripture is not practical or effective. Some changing of vocabulary, sentence structure and story length is necessary to transform a story from a written narrative to a good oral story, especially since what is recorded in Scripture has already gone through at least one filter of translation from a foreign language. To see the best results, this process takes time and many revisions will undoubtedly be necessary, but what is called for is a commitment to the integrity of the Biblical narrative.

In the process of developing oral stories I have had to struggle through this. For instance, as part of a story set for evangelism, I wanted to include the story of Jesus' birth as one story among thirteen stories and one poem I produced as a story set for evangelism. As you know, there are two different accounts of this story in Scripture, offering a variety of information. To take the information related to the story from each narrative and combining it all into one oral story would have made the story too lengthy and very difficult to manage. The challenge was to significantly condense the story without compromising its integrity–the story was to remain largely unchanged. My solution was to tell a part of Jesus' birth story as a stand-alone story, starting with the engagement of Joseph and Mary and ending with Jesus' stable birth and fulfillment of Old Testament prophecy, not leaving out any pertinent details. What is not included is the prior story of the angel Gabriel speaking with Mary and Mary's visit to Elizabeth, nor the later stories of the shepherds or wise men who visited Jesus and King Herod's subsequent murder of the baby boys of Bethlehem. That does not mean that these stories are not important or that they should be ignored, only that the most essential story needed to be told in the initial stage of leading people to Christ. The telling of the rest of the related stories must happen but should be postponed until after the evangelism stage is over to avoid making the process of evangelism too extensive. Some chronological Bible story sets err in this way by including too many stories. Although they are useful for discipling new believers, they are not effective for evangelism because it takes too long to bring the listener to the story of Christ, the cross, the resurrection and salvation.

Layering

That brings us to another consideration in developing a systematic process of telling Bible stories. Through much trial and error I have concluded that systematically telling Bible stories effectively requires layering. Layering involves the telling of selected Bible stories and other oral communication methods like poetry and song, in a chronological sequence to bring people who are at a certain stage in their faith in Christ to an understanding of Biblical truth. Although many different layers can be developed, I have envisioned and begun to develop story sets for three distinct layers: evangelism, discipleship and leadership training.

In my evangelism story set, there is one poem and thirteen stories. The evangelism layer highlights the most essential stories necessary to bring someone from a total lack of spiritual understanding to a place where they can make an informed decision for Christ, particularly in the Khmer-Buddhist context. These "stories" are arranged in chronological order, beginning with a poem entitled, *Who Is God?* Following that there is a story reflecting Paul's address to the Athenians from Acts 17 with an exhortation to respond to God's invitation to turn back to Him, then a story about the creation of heaven, hell and the angels, the creation story and on through to the story of man's fall into sin. Then, there is a "bridge" story, connecting the stories of ancient times to the stories of Christ's birth, life, death, resurrection and ascension. In this layer I have intentionally left out all the stories of the Old Testament after Genesis 3, but have used the bridge story to summarize man's continued slide into sin and death, as well as the emergence of man's attempt to deal with sin through religion.

Then the second layer is the discipleship story set which includes these same evangelism stories (to be reviewed by the new believer) with about thirty additional stories that fill in some of the gaps left by the first layer, including the story of Cain and Abel, Noah, The Tower of Babel, etc. Many of the most important Old and New Testament stories are included in that set. Again, these stories are all told chronologically so as to build a framework of time for people to understand the history of God's story of redemption.

Finally, the third layer is leadership training stories which includes other significant stories to fill in more of the gaps. By this time it is not essential to tell these stories chronologically since a framework for time has already been established. Rather, stories can be selected based on the specific need for training at any given time. A specific set of stories has not been pre-selected for this layer since training needs differ depending on context. Also, in order to maintain growth in leadership skills it is necessary for leaders who are POLs to have access to someone who can read Scripture to them on a regular basis, as well as have input from other ministers. By this time, a leader who is a POL should be able to hear the written Word read aloud to him and transform what he hears into an oral story that can be shared and reproduced.

Objections to a Chronological Storying Approach

At this point it would be beneficial to discuss some objections to using a chronological storying approach. Some have suggested that since the Buddhist worldview is largely cyclical in regard to time, teaching Bible stories in a linear or chronological way is not going far enough in contextualizing the gospel. Examples of this cyclical view of life are seen in the practically unending circle of birth, death and reincarnation as well as the agricultural cycle of plowing, planting and harvest.

Although this objection is worth ongoing consideration and discussion, I would like to make a couple of comments. I have never heard anyone suggest a specific alternative or contextualized gospel message that reflects this worldview, with the exception of simply using the parables, illustrations or Biblical narratives that inherently contain these concepts, such as the Parable of the Sower (Mt. 13:1). Quite frankly, it is my opinion that this Buddhist worldview of time (if, in fact, it truly does represent their understanding of time) stands in direct conflict with the Biblical worldview that time is in fact linear, with a starting point of creation and an ending point of judgment. I can find no way to take the story of redemption and "marry" it to a cyclical worldview.

Another objection to a focus on chronological Bible storying is that it is weak in highlighting other important teachings of Scripture which are not inherently narrative in style. This is a good objection and should be considered by all who are serious about communicating the gospel to POLs. One of the weaknesses of the "Oral Bible" is that it is only oral! We must recognize the limitations of oral approaches and seek to find ways to incorporate the wealth of the written Word among POLs. We must also seek to utilize other oral communication methods besides storying. No one approach is going to cover all the ground of Biblical teaching, and POLs and literates alike must find ways to work together in this great endeavor of communicating the gospel.

Other Important Methods of Oral Communication

In addition to Chronological Bible Storying, there are a number of other effective methods of oral communication. Not only do these methods compliment the Bible-Storying process, they are in fact critical supplements to the communication of the gospel, especially in regard to making disciples. As previously stated, approximately seventy percent of Scripture is narrative, leaving thirty percent of Scripture in some other style of writing. We must find ways of communicating non-narrative Biblical truth in order to be faithful in communicating the whole counsel of God.

One method that has proven effective among oral cultures is poetry. In fact, I found it necessary to use poetry to deal with some specific problems in developing the evangelism story set. Because of the lack of a concept of God in the Theravada Buddhist mindset, I considered it essential to develop such a concept as the first step in evangelism and for some time I struggled with creating a story about God. It seemed an impossible task since there was no Biblical narrative or foundation for such a story. So I turned to poetry instead. It seemed to be a natural solution to the complex problem of describing God. In one short poem I was able to touch on what I considered to be the most critical aspects of God necessary to understanding the gospel. Here is just an excerpt (only two of five verses) of the English translation of the Khmer poem, *Who is God:*

God is sovereign, pure and holy,
almighty in power, unchangeable,
no beginning and no end, eternally alive,
purely Spirit, then, in complete darkness
ready to create.

Life was waiting, in the heart
and will of Supreme God,
waiting for God to proclaim, with one word voiced,
then, born quickly, appearing thickly
all over the universe.

Another helpful oral communication tool has been Scripture in song, songs entirely from specific passages from the Word of God. This method is particularly helpful for teaching passages such as the Sermon on the Mount or other teachings of Jesus or the apostles that were not in the form of stories or parables. We have been actively developing this facet of our Oral Bible and have more than one hundred songs in the process of being written and edited, most of which focus on the commands or the teachings of Christ. The potential of this highly effective tool should not be overlooked.

Music and the Arts

The final oral communication method that I would like to note is the use of music and the arts. Music and songs in various forms including theater and dance are also very powerful means of communication. Although not as central to discipleship and training as the other methods, the arts are obviously a powerful tool for evangelism among POLs. Quite possibly the great potential of these media have yet to be fully explored.

Some Encouragement, Some Concerns

My journey into the world of communicating the gospel to the POL has truly been an adventure, bringing me the joy of seeing fruit as well as the disappointment of failure. I have learned that in the process of teaching and communicating, the road often leads to barriers which must be overcome and occasionally leads to wrong turns and dead ends. Surely it has been a joy to perceive that POLs understand the message as oral methods are applied, but for me, the true litmus test of success is whether lives are changed and the message is reproduced by sharing it with others.

"Bible stories are essential to have a foundation for understanding truth," remarked Koy Sarun, a Khmer pastor and teacher who has been using stories to evangelize and disciple people. He also noted that the only drawback he has found in using stories is that at times he has not made it clear whether the story was from Scripture or from personal experience, leading to misunderstandings (Sarun 2006). We need to remember that there is a danger of confusion when working with illiterates who are unable to verify teachings by checking Biblical references. There is always a concern for heresy as a written Biblical standard for truth is not available to many POLs. Therefore the existence of a strong relationship between a POL congregation and a Biblically literate person is essential.

Sarun also shared about one church member who, after hearing the story of Paul's shipwreck on Malta and his divine protection from a viper's bite, shared the story with the family of a sick person who was unconscious. Then, after laying hands and praying for the sick man, he regained consciousness and was healed! They all had goose bumps as they saw a demonstration of the power of God (Sarun 2006).

Yeth Ye, another Khmer pastor and teacher, also echoed Sarun's perspective, "Cambodia's rural illiterates desperately need to hear the gospel in story form. For them, listening to 'point' sermons doesn't make sense; they need to know that what the Bible teaches is for real life . . . I personally was touched as I heard the story of Jesus calming the sea. I saw how powerful Jesus really is!" Ye also shared that he believed it important for stories to be shared over and over. He commented, "The first time an unbeliever hears a story, he only catches about twenty percent. Those who have been believers for a while can understand fifty percent" (Ye 2006). I must admit, that no matter what method I have used in evangelism, what Ye is saying is true. I have tried many times to simplify and rework stories to try to achieve better understanding and often with the same results. Certainly the work of the Holy Spirit to illuminate the mind of the unbeliever and draw him to the Father is an essential part of the process and to simply rely on various methods, tools or approaches is never enough. More important than any approach is the work of the Holy Spirit within a person to convict of sin and draw the unbeliever to Christ.

Another concern in this process for me has been the differences I see in how people respond to oral approaches. Some seem to quickly understand the stories I have shared and can immediately retell them with uncanny accuracy, while others have a hard time, especially in remembering the details of a story. Despite the disparity, Sok Leng, another Khmer pastor and teacher says, "People understand far more through hearing stories, singing songs, listening to poetry and watching drama than listening to a sermon. Some are more gifted in storytelling while others are more gifted in poetry and song. I have studied TEE [Theological Education by Extension] and have gained information and knowledge, but when I hear a story, I can commit that knowledge to memory instead of needing to refer to a notebook" (Leng 2006). Again, not one approach works well with everyone. We must discover a variety of approaches to be most effective.

Finally, probably the most encouraging story of hope with oral communication approaches among POLs, and especially using the tools that I've developed comes from a Thai missionary working in Cambodia's northeastern-most province, Ratanakiri. Bee Pinthammarak has been working among tribal groups, focusing on training storytellers and translating the evangelism story set from Khmer into four different tribal languages. She just happened to call as I was preparing this article to report some exciting developments with her oral communicators. They have been evangelizing in new villages using Bible Storying and were originally meeting with people twice per week. The villagers have been asking for more and now they are meeting almost every evening. One granny among the villagers has been listening to the stories and repeating them to those who could not attend the meetings, and she is not even a believer yet! In each of the four tribal languages many people are coming to Christ and the church is thriving. It is in this province where we are seeing the "first fruits" of oral communication truly being reproduced through Bible Storying. They have plans to start translating into a fifth tribal language soon (Pinthammarak 2006). Next week I am planning to visit to give further training to the storytellers and translators, encouraging them to continue the great work.

Conclusion

For hundreds of years the preferred means of communicating the gospel has been through various literate methods (although for over a thousand years communication has been through oral tradition – even in the church). Over the last few centuries we have rightfully seen the restoration of the prominence of the written Word of God as a standard for faith and practice as it has become available to the literate populations of the world. Now, we have the great opportunity and challenge to bring the Word of God one step further (and one step back): to see the creation of Oral Bibles in every language and for every nation, so that the great POL majority will also have available to them what has so faithfully sustained so many of us. It is time to begin moving towards oral communication of the gospel.

9

COMMUNICATING THE GOSPEL THROUGH STORY AND SONG IN CAMBODIA

Barnabas Mam, as told to Bruce Hutchinson

Cambodia is still recovering from the trauma of the extreme Marxist Pol Pot era of the seventies, and only since 1990 has the church of Cambodia begun to experience relative religious freedom. This has brought new challenges and lessons for missiologists and nationals in communicating the Gospel message effectively to what remains to be primarily an oral society, particularly in rural Cambodia. Much has and is being done by many to reach and influence the nation's unreached. The purpose of this article is to provide missiologists with a better understanding of Cambodia and how the Christian message can be communicated within a predominantly folk Buddhist Khmer culture to generations undergoing dramatic social change through adapting stories, songs, melodies and even rituals of the people. This article seeks to provide a glimpse into the mind, heart and culture of Cambodians, through the sharing of interviews, personal experiences and lessons learned through trial and testing in the crucible that is Cambodia, past and present.

How does the church effectively reach out and communicate Christ to a nation which gets its sense of identity and nationhood from a seven-headed serpent–the *naga* of Hindu mythology–and a humanistic philosophy that is a counterfeit to all that Christ offers through the completed work of the Cross? As Jesus used familiar words and scenes from nature and the rural culture to convey the heart meaning of the Gospel and the Kingdom of God, weaving them into powerful and memorable stories that embed spiritual truth into the searching heart of the listener, so word pictures from the culture and countryside, inspired by the Spirit of God, tell of His reason for coming to Cambodia.

The Miracle of the Cambodian Christmas Carol

One night before Christmas 1993, my friend Paulerk Sar and I journeyed together to Tuol Klote village, Svay Rieng province, to join a local pastor and his small band of believers to celebrate the event in a land not long set free to receive its message. That night we slept on a stack of rice straw outside pastor Yeung's stilt house because there was no room left inside. I had recently returned from a refugee camp in Thailand's Prachin Buri province, bringing an album of songs I had composed there. Among them was a Christmas song in Khmer called "Angels' Songs of Blessing," set to a classical Bassac operatic melody. Bassac music is a style related to the Hee of China and the Cai leoung of Vietnam, performed with an accompanying ensemble of five traditional Khmer instruments, small drums (*skor*), sitar (*khim*), a two-stringed violin (*tro)*, and a wooden box and stick (*pun*) (Hun 2004: 85).

On this night the song was played over loudspeakers tied to a palm tree so the whole village could hear. The words of the song, accompanied by traditional Khmer instruments playing the Bassac melody, carried through the cool still night. They became an operetta that told a story of hope, peace and goodwill through Christ the Savior born to all Cambodians.

> It was a clear midnight with shining moon when the angels sang . . .
>
> Let the earth be filled with joy and peace that Christ has brought . . .
>
> Let the earth be relieved from fear, grief, suffering, mourning
>
> And enjoy peace forever; Halle, Halle, Halle, Hallelujah.

Early the next morning we were greeted by a group of about a dozen elderly villagers bearing gifts of fruit and cooked rice. As they sat down to enjoy breakfast together, one of the villagers said, "We were so delighted to hear that Christ is not American or French, but the Son of God who came even for Cambodians. We understood the songs. We appreciate that Christ came for us and we want to receive Him now." The familiarity of the Bassac music had attracted them to listen to the whole album and their words of new life and hope in a Savior born for them, and Christ was born again that morning in the hearts of a dozen Buddhist villagers.

A Prodigal Son Comes Home

I was raised in a devout and respected Buddhist family skilled in story-telling. By the age of eighteen I was a Buddhist master of ceremonies and healer. I was attracted to communist ideology but surrendered to Christ in April 1972, at the age of twenty-two, while spying on a World Vision rally in Phnom Penh for my former communist masters three years before the fall of the capital to the Khmer Rouge. My heart was deeply touched by the story of the Prodigal Son, and of a heavenly Father who would later guide and keep me miraculously through the ensuing years of Cambodia's Killing Fields, during which my father and six siblings died. The speaker that night was Dr Stanley Mooneyham, director of World Vision International (Sloggett 2005:28). I was caught up by the power of the Word and the Holy Spirit to see myself as the prodigal son. Communism trained me never to cry. It was a sign of weakness, but that day the Word of God moved me to cry over my sins. I went into the convention centre as a Communist and I came out a born-again Christian.

During the genocidal Pol Pot years from 1974-79 and the year of famine that followed the relatively small but rapidly-growing Christian Church, along with all other religions, including Buddhism and the indigenous Muslims, the Cham, was all but wiped out, along with so many educated and professional people or those who had not fled the approaching holocaust (Lockerbie 1976), while suffering and persecution continued under the subsequent Vietnamese Communist occupation of the 80s.

Early Obstacles

The first obstacle I faced was the disapproval of my uncle with whom I had lived while serving in the local *wat* as a temple boy, After that was my father who had been a monk for fourteen years. God provided both food and words of grace and wisdom. The fire within me pushed me to go to church where I was warmly welcomed. The communists often sang of brotherly love, but I found the community of brotherly love I was looking for at church. In church I was taught to honour my parents so I told my father, "I'll honour you when you're alive. Why wait until you're dead to pay offerings?" He replied, "It's not bad if you still obey."

A year later I met Major Chhirc Taing, who had returned from England in 1973 to lead the Cambodian church for two eventful and tumultuous years only to be martyred along with other leaders shortly after the city's fall on April 17, 1975. The night before that event, I was with him, praying along with about sixty other leaders, and was encouraged by his final words, "Be faithful unto death." Major Chhirc also preached on the mantle of Elijah, challenging the church of Cambodia to rise up as the Elisha generation. We spent the night in prayer together with about sixty leaders. Early next morning, April 17, the Khmer Rouge seized Phnom Penh and in three days more than one million people were evacuated from the city.

Chhirc said his goodbyes and exhorted us from Romans 13:1 to submit ourselves to the governing authorities and that God would guide and protect us. He also told us to learn to be as gentle as doves and wise as snakes. Knowing this was the end of his life, he went out and began witnessing on the streets. I saw him being arrested and then assassinated. I loved to hear his messages. His life, however, spoke louder than his words. He was a man who lived out the Word. He became my Elijah. I didn't know that one day I'd become his Elisha. He discipled and mentored me, and we spent much quality time together in ministry.

Stony Ground

From the beginning of Protestant missionary endeavor in Cambodia in 1923 until 1970, Cambodia was rated as one of the world's most difficult and unyielding mission fields, but between 1970 and 1975 the number of congregations swelled from three to twenty-seven, from 300 believers to 4000 (Lockerbie 1976:210). The questioning of old religious ideas and ideals continues into a new generation of seekers who have become the harvest field of the third millennium, and who are also seeking something more.

Those who escaped to Thailand or remained behind during the Pol Pot era became the source of a revival that swept the refugee camps, from out of which many thousands were resettled to other countries or repatriated back to Cambodia in 1993. I was one of those involved. In 1975 I had remained in Cambodia to be one of the few believers alive while the Khmer Rouge conducted their reign of terror and murder on a grand scale. As many as 2.7 million -- or nearly one third of the entire population at the time -- died through direct killing, sickness or starvation in the following five years. God kept me alive through these desperate and dangerous times, including imprisonment, sickness, and threat of torture and execution.

Seeds of a Worshipper Sown

After the fall of Phnom Penh in 1975 I walked with the rest of the city's swollen population of around one million herded into the countryside as it was turned into a giant slave labor camp. After I was caught I was put into a hard labor camp in the east of the country for re-education for more than fifteen months. I kept track of the dates with daily prayers to God. I found comfort in Psalm 23. God indeed showed himself as provider, shepherd, and even led me through the valley of the shadow of death when I thought I was to be led off one night to be executed.

During my time in the labor camp the Lord sowed the seeds of a worshipper in me. I only knew the hymns that we sang in church, so when there was a thunderstorm and it was raining heavily I would stand by the window and sing How Great Thou Art out loud in Khmer, English and French. I'd have visions of the church of the multitudes worshipping with me.

My faith in God, and usefulness in speaking English (although the latter usually resulted in an instant death sentence), kept me alive. I was even appointed as personal assistant to an unusually caring, illiterate but smart Khmer Rouge leader. In February 1979 the KR fled westward in Pursat province from advancing Vietnamese forces; many were being ordered executed by paranoid KR leadership. I finally challenged my leader with the thought of answering for the lives of all us in the group if he had to face God one day. As others advanced into the killing fields this man allowed about five hundred of us to linger behind until we were able to turn toward the liberating forces.

I returned to Phnom Penh to start over, attending an underground church. I met Boury, a widow with six children whose husband had been killed by the Khmer Rouge a few years earlier. We were married in 1980 and a year later the Lord blessed us with a baby girl, Shalom. In January 1985, under threat of death for illegal Christian activities, I was forced to flee to a Thailand refugee camp with my wife and three daughters. I was initially captured and imprisoned as an illegal alien and kept apart from my wife. We remained in the camps for eight years until March, 1993. During that time we planted fifteen churches, equipped fifty Christian leaders, pastored a Vietnamese church, and started an English school. When the Paris Peace Accord was signed, we were welcomed back to Cambodia for the UN-sponsored elections.

When we first returned to Phnom Penh in 1979 the new church had already been flourishing in the Thai refugee camps among thousands of traumatized Cambodians whose lives, families, nation, and culture had been shattered. In three years following the Khmer Rouge takeover Thailand Southern Baptists alone baptized 2,100 Cambodian and Vietnamese refugees (Smith 2001:58). I had begun developing singing and story-telling to more effectively reach out to the hungry souls left in Cambodia as well the camps and continued this work in Thailand, writing many songs while locked up.

As a result of this early work and its continued development the Cambodian church now has many poems, hymns, and contemporary songs of praise and worship. I have written, composed, or translated into English more than 400 hymns, poems, and contemporary songs since 1981. Together with Cambodian author and poet Uon Seila (co-chairman of the Youth Commission of the Evangelical Fellowship of Cambodia) we produced an initial collection of about thirty songs. Seila gives a New Testament twist to a Cambodian story of the bamboo, and how when it flowers it is no longer any use. This resembles pride, the opposite of the humility God requires of His followers to be of use in serving Him and others.[1] Another gifted songwriter and composer was Sam Sarin, who was also a refugee camp church leader who had become

---

1 Uon Seila's story and his writings on bamboo are recorded in *Honeycomb* 2/2 April 2001.

a Christian in Kao I Dang Camp, Thailand, in 1980.[2] He compiled the first Cambodian hymnal which included some of my songs and hymns, in conjunction with long-serving OMF missionary Alice Compain, who returned later to work in Cambodia (Cormack 1997:368). Sarin resettled in Australia.

My early songs were not initially accepted by conservatives, and we struggled for a decade. Some even called me a son of the devil. Eventually the songs became popular as they struck a chord with many new believers. They are now used in the prisons of Cambodia as they touch the heart of many in similar circumstances.

In 1994 at a time when Khmer Rouge strongholds were still operating, an anonymous KR officer wrote a letter to FEBC saying how much he enjoyed listening to FEBC Cambodia because he had found that Christians in Cambodia were aware of the need to preserve the Khmer folk songs, so he did not see Christianity as a betrayal of Khmer culture. A respected authority on Khmer culture, when asked if he thought Christian hymns set to Khmer tunes were distorting them, he said no, and that he felt they helped preserve them. "They are much better than the Khmer Rouge who used the same tunes but with lyrics that stirred up anger and hatred, whereas the Christians use them to promote love and unity," the man said.

Now I encourage a new generation of Christian songwriters and musicians to record their own albums on CD that appeal to young people as well, and a ministry has been established to facilitate this. Contemporary song-writers whose music is being used and recorded include one of my former tutors, Bin David, pastor of the Khmer Evangelical Church (C&MA), Bun Sambath (Church of Christ), and Heng Piset (New Life Fellowship music director), and

---

2 Sam Sarin's autobiography, *Honeycomb,* July 2001, P 100 (English and Khmer).

also my own granddaughter, Or Angkeara. (Living Hope in Christ Church). These people can work together as a team.

Inspiration for Song-Writing

I started writing songs in 1982 in Cambodia when the church had been forced underground during the Vietnamese occupation. I had received a letter from Alice Compain asking me to find someone who could write songs in a Cambodian flavor so that the new believers in the border camps in Thailand could sing along.

How could I, unlearned in music and clumsy, do this task? The Holy Spirit gave me the grace and ability. I had been inspired in 1980 after reading a story by Brother Andrew about a Russian Christian song-writer who had led many to Christ through his ministry and who had been incarcerated in a psychiatric institution. I asked the Lord, "Who is it that you would raise up to lead your church in Cambodia to worship you?" The answer came as a strong impression in my heart: "It's you." I decided to learn the flute and guitar and to read music.

My wife, Boury, agreed that this was my calling and decided to pay for my music tuition fees. My tutors included Yin Dikan, a Cambodian flautist and songwriter, who was not a believer, Bin David (later to become a believer and pastor of the New Jerusalem Church), and the great Cambodian lead guitarist Minh Sothyvan. I was able to use the flute to make melody and the guitar to write the chords. I practiced writing music on the table of a local breakfast restaurant using a toothpick and tea.

My early inspiration for song-writing came from the late Rev. Sem Bun, who served one term as president of the Khmer Evangelical Church in the early seventies and who wrote the first simple Khmer song of praise with a Cambodian melody, *Jesus Came to Seek and Save the Lost,* to add to a book of translated English hymns. My early mentor, Chhric Taing, also wrote a song that inspired me, *Who is it?* based on the story of Jesus' birth and which was used at the 1974 Christmas celebration in Phnom Penh. This song, with additional verses, is number sixty-eight in the Cambodian Hymnal. The method of song-writing used is typical of the Cambodian question-and-answer style where the man asks a question and the woman answers. In this case, the child who was laid in a manger is Christ the King and the listener is invited to welcome Him and give their hearts to Him.

I wrote and sent off to Alice the first dozen songs, anonymously because of the danger at the time of identifying me in Cambodia as the author and connecting me to the compiler, Sam Sarin, in Kao I Dang camp. Some hymns in the hymnal used today remain anonymous. They were originally published by OMF and later by CAMA Services. I wrote or translated close to 200 hymns and songs in the Cambodian Hymnal, which is still used and updated regularly.

When I fled with my family to Thailand in 1985, the Lord continued to stir me to produce a more contemporary style of worship music based on the Scriptures. This was at a time when I went through many different holding centers on the border. I suffered badly from internal hemorrhoids and was unable to sit, so I wrote or translated many songs lying on my stomach, also translating the picture Bible that way. From 1985 to 1993 I translated many songs, mostly from Integrity/Hosanna Music and Vineyard, which the younger generation enjoyed so much. It made the worship very vibrant and relevant, making worship songs and scripture available at a time when distribution of Bibles and

Christian literature such as hymnals was greatly restricted. New songs were very helpful because the refugees were able to learn them by heart.

When I came back to Cambodia in 1993 I wrote more songs on the grace of God, as well as translations of other songs. I work now more on the grace and mercy of God. It fits very well in opening the heart of Buddhist people to the Gospel. I also translated Hillsong music into Khmer for the young people. Both are very effective, one for young people and one for the common folk. Contemporary Khmer style songs are very effective for older Cambodians.

All my hymns and poems are based on scripture, for example a prayer poem based on 1 John 5:14-15. A Cambodian Lullaby has been used by Cambodian parents to sing their children to sleep and sooth them for hundreds of years. Prime Minister Hun Sen used his own version in "The Life of a Temple Boy." I wrote another version for Christians, *Jesus Loves You Little One*, in 1999 to be used at child dedications, which talks about how important it is to be protected by God, to be secure in His arms, how important it is to raise a baby in accordance with (the parent's) faith, and how the parents admit they can do nothing but entrust the child into the love of the Everlasting Father.

Jesus Loves You Little One

Dale Jones, translator

1. Oh, little one, God loves you
He gently cares for you every day (2X)
From when you were little
Oh, little one, there's nothing that can harm you (x2)

2. He carries you in his arms
He warms you in his kindness (x2)
He loves you so much
He's exchanged his life for his precious one(x2)
3. Surrender yourself, little one, without regret
Your parents have nothing to make a guarantee (x2))
Living with God means stability
Live with your God, little one (x2)

4. He accepts you, little one, as his child
He has prepared a supreme kingdom (x2)
A glorious, unfading kingdom.
Little one, believe Him, you'll live forever(x2)

A funeral service is a good opportunity to bring people to the Lord. I use a poem about what life on earth looks like, called *We Will be with God Forever: Human Life is Worth More than Flowers* based on Psalm 90. It just looks like grass. And what makes it different? The dichotomy of life. Not just soul-eternal-soul and then just temporary body. Human life living on earth is like flowers of the field. In the morning it is in full blossom, but in the afternoon it all fades away. In stanza two it says there are all kinds of flowers with all kinds of aromas and some without aroma, but all face the same destiny, and then human life on earth cannot be better than flowers if we are without Christ. We live and blossom for a short while, and then fade away. So, we need a savior who will give us wholeness of life so we can live our bodily life, our soul life, and our spirit life. Then one day our bodies will become ash, or embers, or return to the dust, but our spirits will live for eternity with God.

We don't think it wise to bring a guitar to the graveside but we can sing this poem at the graveside in unison.

This song was used on one occasion in 1993 when a woman came to see me about nine in the morning asking me to help resolve a dilemma. The woman's husband had just died, but had received the Lord at a hospital before he passed away and his relatives had summoned the Buddhist MC and laymen to fill her house with the chanting of the *dhamma.* At the same time Christians from her church had gathered and were singing "Amazing Grace" in another room. While the Christians stopped singing and started praying quietly, I negotiated with the Buddhist family members to work out a way that the Christian funeral service could continue the next day in a nearby Buddhist *wat* (temple) without offending the Buddhist relatives and friends, who also loved and cared for her and her family. More than 300 believers joined and Khmer hymnals were brought to the Buddhist crematorium about two hours drive from the deceased's home, then I led a choral singing of the poem "We Will Be With God Forever" without musical instruments and in front of the Buddhist monks, nuns and lay people. A friend preached a short message of encouragement. Immediately afterwards an elderly Buddhist nun got into a van with the Christian leaders, knelt down and asked them to lead her in the sinner's prayer, while the other Buddhists were declaring "Christianity is not alien to us any more!"

I looked around and also heard the Christians saying how wonderful it was that they could all sing Christian poems together while conducting a Christian cremation--two things they learned that day. "It was done in such a way that it was acceptable to both Christians and Buddhists. That's the key."

While my wife, Boury, was in a separate prison after we fled to Thailand in 1985, I wrote a song based on The Lord's Prayer (Matt. 6: 9-13) as a prayer from the heart. *In Jesus Hands* was another I wrote from my own need to feel secure in God when I was in his house in Phnom Penh suspected of being a CIA agent and in danger of being arrested and interrogated at any time.

Our church (Living Hope in Christ) is a worshipping church, and we teach by our lifestyle. Churches that teach only contemporary Western Christian music, even though translated, tend to be regarded as American. This is good if you reach out only to young people, but my fear is that they develop their own culture and will not be effective in assimilating with the Khmer culture or fellowshipping with other Khmer churches that do not use this style of music. Most churches in Cambodia use the Khmer Hymnal. It is wise to train young music teachers and worship leaders to use all styles of songs, including the old translated hymns with their theological richness and profoundness.

Ceremonial Music, Instruments, Dance and Rituals

There are some sorts of musical settings that are used just to celebrate, such as weddings or dedications of new houses, and also for blessing people, for example the classical ballet, *The Blessing Dance*, to wish everyone a good future. There are also certain types that are totally dedicated to the invocation of evil spirits, so as a minister of the Gospel I prefer not to use that kind of music because it will invoke the evil spirit, even though we change the lyrics. When we sing the song the people still think of the work of the devil. So I find it is more helpful to use those music styles that bless or celebrate to incorporate or integrate with scriptures in song with a Cambodian flavor.

In Khmer weddings I don't encourage the groom to perform the tradition of taking up the train of the bride because it represents the Princess Naga's tail. In Khmer legend the princess brought her first groom, Preah Thong, known as the first king and national groom, to visit her father, carrying her tail. The man must be the head and not the tail in a marriage relationship submitted to God.

In Khmer dance, I don't have any problem with traditional folk dancing, which usually reflects ordinary life, but I do with copying snake-like movements that are used to invoke or appease the spirits, or imitate the *naga*, as used by dancers who imitate *apsaras*, or heavenly nymphs that Hindu legend of creation says were created by the 'sea of churning milk' in a struggle between good and evil spirits. I feel that any dance used to imitate the *naga*'s behavior or nature is deceptive or seductive.

Khmer folk dancing and Bassac drama to present pivotal Biblical stories such as the Nativity or Easter story is becoming more popular among Cambodian churches and institutions as they realize how effective the Khmer cultural style is in communicating the Gospel to the heart of Cambodians. It can be described as a movement across the nation. Folk dance has even become a focus of life and ministry at Christian orphanages in Cambodia, such as Unicas.

The Importance of Story-Telling

From my experience as a Cambodian among Cambodians I believe storying is the key to communicating the Gospel most effectively in a culture that is predominantly rural and semi-literate at best. More

Cambodians are learning to read and write in their own Khmer language, while English is becoming more popular and necessary particularly among city dwellers and the young, or those born since the Khmer Rouge era who comprise more than half the population. I use a lot of the parables of the Kingdom along with other more homegrown stories with the same kingdom values.

A UNESCO/UNDP report of 2001 estimated only thirty-six percent of the population of Cambodia was functionally literate (able to use their literacy skills for everyday life and income generation). Another thirty-six percent were illiterate and twenty-seven percent semi-illiterate. Sixty-three percent of the nation's population, or 8.8 million, have literacy skills below the functional level (Rosenbloom 2004:3). Rosenbloom comments that estimated literacy skills in Cambodia vary depending on survey methodology and definition of literacy. In spite of state and private literacy programs available in 2000, only two per cent of the total adult illiterate population was being reached at that time.

An experienced C&MA missionary and Christian publisher in Phnom Penh, Steve Westergren, from a long-established Cambodian missionary family affirms these conclusions from his own experience. In an interview with the author, he said it was likely these figures also applied to the church.

> There is a significant number of Cambodians who don't know what they are reading, and a significant sector of society that is essentially oral in the way they communicate. This society is not prone to read. There's been a skipping of generations from those who read to those who are very technologically-oriented who prefer to watch television, videos or listen to music than read. I also know that most high schools and even universities do not teach Cambodian classical literature, therefore there is an inherent

> difficulty in understanding what good literature is or to assimilate what the written word shows, so they have not developed god reading habits because what is available is generally not good literature. My challenge as a Christian publisher is to be a catalyst to growing a society that likes to read and write good literature and we have to begin with the children and young people (20 December 2006).

Protestant Christianity is a relative newcomer to Cambodia after a very slow and hard start in the 1920s by CMA missionaries the Ellisons and Hammonds. Arthur Hammond produced the first Khmer language New Testament in 1933 (Cormack 1997:446). Only two translations of the Bible have been in use until recently, the more formal Khmer Bible, translated in turn from the English translation of the King James Version and completed in 1951, and the contemporary Khmer version translated from Greek and Hebrew.

A Khmer language publishing house, Fount of Wisdom (FOW), was established in 2003 by Westergren to raise up Christian Khmer writers, editors and translators and to foster more indigenous material rather than rely on translations of foreign literature often inappropriate or too Western for the indigenous believers, or which suffer from translation inaccuracies and misinterpretation. Seila and I contributed to the first seminar organized by FOW and sponsored by World Vision through Russell Bowers and Training of Timothys to encourage Cambodian writers to produce indigenous material, and a subsequent series of monthly writer-training modules as part of a "writers' club" to encourage a variety of writing styles. Several publications have been produced directly by FOW and more are in the pipeline. One tool to reach those with low literacy skills FOW has produced recently for the Bible Society of Cambodia is a series of five illustrated booklets on the life of Christ for Khmer teachers entitled "Gospel for New Readers," while an audio tape series, accompanied by picture booklets, entitled "Look, Listen and Live" has been produced primarily for Cambodian women to reach and teach new believers.

Stories with Relevance

Because this generation of Cambodians does not like to read, we must present the stories of the Gospel in a relevant and interesting way, through story-telling, television and radio programs, drama and music, all of which are being used to good effect in Cambodia even through State media channels by Christian program-makers. An example of meeting the need of the younger people would be the EFC Youth Commission's annual youths camps at which Gospel messages are sung accompanied by the *cha pei*, a long-necked three-nylon-stringed Cambodian guitar, or *ayai*. The songs are sung by two minstrels, the woman asking a question and the man answering. The lyrics were written by Uon Seila.

After twenty years of experience in neighboring Thailand, Alex Smith observed that the use of parable, symbol and analogy is generally more acceptable to the Buddhist mind than strictly focused arguments. Word pictures can be employed to great advantage, and it is important to let the meaning shine through as the Bible does so well with its rich stories and simple parables, rather than try to over explain things. "Studying the indigenous process of communication and utilizing these principles for proclamation and teaching will probably be a crucial issue in effective evangelism and theological education, both for national church leaders and foreign apostles," Smith says (2001:47).

Storying of Biblical truth is more effective if the story is familiar with people in the audience. There are many examples from Khmer culture that can be applied in presenting the Gospel effectively in the Cambodian context.

The Blind and the Lame

> There are two friends. One is blind and the other lame. There is an *asura* or titan -- a giant cannibal that kills and eats people every day who is a real threat to the kingdom. He makes a deal with the king: "If you give me your daughter, then I will stop eating everyone in your kingdom."
>
> The king loves his daughter very much, but also loves his people and can not bear seeing them killed every day. He advertises for any courageous young man who will rescue his daughter given as a living sacrifice to the asura and to anyone who can rescue her he will give his daughter in marriage. Along come the blind and lame men. Because they cannot see how big the asura is, or run from him, they are not afraid. After failing to frighten the two men with many tricks, the asura goes away, the king's daughter is rescued and everyone in the kingdom is saved (Ref?).

If one human life can result in so many people being saved how much more precious is the life of the Son of God who was crucified and buried then resurrected by the Father? By telling this story a lot of people come to the saving knowledge of Jesus Christ. Every Cambodian school child and every elderly person in the village is familiar with this story.

Church Planters Trained in Storying

I have produced Khmer-appropriate church planter training modules which incorporate stories and a teaching style developed in the field over the years, and discipled others in the art of story-telling. The teaching is presented with graphic-heavy visual PowerPoint images and Khmer text to emphasize the oral teaching style, reinforced with stories the trainees have to memorize so they can in turn tell them to their small teaching groups and seek their responses so that their questions can be answered.

The Prince and Neang Chaeh

> The prince is sent by the father, the king of the land, to walk across the kingdom to ask the people to welcome him so they can live as family. He goes from one village to another in pauper's clothes seeking those who would receive him, and only a poor girl with a hare lip (Chaeb means hare lip in Khmer) opens her door and invites him in to her home and heart and feeds and cares for him. At the appointed time the prince is taken back to see his father by a parade of dignitaries, representing angels, and takes with her the girl with the hare lip to meet his father, who receives her as his own daughter, heals her disfigurement and sends her back to her village as a princess. She becomes a different person with a new name and new attitude toward herself and others as she enjoys her new life (Mam 2006).

I thank God I am rich in the Khmer culture because of stories told to me by my mother and father. I adapt folk stories, Buddhist stories and Khmer classics, as my own modern parables. This is why the church planters who we train in our Institute of Church

Planting Cambodia are so successful in evangelism and church planting.

I find it more effective when I teach with groups of no more than thirty people; for interaction, for interrelationship, and especially for group discussion, and also when they minister to one another in prayer. People are more sincere to one another in smaller groups. I believe my church grows spiritually, numerically, culturally and socially, especially in evangelism, mission and church planting, because we run discipleship groups.

Contextualization and Rituals

There are pros and cons to contextualization in presenting the Gospel stories, for example when the Bible says "for the kingdom of God is not eating and drinking, but righteousness and peace and joy in *the* Holy Spirit" (Rom. 14:17 MKJV), it gives the impression that if you drink you never lose your salvation but you lose your reputation and respect and you will die young. But with some tribes if we say that it is okay to drink, they say "No, it's not okay. Every cup that we drink we offer it first to the devil." So their culture says that the devil is in every cup that you offer to someone. It's all spiritual. If you bring something from the Western way of thinking that drinking is OK it will harm the whole community because every cup that you give to your visitors is offered to the devil.

We need to be very sensitive to what extent we can please or improve the culture to elaborate the Gospel in such a way that they see Christ is superior to all culture but to some extent we should avoid culture that never brings honor or reverence to Christ. A lot of good things have been done by way of contextualization, for example the Khmer Hymnal. I think we are number two in Asia after the church in China in compiling our own songs of praise and worship, worship poems, and the contextualization of wedding and funeral ceremonies. But it can also become a tool for the devil to use if the officiating ministers are not well trained in worship and of the need to redeem instruments back to God.

I am often asked by Christians when I am at wedding ceremonies in rural areas, especially by the middle-aged or over, to perform something such as the *Chong Dai,* or the tying of the wrist of the newlyweds, similar to the tying of the forehead in Thailand. And I say no, because the marriage will last longer when everyone is tied by the unbroken cord of peace and joy, not just by a few pieces of thread (Eph. 4:3). It may work in some cultures, such as among the Isaan of North-East Thailand (De Neui 2002:160) and even in tribal cultures in Cambodia, but not among urban Khmer believers. My conclusion, having been brought up as a practicing Buddhist for twenty years, is that there is a need to be very cautious. This is a stumbling block to me because it is practiced widely here, and if Christians are seen to be wearing a red or white thread tied around the wrist, other people will think they had been to a spiritist. The Bible says we should "abstain from every *appearance* of evil" (1Th. 5:22 MKJV).

But at the ritual of washing feet (used in many Cambodian Christian wedding ceremonies) the parents of both the bride and the groom cry for joy because Christians can show them that it is not only the bride that washes the groom's feet, but the latter is also to wash the feet of the former. Washing one another's feet is serving and supporting one another; so we can introduce the Biblical culture of 'one another' through a Cambodian wedding ceremony. It makes everyone happy by preserving the Khmer culture that is in line with Biblical values.

Understanding Buddhism in Cambodia

There are three schools of Buddhism worldwide: Mahayana Buddhism (liberal and lay oriented) is called the "greater vehicle" and is found in China, Japan, Korea, Bhutan, Taiwan and Vietnam. Vajra Buddhism (the most esoteric) is called the "diamond way" and is known as Tibetan Buddhism, Tantric Buddhism and Lamaism. The Theravada school (monastic and conservative) also called "Hinayana", is found in Cambodia, Sri Lanka, Myanmar, Laos and Thailand. In Cambodia Theravada Buddhism has two orders: Mahanikaya, which comprises the majority of Theravada believers, and Dhammayuta, which uses the ancient Pali language only and is stricter and more legalistic in keeping the Buddhist disciplines. In Mahanikaya there are more sages, or wise men. The Royal family belongs to the Dhammayuta order.

Folk Buddhism in Cambodia is more orthodox to the original Theravada Buddhism than in Thailand, which is more magical and radical. For example in Cambodia you will find statues of Buddha everywhere but in Thailand you will find statues of the living and people such as abbots they admire who could bring them good luck. We don't see things like this happening in Cambodia yet. We only see statues of the Buddha or other gods.

According to "Jataka," the legend of Buddha's past lives, he claimed to live through 550 lives. This view affirms the belief of "Samsara" (cycle of rebirth and reincarnation). He lived the life of Sasapandita the rabbit, the life of Bhuridatta the Naga and the life of Vessantara the prince just to earn more merits for his Buddhahood.

Buddhists are agnostic and atheist in one way but polytheist in another. They do not believe in God but claim to have contacts with many gods: Brahma, creator of the universe; Indra, king of heavens;

devata, or angelic beings (male and female); Yomaraja, king of hells; Nagaraja, king of *nagas* (five-headed serpents). Six realms of existence are mapped out from the experiences of the Buddha and his enlightened disciples beginning with the superior and progressing downwards, into which one may be born according to one's karma: *deva* (gods), *asura* (titans or giants), *manussa* (human beings), *preta* or *peta* (hungry ghosts), *Tiracchana* (animals), and *naraka* (hells).

Advice for Evangelists

In sharing the Gospel with Buddhists use terms that they can understand so avoid Christian vocabulary that may confuse them. Focus on personal stories of righteous living, complete forgiveness and God's compassion, for example the story of the prodigal son. If we use contemporary stories and quote from Christian heroes from the Western world folk in the rural areas do not know who they are, so sometimes I find it is not so easy quoting the modern story of the modern disciple of Christ. The strange names and the strange places are difficult to remember, but if I can find some story that is a folk story with the same Biblical values, they will remember it forever.

Be able to show them the difference between Christ and Buddha. To tell this in story form, I say that for me, as a former Buddhist, Buddha was like a swimming teacher who taught me how to swim but was not a rescuer. But Jesus didn't give me swimming lessons--He jumped into the river where I was drowning and rescued me, then taught me how to swim later. I use this story with Buddhist audiences, because when a Buddhist faces a crisis, Buddha says "rely on your own self ... I show you eight right ways, five practical precepts." But people in crisis cannot do them. However, Jesus goes straight into the crisis and carries you, hugs you, and gives you all the warmth of His acceptance.

Religious leaders are good people, good teachers who see you in the river drowning and then give you a swimming lesson. They tell you how to breathe in and out; how to stretch your arms. But you cannot move your body, so what is the use of giving good lessons on swimming while you cannot swim?

Some times people question me on Christian living. "I want to accept Christ, but Mr. So-and-so cannot prove to me that he is a born-again or transformed Christian at all." It took the insight and wisdom of the Lord to answer such a pointed question, because I was also frustrated with my Christian life and that of other friends of mine who stumbled many times. Then the Lord gave me a new parable that has become an effective evangelistic tool:

The Three Friends

> Three friends were swimming in a river and two were fighting to get out onto the muddy bank. Their bodies became muddy and dirty, but the other one who was still in the river was clean, and mocked the others trying to get out, saying "You are so dirty!" But is it the end of the story? No. Finally the two friends are able to get out of the river with their dirty bodies and arrive home. Then they realize they are dirty so take a shower, and are clean--and alive. But the other one drowns in the river with a clean body.

After telling this story I challenge my listeners, "Do you want to be clean and die, or do you want to be dirty and alive then take shower and be clean, and then every day take another shower and be cleaner and cleaner?" And people will say, "I also want to be like the two friends." A friend, at the time a non-believer, had asked me this question. He encouraged his staff to go to church but was reluctant himself to accept Christ because he had seen two pastors on his staff disagreeing every day. That night I asked the Lord to give me an answer for him, told him the story then asked if he wanted to be like the man who died clean and he gave his heart to the Lord.

Show how good the law is--the precepts, the eightfold path--but how sad it is that one cannot keep the law, for example, climbing steps or running a race (Mills 1999). Explore the concept of one's ultimate destination: What is *nibbana*? What is eternal life? What if a Christian fails to obey the law? (1 Jo. 2:1-2). Tell a story of God's amazing grace (Gal.3:13-14). The five precepts are good – no stealing, lying, sexual, immorality, drinking, or killing any living creature -- but ask, "If you follow them perfectly, what will happen in the next twenty days?" For example, the precept "don't kill any living creature" – even an ant or a worm or a bug everyone would stop existing. You cannot dig ground because you would kill worms. You cannot dig for potatoes or plow the land, for you would kill so many frogs and crabs. In Buddhism there is unintentional sin as well as intentional sin, so you cannot even boil or mix soup with green vegetables because you might kill thousands of bugs, so there are the shortcomings. You break all the laws.

For me, Christianity is a story of walking the journey. I may stumble and fall. Then my Father picks me up and teaches me to walk. There's no need to go back to step A or B. I start at A, try to walk at B, then I rise up and continue walking at C. But for the Buddhist you have to start over again every day and go through step A, B and C once more. So which one do you like? Climbing the stairs or walking the journey? And (the listener) will say, "walking the journey!" This is my approach in evangelism.

Show them prophecy about Christ because people believe in prophecy. Tell them that each prophecy is fulfilled: Define the Messiah, the Christ (the Anointed, Enlightened One) mention the virgin birth (Isa.7:14); the place of birth (Mic. 5:2); the crucifixion (Ps. 22:14-18); bodily resurrection (Ps. 16:10). And, most important, pray for them (2 Co. 4:4; 2 Co. 10:4-5, 2 Ti. 2:25-26).

Telling about the superior promises and prophecies of the Bible is a very practical way of storying the Gospel. But if you talk about miracles, the Buddhist spiritists perform a lot, so we need to prove that God is real and working in us, through us and for us. Don't just talk about it--prove it. I often share my personal experiences. I have a story about Yen, a medium and traditional birth attendant in Oudong District, north of Phnom Penh (now deceased), who came to faith in Christ through a power encounter when she was delivered of twenty-one evil spirits. In another incident a village church was born as a result of the deliverance and healing of Pun, a woman who spent her life in a graveyard like the demon-possessed man Jesus set free in the Gadarenes (Mk. 5:1-20). Like the demoniac she told others the story of how Jesus had set her free and others believed as a result of seeing the miraculous change in her life and the church of Srei Chenda was formed as a result.

At a wedding I was attending the mother of the groom who opposed him marrying a Christian girl came armed with a knife with the intention of intimidating him by threatening to kill herself. The situation was turned around when the groom humbled himself before her to pay honor to her by giving thanks for her love and care in raising him to reach manhood and enable him to marry a bride, and asking her to accept her into the family. This ritual is performed by the bride and groom and is a way Christians can honor their parents in a Biblical way. The parents cry for joy.

God at Work Among the Tribes

The Khmer Hymnal has made the Gospel more accessible to Cambodians by using traditional folk tunes with scripture messages, which appeal to the heart music of the Cambodian people. Other factors include the use of indigenous tribal instruments and music in worship by the indigenous minority people of the northeast, such as the gongs, *chai pei*, *khlok,* and *tro*. Elders of the Kreung, Preuv and Jarai are accepting the Gospel because they see that the Christians value the culture of the people and give it new meaning. Translation of the Bible into the contemporary Khmer language and indigenous minority languages such as Kreung, Preuv, and Tampuen, is another factor. The Jarai are using the New Testament in their own language using the latinized scripture from Vietnam. Christian-owned radio stations broadcasting holistic Gospel songs and messages are another factor in the greater availability of the Gospel in the countryside.

Listening and group discussion as effective teaching tools have been developed among the animist tribal people as a result of ministry visits to Ratanakiri province. Arriving late one night for a training session after a long journey, I simply asked the group to share their needs and then answered their questions. At the end they said it was the best training they had ever received because no one else had come to listen to them. I had brought the food they needed. There is always good attendance, participation, and good fruit when I go there now. I see a lot of transformation in their lives. They are slow learners because Khmer is their second language as they have their own primary tribal languages, so I listen more and then address their real needs. I don't give as much as I can, I give as much as I feel they can take.

There has been repentance from dead works, more commitment to church and community service. Some Christian leaders have become community believers as well. They have developed an ability to preserve those noble aspects of their cultures containing Biblical truth and to do away with those without Biblical truth. They have formed groups of intercessors with a heart for the nations and so have become part of the global prayer network. They use songs of worship in their own tribal languages and tunes, using their own indigenous instruments more and more.

Breakthrough Experienced

A long-term missionary, community worker and elder of the Banlung church in Ratanakiri told the author that a breakthrough had been experienced in the use of traditional instruments in worship since 2004. This had released the church from a period of spiritual dryness. In a district where buffalo sacrifices were practiced routinely to ensure success with crops, local believers now understood the significance of Christ's atoning sacrifice. Christians had changed the sacrificial ritual to "harvest festivals" in which the first fruits of the land were presented to God in an act of thanksgiving for His provision and protection rather than to appease the spirits. Animals were not used, but instead symbolic rituals such as "wave offerings" using sheaves of rice were conducted as part of worship. In adopting this practice the local governor was able to understand what Christianity was all about.

Among the Kreung tribe, storying of the Gospel is being regularly practiced, as significant portions of scripture have now been translated into their native tongue. Story-telling has become the primary means of evangelism and discipling, and Khmer-speaking evangelists are able to memorize stories adapted from the scriptures and share these orally with the other people in their tribal tongue. The churches are also active in planting new groups. The Kreung now have their own songbook comprising a collection of about two dozen traditional songs, written by several local Christian songwriters, with new songs based on the scriptures being added progressively. In the northeast, as in other rural areas, changed lives as a result of the impact of the Word and work of the Holy Spirit are the most effective witness.

Westergren also commented that it had been the verbal and practical witness of lives lived out that had made the most impact within Khmer communities in Cambodia This lesson was learned by the C&MA after they stopped paying local pastors' salaries in 1955, a decision that radically changed the methods of the spread of the Gospel in Cambodia when many Cambodian pastors stopped serving the Lord because there was no subsidy. This curtailed progress of the Gospel, but at the same time developed a firm foundation of Cambodians who truly wanted to serve the Lord because of their love for Him. This made their words more authoritative and practical for Cambodians who heard them proclaim the Gospel. The church remained small, but stronger. The impact was primarily in the countryside, where most Cambodians were not well educated. They saw the true love of God in the lives of Cambodian Christians who were in contact with them. In this case it was a result of verbal witness and life lived out that had the most impact and that is so today.

A Mother Comes to Christ Through the Word and The Spirit

"Share the story and let God's power work," was a lesson learned in Thailand by Rev. Tongpan Phromedda (De Neui 2001:14). In 1993, this story happened after my family was reunited in 1993 with my mother.

My mother, Oun Yen, had become a widow during the Pol Pot years when my father, Mam Diap, died of starvation. Six children – my three brothers and three sisters -- were also killed and she, my two sisters and I are the only family survivors of the Killing Fields. My mother stayed behind in Phnom Penh with one of the daughters in 1985 when he went to Thailand, and the Lord gave me the passion to pray and fast for her salvation. I returned to Phnom Penh eight years later, in March, 1993, when my mother was seventy-four years old.

She was so excited to see us she cried. The first words I heard from her were, "Son, it's so good to see you come back. I have prayed to hundreds of gods (Hindu, Buddhist and even the Christian's God) – that they would grant my wish to see you for the last time, then I could die in peace.

I said: "Thank you for praying for us, for our reunion. My wife, three daughters and I have prayed and fasted to Jesus to grant our wish to see you and meet with you for eternity."

Then my mother asked, "How can we meet for eternity?" I led her through the story of salvation; of the bodily resurrection when Christ returns, and of those who receive Him sharing fellowship for eternity. She answered: "It sounds so exciting, but who will give the offering to the spirit of your dad if I ever become a Christian like you?"

I asked her where she thought dad was now, and she felt that because he had done a lot of good things he would certainly be in heaven. But after further leading questions, she broke down and wept, fearing that while he had done a lot of good things and had been loved and respected by the community, according to the Buddhist law of cause and effect he would be in hell being punished for eternity because of a particular sin he had committed.

I asked, "How many days a year, mum, is the spirit of the hungry ghost of my dad released to wander the earth in search of food offered by you on behalf of your loved ones?" -- a reference to the annual Cambodian Pchum Ben, or Festival of the Dead (Bowers 2003:48). And where is he supposed to find the offering?" "In seven wats (pagodas)" she replied.

I said: "What is the use of offering food to him every day of the year if he is released only fifteen days of the year, or at home if he is only allowed to look for food at the temples? What is the use of offering food to the hungry ghost in the urban temples when he knew only temples in the rural areas?"

She acknowledged she had not known my address in Thailand to send anything to me – and neither did she know her husband's address to send offerings to him. Then she realized then that it was too late to give him offerings any more. I said: "Mother, Jesus teaches me to honor my parents while I am alive, and the Lord will give me long life and prosperity."

She said: "I know that. You have shown me this since the first day of your conversion. You are a good boy to respect your parents. "But can I ask another question before I make my decision? "Can I still be friends with the Buddhist monks, nuns and lay people?"

This is a very important question and a stumbling block to many. What if a monk comes and stands in front of my place begging for food? And I said: 'You can still give food to the monks -- not for merit-making, but out of love, and make sure that when the lepers and the beggars come asking for food, also give it to them and ask Jesus to bless them. Jesus is very pleased to see you doing such acts of love" (Eph. 2:10).

My mum smiled. Now the stumbling block had been removed, and she asked: "What can I do to become a Christian? Is there any *dhamma* (law) to learn?" I replied: "Just to be born again as a new baby – by confessing your sins, your need for a savior, and confessing that Jesus is your lord and savior. Then His Spirit will guide you and keep you, as you guided and kept me as a baby. She said: "Wonderful!"

Two years later when she was a sick and being carried on her bed to hear me preach to some villagers, she asked to be baptized in the river. A miracle occurred after she came up out of the water: she walked back up the steep bank without asking anyone to help her. Jesus had healed her and set her free. And she is still loved and accepted by her friends and many other monks and lay people in her community.

This story has never been written until now, and I pray it will be used to reach many others to open their eyes. You can see in this story how pre and post-evangelism was the key. My mother was a polytheist and I was a monotheist, but she was delighted and touched when she learned we had prayed and fasted for her. This is a model of the power of the Gospel being presented well with gentle questions designed not to embarrass but to honor--a demonstration of word, works, and wonders together.

10

GOSPEL COMMUNICATION IN TIBETAN SONG

John Oswald

Tibetan Christian songwriters are joyfully intent on sharing their Christian faith within a largely Buddhist environment. Their songs are markedly different in this respect from contemporary western Christian songs. This article examines Tibetan Christian song for its approach to gospel communication. First, two common Tibetan misunderstandings of the Christian message are pinpointed; then the role of song in culture is introduced along with the importance of heart music for Christian worship and proclamation. The remainder of the article is devoted to an analysis of Tibetan Christian song and the way in which its musical, poetic, and textual features communicate gospel truths to Buddhist Tibetans. Several examples of song texts illustrate distinctive features and communicative patterns quite different from contemporary western Christian song. Finally, the cultural values demonstrated by these Tibetan songs seem to compare well with dominant cultural values in the Buddhist nation of Thailand.

Tibetan Response to the Gospel

Striding into my room with the warm smile and gentle swagger of men from the Eastern Tibetan Khampa race, my new acquaintance and I fell into conversation about the gospel of Jesus. Perhaps out of curiosity or because of his background as a Buddhist monk, he seemed unusually interested in what this language student had to say. I severely lacked the language ability to do justice to such a topic and within a short space of time I had exhausted all I could convey, aided greatly by a few simple pictures. I expected him to be confused, amused, amazed or annoyed but, on hearing of creation to final judgment, this fox hair hat bedecked young man beamed and declared, "It's just the same as Buddhism!"

Sixteen years later, I now anticipate this reaction. Regardless of the language ability or ethnic background of the communicator, this is one of two common responses to the gospel among Tibetans. The Buddhist thought world of Tibetans has an ability to absorb everything into its orbit; such is the power of worldview. Little wonder they see Christianity as "just the same." The other reaction is, "It's the foreigners' (or westerners') religion." This second response is superficially more predictable since Buddhism of any color is referred to as "insider religion," rendering other faiths outsider religions.

Among Buddhists, these misunderstandings are not restricted to Tibetans. The Lausanne Occasional Paper on "Christian Witness to Buddhists" illustrates the same problem in Thailand where the Thai word for sin (*baap*) means something quite different from the Christian understanding. The same is true of the Tibetan term (*dig pa,* <u>sdig pa</u>[1]). The report concludes, "While the Christian understands the new meaning given to these words, he cannot take

---

1 Throughout this paper, the accepted Turrell Wylie system of transliteration of Tibetan terms, shown here with <u>underlining</u>, is included alongside a more easily pronounceable phonemic form of Central Tibetan in *italics.* Use of the transliterated form is for more accurate literary and cross-dialect reference.

for granted that his Buddhist audience makes adjustments to the Christian meanings unknown to him" (Mini-Consultation on Reaching Buddhists 1980:8).

A significant prerequisite, therefore, in gospel communication, is to allay these reactions. Clearly they are misunderstandings: doctrinally, the biblical perspective represents a way of looking at life and death that is rooted in a form of Hebrew monotheism that is closer to Tibetans culturally since it is more Asian than western.

The Role of Song in Addressing the Problem

While verbal communication is primary in addressing the detail of such profound differences in concept between Buddhists and Christians, music and song can serve to pave a pathway through the complexities of this process. This is no new observation in discussion about communication with Buddhists. The 1980 Lausanne Paper summarizes:

> In many Asian cultures, especially rural and tribal ones, oral communication forms tend to predominate. The electronic and print media in such populations usually have low impact as local communicative media. Each culture has its own primary communication systems, such as indigenous songs, dance, drama, music, and other arts. The best media for each culture should be used in evangelization. Use and adaptation of local media should be encouraged in all evangelism...... Christian communicators should carefully study the principles and process of indigenization behind the acceptance of such media, and not glibly follow western modes (Mini-Consultation on Reaching Buddhists 1980: 8-9).

The issue, therefore, is not only what to communicate but via what media the gospel will be best received and understood. We will look at several roles that song plays. It preaches; it can express things we cannot say; it is often the first means by which the gospel is heard and the musical form itself conveys its own message.

Music Preaches

"Music is theological; it talks about God and our relationship to him and our world, and answers one basic question: what is the good life, and how does one attain it?" So writes J. Nathan Corbitt. By this he means that songs express worldviews:

> This theology held in song has power. Music was preaching for Martin Luther; music was a testimony to John Newton, the writer of "Amazing Grace"; and music was the "soul of the Civil Rights Movement" to Martin Luther King Jr. Hymnbooks are the theological compendium of the literate church. Congregational song is the oral theology of the Emerging World church. Popular songs are the theological creed of secular society. (Corbitt 1998:173)

If this is true, then song is a powerful medium through which to express belief. Tibetan Christian song undoubtedly expresses the oral theology of the Tibetan church as a statement of what is most important to them as believers. Secondly, it is an example of what they want to communicate to their fellow Tibetans and, perhaps of equal importance for the wider discussion of communication among Buddhists, of the manner in which they do so.

We Can Sing What We Could Never Say

Song can be far more socially acceptable than speech for certain topics. Alan Merriam writes, "One of the most striking examples [of the special functions of song] is shown by the fact that in song the individual or the group can apparently express deep-seated feelings not permissibly verbalized in other contexts" (Merriam 1964:190). Expressing something in song leaves hearers free to decide whether to hear it only as music or as a message. Marion H. Duncan, a missionary resident in Batang (the Kham area) between 1921 and 1936 wrote in his introduction to a set of translations of Tibetan songs:

> "The deepest and most concealed thoughts of a people usually are found in their songs and proverbs, which express sometimes in veiled forms, that which is too sacred or too revealing, or perhaps at times too dangerous to be expressed in prose" (Duncan 1961:8).

Music also helps to build bridges of relationship and perhaps for this reason song is also frequently the first medium through which people hear the gospel; it is accessible and aesthetically appealing. Music that touches the heart draws from a deep emotional stream that culture insiders love to drink from. The message may be strange but the medium is familiar.

Some years ago, a Nepalese Christian leader recorded a few Tibetan Christian songs accompanied by the Tibetan lute. Cassettes of this recording ended up in a remote Himalayan Buddhist community of trader-nomads, taken by Nepalese evangelists. The locals could understand the words and so loved the songs that, on the evangelists' next visit, they requested more cassettes because they had passed on their own to their trading partners across the border in Tibet. Almost without doubt, those who listened to these songs in Tibet were hearing of Jesus for the first time.

The Music Itself Conveys a Meaning

As with any ethnic community, all the different musics that make up the Tibetan musical universe convey specific meanings. The Himalayan group above loved the sound of the lute and the songs because they heard it as familiar; it was like their own music.

Keila Diehl states, "particular musical genres are, in fact, perceived by most Tibetans as aural icons of particular places and cultures." She describes the "geographical and conceptual mandala" of younger refugee Tibetans in India. Tibetan folk music represents the authentic; Lhasa pop music bears all the hallmarks of Chinese "colonization"; Hindi film songs provide superficial entertainment in their land of exile, while western rock, reggae and blues evoke freedom. (Diehl 2002:27).

In other words, the refugee Tibetan identity is multi-layered; musical and extra-musical associations of different musics all play a part in how they are perceived. Afghan music specialist John Baily writes this of the efficacy of music to embody, evoke, invoke or even create identities:

> Music is bound up with identity and memory in a special way, for music is not only a ready means for the identification of different ethnic or social groups, it has potential *emotional* connotations and can be used to assert and negotiate identity in a particularly powerful manner (Baily 2005:216).

This is precisely what is happening with the different musics Tibetans are exposed to. All of these form part of, or are antithetical to, a deep-rooted sense of self-awareness.

With regard to religious music, Ter Ellingson identifies a continuum of chant genres with three levels of Tibetan Buddhist chant in an ascending hierarchy: recitation chants, melodic chants, and tone contour melodic chants. In this ranking, recitation chants are the fastest, more frequently performed and easiest and hence the least valued. Melodic chants are of medium speed, frequency of performance and value; while tone contour chants are the slowest, least frequently performed, the most skilful, most attractive and most ritually effective (Ellingson 1979:112-117).

Implications for Gospel Communication

If musical genres implicitly convey particularized meanings and associations and thus attract values and rankings within a culture, one of the most important conclusions to draw is that the choice of musical style is paramount for gospel communication. If we are to address the problem of perception noted above, that Christianity is seen as similar to Buddhism yet foreign to Tibetans, it is important to choose a musical style that conveys Tibetan-ness and authenticity without confusion with Buddhism.

Heart Music

Christian ethnomusicologists are discovering that, alongside use of the mother-tongue language, gospel communication is best assisted by what is termed "heart music," styles of music that most fully express the emotions of a culture insider. This will certainly help in looking for an authentic musical voice.

Heart music has been promoted by the movement for indigenous hymnody that gathered increased momentum through the formation in 2003 of a network called, the International Council of Ethnodoxologists. The identification of locally appropriate heart music lies at the root of the astounding success of this movement in the last few years to facilitate or assist in the creation of indigenous Christian music across the globe. Since heart music is usually learned in one's childhood and teenage years, this may result in the use of traditional genres or it may reflect a synthesis of these with contemporary tastes. Almost universally, the response is a feeling among national Christians and non-Christians alike that this music "belongs to us". Bruce Smith writes this report of recent song creation workshops in the Philippines:

> It is always a privilege to see new songs "born" among different language groups. In the last six months I saw this happen for churches in three areas of the central Philippines. In some cases the new compositions were the first worship songs ever to be composed in the local language at all. Many multi-lingual people assume that they must approach God using a foreign language. What a joy to see these workshop participants realize that they can worship using their own language. (Smith 2005:1).

As a result, the gospel is often not only heard but welcomed for the first time and in some places where the gospel has normally been seen as foreign, new churches have been started. Frank Fortunato reports the effects of Chris Hale's use of the bhajan style of devotional song among Hindus in North India:

> A North India Christian leader described the effectiveness of this indigenous artistic approach for the upper class Hindu from an event that took place recently in the city of Lucknow. This leader teamed up with Chris Hale for an evening of cultural music. The forms and the sounds and the presentation were totally Hindu. By tapping into the music associated with religious longing and yearning of philosophical Hinduism, (the musical genre known as bhajans) and infusing the sound and form of this religious music with the truth of the Gospel, the presentation reached into the very depths of those attending the devotional

> music concert. ...Following the three-hour presentation, friends who had befriended these Hindu people continued to develop relationships with them and further explained the truths that were portrayed in music and narration. As seeds of the Christian message were planted, relationships continued to develop and eventually these Hindus decided to follow Christ. Two churches were eventually started (Fortunato 1999).

Tibetan Heart Music

Tibetan Christians have been fortunate to identify their heart music so easily. By the mid 1980s there was a small but widely spread network of Tibetan Christians in North India and Nepal, of whom some wrote songs in Tibetan. At that time, a Tibetan pastor put together a landmark songbook, *Chamba Chöling Hymns* (byams pa chos gling mgur ma), that included fourteen Tibetan style songs in the Central Tibetan folk style. In the early 1990s collections of these songs were supplemented with songs written by new Tibetan believers from several dialect areas who found themselves in India. Among these Tibetans, traditional and folk-based modern song styles were intuitively identified as the most suitable genres to express heart-felt worship in a group setting. Buddhist monastic music is distinct in almost every way from Tibetan non-monastic music. Because of the secular associations of folk instruments they are "barred from monastic ritual use" (Collinge 1993:31). Thus, the genres chosen for Tibetan Christian use are all of the non-monastic form, accessible to more people and adaptable to a wide variety of subject matter. This heart music covers a spectrum of genres that convey Tibetan-ness, authenticity and avoid confusion with monastic Buddhism.

As a lute player in a local Tibetan song and dance troupe, I had the opportunity to witness the effects of Tibetan heart music first-hand. On one occasion when an electricity power cut interrupted an evening dance practice, group members gathered round tables as candles were lit and tea was poured out. Unannounced, they started to sing a popular group song. Such was their wholeheartedness in song that it was difficult to resist the conclusion that they had moved from rehearsal to the communal uplifting of hearts; a form of praise was being offered. This was not the worship of Jesus, but praise to the Tibetans' exiled spiritual leader, the Dalai Lama. Undoubtedly, this modern folk-based genre was their heart music.

In Mongolia, the earnest search for a suitable indigenous heart expression of worship has recently begun to take wings, encouraged by Frank Fortunato and Paul Neeley. According to the reports of recordings, workshops and concerts in Mongolia, it is energetic young Mongolian worship leaders and singers, some with a western rock background, who are leading way to take up Mongolian instruments and genres (Fortunato and Neeley 2004).

Features of Tibetan Song

Fundamental to an understanding of heart music are musical style and tone and use of language. Tibetans define this as *nyen po* ("attractive to the ear", <u>snyan</u> <u>po</u>) and inbuilt into this are musical and linguistic expectations. Regardless of regional distinctives, folk song or modernized folk song that is *nyen po* usually has the following features: a) a "calm" quality (*jam po*, <u>'jam</u> <u>po</u>) of sound production (i.e. not harsh); b) flowing or "steady" (*den po,* <u>brtan</u>

po) melodic movement (not sudden); c) ornamentation and often glottalization (*dring gu,* mgrin 'gug) of the vocal line (not plain); d) poetic textual style (also not plain); and e) lyrical content that is sentimental and emotionally linked to one's identity (Oswald 2001: 96-97). Further features might be identified, such as melodic patterns that synchronize rather than syncopate with the primary beat structure.

Tibetan-composed Christian songs match all these six characteristics, while translated songs occasionally fit three, somewhat inadequately. The implications are clear: only certain western Christian hymns and songs transfer either linguistically, culturally or musically into Tibetan with any sense of ease. In fact, certain hymns of the early 20th century American revivalist genre fit more easily with this Tibetan profile than contemporary worship songs. The common attributes of revivalist and Tibetan profiles are non-syncopated, flowing melodies set to a metrical poetic style that is often sentimental. This may explain the enduring popularity of some of these older hymns among Tibetan believers.

The Tibetan Songbook Illustrates Heart Music

In 1995 a Tibetan Christian worship book was produced called "Offer A Praise Song" (*Döyang Pü Shi*, bstod dbyangs phul zhig). This is a compilation of one hundred songs of which fifty-five are in Tibetan musical styles, ranging from traditional to more modern popular melodies and spanning several regional styles across the vast Tibetan plateau. The songbook has now been adapted in its entirety into five other Tibetan languages and used in part of the songbook of at least one other. This popularity might legitimately be attributed in part to a paucity of comparable material but it also reflects the broad reach of the heart music genres chosen by the songwriters. Now, national believers are adding new songs to this repertoire in more regionally distinct dialect styles. Heart music focused on Christ and his gospel is quietly on the increase in these mountain lands.

The Role of Song Texts

Quite apart from purely musical considerations, song texts encode cultural values in their content and poetic style. Ethnomusicologist Alan Lomax writes, "Song style reinforces and expresses the major abiding themes of culture" (Lomax 1968:75). Corbitt defines this further:

> ‘We sing to identify, express, or proclaim our viewpoint and loyalties. Songs function as guideposts to the deeper issues of life. They provide information that is otherwise inaccessible - the hidden or unconscious worldview. They are a map of a worldview, telling the “basic assumptions the people have about the nature of reality and of right and wrong.”’ (Corbitt 1998:179)

Tibetan Song Texts

These descriptions are abundantly true of Tibetan song, where lyrics are arguably the most important aspect of aural beauty. In my experience, this is what Tibetans listen for in a song. Diehl agrees, “Tibetan audiences never complain if an instrument is out of tune..., but they leave a concert disappointed if they have not been able to understand the words of a song… disappointed not to have clearly *heard* the words.” (Diehl 2002:211-212). Tibetan lyrics generally deploy a range of metaphors associated with a set of common song themes: one's mother, family, homeland, lama, lover, nation, and religion. In the act of singing and hearing, participants are reengaging with what Corbitt described as the “basic assumptions the people have about the nature of reality and of right and wrong". In the refugee community these are focused on the land of Tibet, the cry for independence (*rang zen,* rang btsan), devotion to the Dalai Lama and poetically coded love songs.

At the same time, some Tibetan song texts may not be readily understood because their poetic form is too far removed from colloquial speech. Literary conventions, rooted in the Classical Tibetan of Buddhist texts, render higher levels of written Tibetan obscure to all but the well educated. In a Buddhist's view this does not devalue them. To the contrary, it is the hearing of the words that transmits the sought after benefit, not necessarily their comprehension. It is enough that the sense of the text is felt, whether that is devotion, patriotism or affection. Applying Diehl's distinction between the *sonic* and *semantic* meaning of lyrics, (Diehl 2002: ch.6), words, and phrases set to melody can be evocative by their sound alone, while their semantic content is only partially appreciated. This may be likened to Christian hymns learned by heart and well-loved but not fully understood or to the uplifting sound of Gregorian chant sung entirely in Latin.

Response to Tibetan Christian Texts

The following three examples illustrate how a variety of Tibetans respond to Christian song texts. These show how familiar word pictures and the high value placed on written Tibetan language within the culture impact the reception of a song.

Appreciation of Familiar Song Language

The first example relates to informal performances of a Tibetan Christian song, *Nyin chik mi chik song ne* (nyin gcig mi gcig song nas; *Döyang Pü Shi* Song 35). The lyrics are replete with Tibetan metaphor. The first verse sets Jesus' parable of the hidden treasure (Mt. 13:44) where the word "treasure" is exchanged for the word for "precious jewel" (*nor bu*), a highly symbolic term for Tibetans:

> One day one man went out (ya la so),
> Saw a precious jewel in a field.
> (He) sold all, bought the field
> And got the jewel.

The second verse transposes the phrase "Lhasa's Norbulingka" from the original text for "this world of beauty" and "Yishe Norbu" (the Dalai Lama, notice the word *nor bu* in this common title for the Dalai Lama, "Jewel of Wisdom") for the "Lord Jesus":

> In this world of beauty (ya la so)
> Don't say there's no jewel (ya la so)
> If the Saviour Lord Jesus
> Is not the jewel, then what is?

In my experience, Tibetans love both the first verse parable story and the second verse adaptation, especially the mid to older generations and they ask for it to be repeated, sometimes for others to hear. The melody is traditional but not one normally set to the original words. Tibetan hearers know all the metaphorical allusions and, in the context of mutual discourse, the unexpected change to "the Saviour Lord Jesus" meets with respect rather than offence. Understanding has been gained through familiarity and well-loved word play. Repeated experience shows that songs like this easily open doors of authentic relationship and genuine discussion.

Respect for the Written Text

The second response reveals another type of respect. Sometimes when Christian songs are being sung a Tibetan has requested a copy of the songbook to place on the family altar. Christians usually discourage this but such a desire shows the value of the document as a sacred book in itself. Those who can read Tibetan enjoy reading these songs aloud and singing along with those who know them. There is cultural value in the act of reading religious texts that are thought to accumulate Buddhist spiritual merit. This provides an opportunity for Christian communicators who, wary of superstition, can easily dismiss such honour as grapholatry instead of discerning in this a pathway to greater revelation.

Songs Texts Gradually Understood

A third example reflects a strong desire by Tibetans to understand song lyrics. While watching some dancers rehearsing steps to a song about creation, an elderly man spun his prayer wheel and poured over the words of the song, discussing them until he felt he understood them. There appeared to be a deep satisfaction in this process, such that the next day he asked for a copy of the words. The first pair of stanzas could be translated as follows:

(Question):
Before the creation of the world, how did this world come into being?
Who is the maker of this world? What was created at the beginning?
Was there any distinction between good and evil?

Singing a song, I've posed the question.

(Answer)

Before the creation of the world, this worldly realm was empty.

The maker of the world was God. Formerly, angels were made.

At that time there was only goodness; evil was not even named.

This Tibetan-composed song is based on a little-known song genre we could call "origin songs" (*lu si pa or si pä chag lu;* <u>glu</u> <u>srid</u> <u>pa</u> or <u>srid</u> <u>pa'i</u> <u>chags</u> <u>glu</u>; <u>Gcod</u> <u>Pa</u> <u>Don</u> <u>Grub</u> and <u>Sangs</u> <u>Rgyas</u> <u>Rin</u> <u>Chen</u> n.d.a: 681, 699) from an Amdo Tibetan area in Qinghai Province and this song is sung by Tibetan believers of that dialect. In the version this man heard the melody and language had been adapted to Central Tibetan taste but it retained the question and answer form and the textual content. The repetition of concepts and phrases from the question stanza in the answer stanza creates a tension-release structure. Each stanza pair starts with the same first line and builds up a series of questions based on Genesis 1, each being resolved in its answering stanza. This progressive pattern was clearly attractive to this man as he sang along and began to grasp the song's meaning.

Reflections on These Responses

These three responses all illustrate the fact that song can pave the way for truth sharing, whether one to one, in a small group or in a larger performance setting.

The first highlights the power of parabolic story, poetical metaphor and partial predictability in textual content. These make a song more intelligible, more enjoyable and more communicative.

The second demonstrates that the mere singing or reading of religious song texts can inspire respect even before comprehension comes.

From the last example we can see the enjoyment that Tibetans derive from the intellectual opening up of a spiritual text such as the creation song. For such people, understanding does not have to come on their first, second or third hearing. An attractive, well-written text with layers of meaning is worthy of attention through its gradual disclosure to its hearers and readers.

Those reared in direct and instant communication techniques may find some of these implications frustrating. I would like to suggest that they provide challenging clues about preferred forms of communication among Buddhists and ways in which God reveals his truth to them. Many parables of Jesus exhibited similar characteristics; they enthralled his audiences but left them asking questions and reaching for their deeper layers of meaning.

A Closer Examination of Tibetan Christian Song Texts

So far, we have looked primarily at poetical and musical form and meaning. We have seen that songs that set Christian themes in familiar poetic forms to a suitable genre of heart music have far greater potential for communicative engagement than forms and symbols that ignore cultural patterns of message sharing. Now we can examine in greater depth the content, the issues chosen by Tibetan Christian songwriters to communicate the gospel through song. The following analysis of thirty four songs written by Tibetan Christians excludes Tibetan style songs where the textual content is pre-determined (i.e. settings of scripture or translated songs) and those written by non-Tibetans. A different treatment of this research is presented in "A New Song Rising" (Oswald 2001:Ch 5), where the issue under view is Tibetan Christian worship. The same eleven features are highlighted but the focus here is on communication.

If the foregoing song examples have not already done so, it will soon become clear that these Tibetan originated songs are quite different in their theme preferences and manner of presentation from contemporary western Christian worship songs. Non-Tibetan Christian communicators will identify in this analysis a distinctive approach by which to assess communication style and content in addressing primary concerns among Buddhists in general and Tibetans in particular.

The Language of Warm Reverence

The language of Tibetan Christian songs demonstrates a deep reverence for God. Built into the language and culture is the vocabulary of respect, honorific language (*she sa;* zhe sa) in which elders, teachers and religious figures are addressed with special terms. This language is eminently appropriate for speaking to or about God both in song and in speech.

Titular language is also used of God. In the songs, titles for God not only use honorific forms for "Father", "Maker" or "Saviour" but such titles are not infrequently expanded to add greater respect. This changes the tone of discourse from propositional statement to worshipful conversation. For example, the songs speak of, "God who abides in heaven", "Our great Father God", and "Our Saviour Jesus who inhabits the heavenly realm." Not every stanza contains such long hand divine titles, but this type of language peppers the lyrics and prayers of Tibetan believers.

This is equivalent to using phrases such as "Our Lord", "the Lord Jesus" and "Our heavenly Father" in English gospel sharing, instead of "Jesus" and "God". In many western contexts today such churchly phrases appear archaic and flowery in normal conversation but in Tibetan this practice is both appropriate and necessary. Such expressions are appropriate because religious figures are usually referred to by their titles. It is rare for a Tibetan use the name "Dalai Lama". Usually, they speak of him as, "Presence", "Precious Conqueror" or "Jewel of Wisdom" (*Kündün, Gyewa Rinpoche* or *Yishe Norbu*, sku mdun, rgyal ba rin po che, or yid shes nor bu). All lamas and historic Buddhist figures have titles. Teachers, parents, monks, uncles and aunts are all addressed by title.

Using titles for God is not only appropriate it is necessary, because this provides a contextual way to define the God of whom we speak. Since the word "God" (*Kön cho(k),* dkon mchog) is also used in Buddhism for the "Three Jewels" (*Kon chok sum,* dkon mchog gsum), definitions are vital and adding qualifying phrases expressed as a title is ideal, such as "The Most High God" (*la na me pay Kon chok,* bla na med pa'i dkon mchog).

A similar range of titles surround, "The Saviour Jesus". Rather than "The Lord Jesus", Tibetan Christians much prefer the title "Saviour". Again, the reason is the title format for high lamas who are referred to as "Saviour". In common language, the word "Lord" (*Tso wo,* gtso bo) is more like an adjective and is not well known as a title.

This language of reverence and title could be extended to other biblical characters, partly to give respect but also to explain their role to those who have never before heard of these figures: King David, the Prophet Elijah, the Apostle Paul, etc.

Audience With God

Tibetans regard a few minutes' audience with a lama as a deeply personal moment of blessing where they are touched by what they conceive as the sacred. A Christian goes to meet with God for spiritual blessing. The same Tibetan word is used for both "meet" and "have an audience with" (*Jä(l);* mjal). This imagery is not unlike the language of the Psalms, where God is seen as " the Great King" and prayer is like going before the heavenly king in his courtroom (e.g. Ps. 96 and 99), or of Moses who went to meet with God in the "Tent of meeting" (Ex. 33:7-11).

One song, in particular (*Döyang Pü Shi* Song 44: *Tang por la jig den di la lep dü,* dang por la 'jig rten 'di la slebs dus), applies this motif to two audiences: meeting Christ in Christian conversion and then in a prayer to one day enter the presence of God the Father. The first stanza is as follows:

First, when I came into this world here
O my heart was so full of suffering
Second, I met the Saviour Jesus
And my heart's suffering was washed away.

This song is a song of a new Tibetan believer, using a popular melody. In the mind of the singer is the common experience of fleeing from Tibet to find freedom and meet the Dalai Lama in India. In this brief audience the new arrival seeks the blessing of the Dalai Lama and a word of advice. In this case, it is the Saviour Jesus who has brought relief to the singer's anguish of heart through faith and the gift of salvation.

Drawing partly from 2 lines of a well-known song verse attributed to the Sixth Dalai Lama (1683-1706; for annotations on this verse see Sorensen 1990: 251), the remainder of the song is a prayer that he/she would be given the “wings of the white crane” (a bird associated with flying high and far) to share the gospel and come at last before the Father.

This song not only reminds us of the power of symbolic language but it also highlights the way in which gospel communication that touches the heart strikes a chord with common aspirations. In this song, it is the desire to meet (have an audience with) one who can wash away inner suffering, a Buddhist concern and a repeated account of Christian experience in these songs.

The Experience of Joy

Besides reverence, Tibetan Christian songs display openly happy praise. Much of this comes from early encounters of the new believer with Jesus, as in the song above. Words for “joy”, “joyful”, “happy” or “happiness” are more prominent in the Tibetan composed songs than in songs translated from English. These songs typically reflect the believer's delight in the gospel story and the power of salvation through Christ. A specially recurring theme is Christ's cleansing, both from our sin and from our heart's suffering. To emphasize the point some songs repeat the refrain, “O what joy! O what happiness!”

Tibetans, like all people, seek joy and happiness and these new believers testify that they have found it in Jesus. Gospel communication that is appropriate for Tibetan Buddhists will not only talk about joy but will demonstrate it and create an appetite for it. Song and dance are obvious ways to express this in Tibetan society.

Request Prayer

Words for prayer are used twice as many times in the Tibetan-authored songs than in other songs in the same volume. Firstly, not-yet believers are encouraged to pray and to take refuge in Jesus for eternal salvation. The second focus is for believers to pray to receive daily needs and such prayer is to be offered "from the heart", "believing" and "in unity". Such expressions portray a distinctively Christian approach to prayer.

Two observations may be made about this in relation to gospel communication. The first is that prayer is a natural part of evangelistic discourse in the Tibetan context. Most Tibetans have a sense of the spiritual and an appeal to pray or a time of prayer in Christ's name is both acceptable and important. Christians are respected for their good works but the spiritual life of the Christian can sometimes be all but invisible to a non-Christian. Despite Jesus' warnings to beware of hypocrisy in prayer, it was far from the practice of the Lord Jesus or the Apostles to separate prayer and evangelism.

Alongside more visible prayer, the second observation is that sung prayer may also be appropriate in gospel communication. In the Tibetan songbook there is a musical setting of the Lord's Prayer that often closes a Tibetan Christian gathering. Another song is a prayer of blessing on a friend (*Döyang Pü Shi* Song 18). I have seen this Amdo Tibetan style song profoundly move the hearts of Tibetan bystanders:

> O friend, in the Lord's name, May the Lord's reply be given (to you).
> O friend, in Jesus' name, may salvation be given (to you).
> O friend, may the Holy Spirit's power be given (to you).
> O friend, to the Holy One, may you offer a praise song.

A Gentle Sense of Order

The poetic structure of Tibetan Christian songs reflects a conservative desire for order and formality. Song 44 above, *Tang por la jig den di la lep dü,* marks time with the words, "first" and "second." This may sound strange in English but numbering is typically Tibetan. In education and public speeches items are numbered in a formulaic manner. Buddhist and secular categories are grouped together in numbers, such as, "The Three Jewels", The Four Vowels", and "The Five Brothers."

In Christian communication such ordering and grouping may help Tibetans to remember what is taught, such as the two Testaments, the three virtues (faith, hope and love), the four gospels, the five books of Moses, etc.

In seeking to avoid "vain repetition" (Mt. 6:7 KJV) western evangelical missionaries may overlook the benefits of memorization and repetition in societies more accustomed to oral learning. In the Tibetan socio-linguistic environment, therefore, the recitation of standard texts like the Lord's Prayer, the Two Great Commandments (Mk. 12:29-31), the Ten Commandments (Ex. 20:2-17), The Great Commission (Mt. 28:18-20) and the Apostle's Creed may assist in the learning process. Tibetan Christians recognize the effectiveness of this method of learning; when a revised Tibetan songbook was proposed it was a senior Tibetan Christian leader who requested that these texts should be included as a supplement to the songs.

Story Telling

Several Tibetan Christian songs illustrate how important storytelling is to Tibetans. Some tell a direct bible story, others allude to bible stories, while some relate a personal story. This is not uncommon in hymnodies around the world and story hymns formed one strand of western hymn writing until the present era when the emphasis in song writing shifted radically and rapidly to a more direct expression of prayer to God.

This fact alone should alert Christian communicators to the beauty of telling the bible story in song and its capacity to illuminate its hearers, if used well. While a rising emphasis in missiology today focuses on orality, storytelling and chronological bible storying, it should be noted here that singers and musicians may wonderfully partner with storytellers to enhance and optimize the potency of the story form to enlighten and challenge human hearts.

Another reason for the inclusion in Tibetan Christian hymnody of bible stories is that Tibetan people simply do not know the bible stories; singing them helps to get them known. Tibetans encode Buddhist belief in stories that they know well and see enacted before them in a host of ways, including in song, dance, drama and narration. As a result, they possess a mental meta-narrative that has a fundamentally different interpretation to that of the bible and it is probably only when they hear the bible narrative as a whole that they will be able to attach more accurate meanings to statements of Christian belief.

Having said this, telling or singing beautifully prepared individual bible stories is not sufficient. In fact, without explanation, it may reinforce a Buddhist interpretation on the Christian story. As with the parables of Jesus, storytelling must lead to the question, “what does this mean?” and the unfolding of the answer in a process of illumination that we see in Mark 4:1-20: story – questions – story – explanation – response (identification with the story).

An Emphasis on Community

Probably the most striking difference between western contemporary worship songs and Tibetan Christian songs is the emphasis on a purely individual relationship with God in the western church and the communal context of an individual's encounter with God in the Tibetan setting. A word count of first person singular words (I, me, my and mine) and first person plural words (we, us, our) in English and Tibetan songs produces an almost exactly opposite profile in the two songs samples. English language songs have a 60% preference for "I", while Tibetan songs have a 65% preference for "We". From more recent analyses, this emphasis on "I" in English language songs is continuing to increase.

Group emphasis is also expressed in words such as, "friend", "brothers", "kinsmen" and "Tibetans". We will see later that such a group consciousness results in songs that are addressed to others, i.e. believers and unbelievers, more than to God.

There are three reasons for this communal focus in these songs. Firstly, it is virtually impossible for a Tibetan to turn to Christ without some reaction from the community or family. Such is the respect that Tibetans have for their elders that consciousness of their feelings is prominent. Where this biblical cost counting is not present, a premature decision is often made and a turning away from Christ is likely at some point.

A second reason is that the new Tibetan believer's response of joy and delight in Christ and his salvation is often accompanied by a desire to share this discovery with other Tibetans.

A third reason for group language is that the new believer now sees himself as part of a believing community and faith is expressed communally.

The implications of this for gospel communication and church planting are profound. In this discussion it is perhaps sufficient to draw attention to the way in which an appeal to follow Christ is expressed in the Tibetan Christian songs. Since these songs are usually sung in a group context the call of Christ can be addressed communally to individuals through song, with appropriate explanation. As was brought to the fore earlier, there are occasions when we can sing what we cannot say and for some the sung form may provide the very means of Christ's call. One such song is explained in the following section.

"Our Great Father God"

Before outlining the remaining observations of Tibetan Christian song lyrics, it would be pertinent to dwell on the full text of an outstanding Tibetan Christian song, "Our Great Father God" (*Döyang Pü Shi* Song 30). The song *Ngantsö Yabchen Köncho* (nga tsho'i yab chen dkon mchog) has been a favorite Tibetan Christian song for many years. This was penned by a Tibetan pastor whose 1980's songbook brought together the existing Tibetan Christian songs and provided a model for future generations of songwriting. The melody is in the Central Tibetan folk song style. The song displays the characteristics that make a Tibetan song *nyen po.* In particular, the melody is flowing, the metre of the verses is the standard 4 lines of 6-syllables each and the text uses an appropriate degree of repetition and variation. A well-crafted modern touch is the use of repeat for the closing words.

In this song many of the hallmarks of Tibetan Christian song can be identified: warm reverence, joy, order, and singing the gospel story to a community, including unbelievers. The story line builds up gradually to an appeal to believe in Christ that is personal yet set within a corporate view of God as “our” great Father God. For gospel communicators it provides a beautiful model of simplicity, clarity and application.

Our great Father God. What a love he showed!
He sent His Son Jesus to this earthly realm.

What love He has shown me. What love He has shown you.
He has shown me. He has shown you.

Our Saviour Jesus, He came to seek me
But not only me; he came to seek you.

What love! He has sought me. What love! He has sought you.
He has sought me. He has sought you.

His own life He gave for me
(But) not only for me He gave it for all.

What love He has shown me. What love He has shown you.
He has shown me. He has shown you.

I have faith in Him and (He) gave me salvation
If you also believe (He)’ll give you salvation

If (you) believe, (he)’ll give salvation.
If (you) believe, (he)’ll give salvation.
If (you) believe, (he)’ll give salvation.

Third Person Language of God

It will be observed from songs like this that those being addressed are human and God is spoken of in the third person. This is more common than not in Tibetan songs and is equivalent to the language of many English language hymns until the modern era.

Diehl relates a conversation about Tibetan love songs with Jampa Gyaltsen Dakton.la in Dharamsala, “Tibetan lovers don’t directly shout, ‘Hey, I love you!’ like Americans, he joked. They always try to give poetic examples from the natural world to convey their feelings” (Diehl 2002:208). Similarly, in my research I have discovered that many Tibetan believers do not feel comfortable about using romantic language towards God, as in English worship songs. They express intimacy and passion in different ways preferring to sing in the third person about God in reverent and joyous ways (Oswald 2001:57), often with instruments and sometimes with dancing.

Festivals

An interest in festivals and group celebrations is apparent in Tibetan Christian songs. Four of the twenty eight songs analyzed from the songbook *Döyang Pü Shi* are written for Christmas, and one each for Palm Sunday and Easter. This emphasis is also found in *Chamba Choeling* Hymns, with songs appropriate for Christmas, Easter and "Founder's Day”.

The singing of songs for festivals like Christmas, Easter and the Tibetan New Year is very appropriate. Christmas provides opportunity for singing and dancing in the context of hospitality in homes, concerts and other programs. Similarly, songs can be sung on certain Tibetan festivals or social events.

The spontaneous singing of words made up at the time and addressed to a particular recipient of a song is another feature of some festivals and social occasions. Although I have yet to hear of this kind of Christian response, gospel communicators who can creatively respond in faith to this challenge may find God's Spirit's opening up new doors.

First Generation Faith

The songs of Tibetan believers reflect the fact that most are first generation Christians. Many songs deal with personal encounters with God, especially how Christ has cleansed us from our sins and "our heart's suffering". Some songs call for a response from unbelievers. Some songs tell of the need to proclaim the gospel. In contrast to most western worship songs, the audience that these songwriters have in mind includes non- Christians.

For gospel communication there is a range of songs appropriate for gospel sharing. Of the twenty eight songs in *Döyang Pü Shi* under survey, as many as one quarter contain a direct gospel appeal for unbelievers to believe in Christ. Of the one hundred songs in *Döyang Pü Shi*, a third are gospel oriented, either relating a gospel story or singing of salvation through faith in Christ. This is a major point of differentiation from western worship songs.

Buddhist Background

All of the songs composed by Tibetans show an awareness of the Buddhist background from which the writers have come. The songs demonstrate two reasons for this: firstly, in songs that rejoice in salvation, the desire to articulate their new faith in ways that help them make sense of the radical change that has taken place in their own lives and secondly, in songs addressed to the Tibetan non-

Christian, as an apologetic response to questions posed by Buddhists.

At the surface level, these songs use words in common with Buddhism. Some of these words are only used in texts written by Tibetans while other terms are used more by Tibetan writers than by non-Tibetans. The following list shows word groups used in descending order of frequency: joy, worldly realm, faith, path, sin, suffering, prayer, realm, precious, compassion, sinful defilements, heavenly realm, and repentance.

At a deeper level, these believers redefine these terms in the light of the gospel, filling them with Christian meaning. For example, their joy is because they have "taken refuge" in the Saviour Jesus and his cross. A new "day of salvation has dawned" for them and it is because they have repented and their faith is now in Jesus, that their sin has been cleansed and their heart's suffering has been removed. This suffering is something believers experienced before coming to Christ and Christ experienced the suffering of the cross in order to save us from suffering.

A clearly biblical theology of salvation is expressed in two songs. One of these is *A Ha La Ni* (*Döyang Pü Shi* Song 93). The title phrase *A Ha La Ni* is no more than a joyful expression of lexically meaningless filler syllables common in Tibetan songs and the melody is stately and reminiscent of the Lhasa *nang ma* style. The author was the late Rev. Peter Rapgey of Kalimpong, a former Buddhist monk and later a Bible translator. His profound experience of spiritual regeneration is reflected in the song:

> Aha Aha Ahalani
> In order to save lost sinners in the darkness of sin, Ahalani,
> Giving up the realm of paradise, Ahalani,
> God took human form.

In your hearts do not forget such endless love, beloved Tibetans.

Aha Aha Ahalani
The sin of your old nature cannot be cleansed by virtuous deeds. Ahalani.
To overcome in the battle against sin, Ahalani,
(You) need a new nature.
Believe in Jesus to receive a new birth in this bodily form,

Aha Aha Ahalani
However serious (your) sin, accumulated from (one's) ancestors, Ahalani,
If (you) repent to Jesus, Ahalani,
His precious blood (will) cleanse (your) sin.
Take refuge in Him (and) definitely receive the way of salvation.

In this song terms familiar in Buddhism appear, including paradise, virtuous deeds, accumulation (commission) of sins, repent, and taking refuge. More significant than mere word use is the deliberate emphasis on the ineffectiveness of virtuous deeds to cleanse sin and the necessity of a new birth and a new nature in this bodily form, not after this life is over. Such statements directly address a Tibetan Buddhist view of the gospel. The way in which Rev. Rapgey's well-expressed biblical thinking touches on a key fault line between Buddhism and Christianity has directly influenced the wording of another song (*Döyang Pü Shi* Song 55).

Tibetan Identity

As the last song shows there is a keen sense of Tibetan identity in many Tibetan Christian songs. In most it lies beneath the immediate text, in metaphor, cultural inference and its appeal to concerns common to Buddhism. In several, however, this surfaces in direct expression. Rapgey calls on "beloved Tibetans" not to forget God's love. Another song says, "Our Tibetan brothers, if we believe in Jesus, he will remove our sin". Elsewhere there are references to the land of Tibet (snowland, snow mountains and grasslands), and the Tibetans (the black heads of the snow mountains).

Such articulation of ethnic self-consciousness is almost unknown in English Christian songs. The difference is that the Tibetan struggle to maintain their cultural identity in the world is felt as keenly by many Tibetan Christians as by Tibetan Buddhists and atheists.

Identifying Key Differences

Throughout this article reference has been made to several differences between the communication characteristics of Tibetan Christian song and standard western gospel communication. In his doctorate thesis, Thai pastor and scholar Dr. Nantachai Mejudhon has identified eight polar differences between the cultural values of the Thai and the Americans: time, work and play, youth versus age, equality versus hierarchy, material versus spirituality, change versus tradition, independence versus dependence and confrontation versus indirection (Nantachai 2005:18).

Many of the values of the Thai closely echo the characteristics of Tibetan Christian songs noted above. According to Dr. Nantachai 's research, the Thai have a long view of time, allowing time for stories and for listeners to come to their own conclusions. The Thai integrate work and play where American missionaries typically approach evangelism as work. The Thai respect age and value hierarchy. They view a simple lifestyle rather than materialism as expressive of spirituality. The Thai value tradition over change, such that conversion of thought and action is likely to take time among Thai coming to Christ. They value dependence over independence and pray for everything. Finally, they prefer "indirection" (sic) rather than confrontation, soft speaking as opposed to direct challenge (:18).

Tibetan Christian song combines almost all of these eight characteristics. Song form allows listeners time to reflect, can attractively tell stories and is frequently a more playful medium than speech. Tibetan Christian song encodes reverence for God, others, tradition and order and promotes prayer as part of evangelism. Song form itself is a less direct way to appeal for response, comparable to soft speaking.

Having said this, song is by no means the only medium of choice among Tibetan Christians. The combination of sung and spoken communication is common while much scope exists for bringing together Tibetan art, drama, dance, music and song or telling extended stories through metrical speech, song and narration.

Summary

This article has examined Tibetan Christian song for the means and emphases it displays in communicating the gospel to Buddhist Tibetans.

The first section looked at the key problem in gospel sharing among these peoples, that Christianity is seen to be both "the same as Buddhism" and "foreign."

The second section drew attention to the role of musical style in conveying a message. Musical and artistic media and song in particular have long been recognized as important in gospel communication but mere recognition of this is not sufficient. If a song form can be found that conveys Tibetan-ness and authenticity and at the same time avoids confusion with Buddhism, Christian communicators may discover ways to set to rest Tibetan misconstructions of the gospel. Around the world national songwriters are identifying their culture's heart musics. Culture insiders perceive this music as their own and thereby the gospel as available to and relevant for their people. This discovery has often led to the joyous response of faith in Christ by previously disinterested social and ethnic groups and the formation or growth of believing communities.

The third section explained that Tibetan Christians have already intuitively identified and appropriated their heart music and that these genres are singularly powerful to stir strong emotions in Tibetans.

The fourth section listed six common characteristics that render a song *nyen po* (beautiful to listen to) from a Tibetan sense of musical aesthetics. These are what make the folk and folk-based popular genres the heart music of the vast majority of Tibetans.

In the fifth section attention turned to song texts and demonstrated that they effectively reinforce the cultural worldview. This is true of Tibetan song in general but in the socio-linguistic environment of Tibetan culture where the written language has to be painstakingly learned, total semantic comprehension of song lyrics is not always possible. Nonetheless Tibetans can still be moved by the capacity of the words to evoke meanings by their sound.

Sixthly, three common responses to Tibetan Christian song texts illustrate that Tibetans respect song texts and appreciate the well-crafted poetry and familiar metaphors used in song. For such people, the gradual process of understanding the different layers of meaning in a song text can be profoundly gratifying.

The next section looked in more detail at key characteristics of Tibetan Christian song from the point of view of their communicative potential in sharing the gospel. Prominent among these are their tone of reverence in speaking of spiritual things, their leaning towards joy, order, prayer and storytelling, their group orientation and the manner in which Tibetan Christian songs address Tibetan Buddhists with concerns familiar to Buddhism, such as suffering and compassion, with an appeal for a faith response.

Finally, all eight fundamental differences between values of the Thai and American cultures listed in Dr. Nantachai's research are true of Tibetan culture and Tibetan Christian song proves to be an art form that can combine at least seven of these values in a communicative medium that is appreciated by Buddhist Tibetans.

Coda

There is a Christian bell in Lhasa the capital of Tibet. It is the only surviving physical evidence of a Catholic chapel that existed there under the Capuchins until its destruction in 1745. Its voice sounds no more; it is cracked and its clapper is missing, having been housed in the most revered Buddhist chapel of all in Tibet, the

Jokhang, before being used or abused during the Cultural Revolution (Marini 2004).

Just as God has chosen to impart his sublime message through the cracked and incomplete means of human language and culture, it is hoped that those interacting with this article will find increasingly appropriate and effective means by which the message of Jesus can sound clear and loud among the Buddhist peoples they love and serve, to the glory of God, or as the Latin inscription on the rim of the bell of Lhasa says:

TE DEUM LAUDAMUS

"We Praise You O God"

La Me Kon Cho Khye La Tö Par Sho!

REFERENCES

Chapter 1

Alaska Department of Natural Resources. N.d. *Totem Bight*. Ketchikan AK: Brochure, Division of Parks and Outdoor Recreation, Harris, Chiang. Personal e-mail. Chiang Mai, 10/23/ 2006.

Google Search. C:\Documents and Settings\asmith\Local Settings\Temp\notesFA9227\~2699140.htm, 10/24/ 2006.

Jewell, Dawn Herzog. "Winning the Oral Majority," in *Christianity Today*. March 2006, 50(3)56-58.

Larson, Donald N. "The Viable Missionary: Learner, Trader, Story Teller," in Arthur F. Glasser (editor), *Missiology: An International Review*. Pasadena CA: American Society of Missiology, April 1978, VI(2)155-163.

Lim, David and Steve Spaulding, eds. 2005. *Sharing Jesus Holistically with the Buddhist World*. Pasadena CA: William Carey Library.

Maquire, Jack. *Essential Buddhism: A Complete Guide to Beliefs and Practices*. 2001. New York: Pocket Books.

McGavran, Donald A. 1970. *Understanding Church Growth*. Grand Rapids MI: Eerdmans.

Moreau, A. Scott. "A Word from the Editor," in *Evangelical Missions Quarterly*. Wheaton IL: EMIS, January 2006, 42(1)1.

Mizuno, Kogen. 1982. *Buddhist Sutras: Origin, Development, Transmission*. Tokyo: Kosei Publishing Co.

Newspaper. *Phu Shian*. 2002. Cebu City, Philippines: Phu Shian Temple Propagation Foundation.

Rhys Davids, Caroline A.F. 1989. *Stories of the Buddha: Being Selections from the Jataka*. New York: Dover Publications.

Schultz, George F. *Vietnamese Legends*. 1965. Tokyo: Charles E. Tuttle.

Short, Greg. Email update. 6/20/2006 08:54am, 1/02/2007 10:18pm.

Smith, Alex G. 1977. *Strategy to Multiply Rural Churches: A Central Thailand Case Study*. Bangkok: OMF Publishers.

________. *Buddhism Through Christian Eyes*. 2001. Littleton CO: OMF International.

________. 2004. "Transfer of Merit in Folk Buddhism," In *Sharing Jesus Holistically with the Buddhist World*. David Lim and Steve Spaulding, eds. Pp.91-124, Pasadena CA: William Carey Library.

Søgaard, Viggo. 1993. *Media in Church and Mission: Communicating the Gospel*. Pasadena, CA: William Carey Library.

Thisbaseballmitt, source of sensitive data protected, 1998.

Totem Heritage Center. N.d. *Totem Heritage Center Ketchikan, Alaska.* Ketchikan AK: Brochure.

Woragamvijya, Sorajet. 1987. *The Sanctuary Phanomrung*. Buriram, Thailand: The Lower N E Study Association.

Zacharias, Ravi. 2002. *The Lotus and the Cross: Jesus Talks with Buddha.* Chennai, India: RZIM Life Focus Society.

Chapter 2

Acoba, E. 2006. "Negative Hermeneutics: An Interpretational Structure for Naming the Christian God for the Underside." *Naming the Unknown God*, E. Acoba, ed. et al. Pp. 44-59. Mandaluyong, Philippines:OMF Literature.

Ahn, Seung-oh. 2001. "Worship: A Missiological Role," *Journal of Asian Mission* 3.2 (September 2001):151-165.

Aikman, David. 2003. *Jesus in Beijing.* Washington, D.C.:Regnery Publishing.

Anderson, Allan, and Edmond Tang, eds. 2005. *Asian and Pentecostal: The Charismatic Face of Christianity in Asia.* Oxford Regnum Books International.

Arterburn, Stephen, and Jack Felton. 2000. *More Jesus, Less Religion.* Colorado Springs, CO:Waterbrook Press.

Atkerson, Steve, ed. 2005. *Ekklesia: To The Roots of Biblical House-Church Life.* Atlanta, GA:NTRF.

Banks, Robert J. and Julia Banks. 1986. *The Church Comes Home.* Sutherland: Albatross.

Banks, Robert. 1985. *Going to Church in the First Century.* Sydney:Hexagon.

________. 1979. *Paul's Idea of Community.* Sydney:Anzea.

Barrett, Lois. 1986. *Building the House Church.* Scottdale, PA:Herald.

Boff, Leonardo. 1986. *Ecclesiogenesis:The Base Communities Reinvent the Church.* Maryknoll, NY:Orbis.

Bryant, David. 2006. "Confronting the Crisis of Christ's Supremacy," *Mission Frontiers* 28.2 (March-April):16-17.

Castillo, Met. 1982. *The Church in Thy House.* Mandaluyong: OMF Literature.

Deng, Zhaoming. 2005. “Indigenous Chinese Pentecostal Denominations,” in *Asian and Pentecostal: The Charismatic Face of Christianity in Asia.* Allan Anderson and Edmond Tang, eds. Oxford:Regnum Books International.

Dyrness, William. 2004. *Reformed Theology and Visual Culture: The Protestant Imagination from Calvin to Edwards.* Cambridge:Cambridge University Press.

Edwards, Gene. 1995. *When the Church was Led only by Laymen.* Seedsowers.

Ehrenreich, Barbara. 2006. “Fight for Your Right to Party.” *Time*, Dec. 18, 2006:80.

Finnell, David L. 1995. *Life in His Body.* Houston, TX:TOUCH Outreach Ministries.

Fitts, Robert. 2001. *The Church in the Home: A Return to Simplicity.* Salem, OR:Preparing the Way Publishers.

Garrison, David. 2004. *Church Planting Movements.* Midlothian, VA: WIGTake Resources.

Gibbs, Eddie. 2000. *Church Next.* Downers Grove, IL:InterVarsity Press.

Goudzwaard, Bob. 1984. *Idols of Our Time.* Downers Grove, IL:InterVarsity Press.

Hattaway, Paul, et al. 2003. *Back to Jerusalem.* Carlisle:Piquant.

International Oral Network and Lausanne Committee for World Evangelization. 2005. *Making Disciples of Oral Learners.* Bangalore:Sudhindra.

Jones, Gordon. 1985. *The Church Without Walls.* Basingstoke:Marshalls.

Kirkpatrick, John. 2001. “Asian Churches: Examining the Love Quotient,” *Journal of Asian Mission* 3.2 (September):231-41.

Kraft, Charles. 2005. *Appropriate Christianity.* Pasadena, CA: William Carey Library.

Kreider, Larry. 2002. *House Church Networks.* Lancaster, PA:Dove Christian Fellowship.

Lambert, Tony. 1999. *China's Christian Millions.* London:Monarch.

Lim, David. 1987. *The Servant Nature of the Church in the Pauline Corpus.* Ph.D. Diss., Fuller Theological Seminary. (Ann Arbor: University Microfilms International).

________. 2003. “Towards a Radical Contextualization Paradigm in Evangelizing Buddhists,” In *Sharing Jesus in the Buddhist*

World. David Lim and Steve Spaulding, eds. Pp. 71-94. Pasadena, CA:William Carey Library.

Loewen, Jacob. 1980. "The Gospel: Its Content and Communication – An Anthropological Perspective." In *Down to Earth: Studies in Christianity and Culture.* John Stott and R. Coote, eds. Pp. 115-120. Wheaton,IL:LCWE.

_________. 2006. "The Shifting God(s) of Western Christianity," *Mission Frontiers* 28.3(May-June):25-27.

MacDonald, Gordon. 1998. *Rebuilding Your Broken World.* Nashville, TN:Oliver-Nelson Books.

Martin, Ralph. 1979. *The Family and the Fellowship.* Grand Rapids, MI:Eerdmans.

_________. 1964. *Worship in the New Testament.* Grand Rapids, MI:Eerdmans.

_________. 1982. *The Worship of God.* Grand Rapids, MI:Eerdmans.

Oblau, Gotthard. 2005. "Pentecostals by Default? Contemporary Christianity in China," in *Asian and Pentecostal: The Charismatic Face of Christianity in Asia.* Allan Anderson and Edmond Tang, eds. Oxford: Regnum Books International.

Olavidez, Henrietta S. 1984. "Church Rituals and Their Relevance." *Christian Forum*, Silang, Cavite: Philippine Missionary Institute.

Ortland, Ann. 1980. *Up with Worship.* Ventura, CA:Regal.

Packer, James I. 1980. "The Gospel: Its Content and Communication – A Theological Perspective." In *Down to Earth: Studies in Christianity and Culture.* John Stott and R.Coote, eds. Pp.97-114. Wheaton, IL: LCWE.

Parsons, Greg. 2006. "What is the Church? (Part 2)," *Mission Frontiers* 28.1 (March-April):22.

Patterson, George, and Richard Scoggins. 1993. *Church Multiplication Guide.* Pasadena: Wm Carey Library.

Petersen, Jim. 1992. *Church Without Walls.* Colorado Springs, CO: NavsPress.

Pierson, Paul. 2004. *Emerging Streams of Church and Ministry.* Thailand: Forum for World Evangelism.

Ringma, Charles. 1994. *Catch the Wind.* Sunderland: Albatross.

Schweizer, Edward. 1961. *Church Order in the New Testament.* London:SCM Press.

Simson, Wolfgang. 2001. *Houses that Change the World.* Carlisle:Paternoster.

Smith, Gordon. 1989. *Essential Spirituality*. Mandaluyong:OMF Literature.

Snyder, Howard. 1983. *Liberating the Church*. Downers Grove, IL:InterVarsity Press.

________. 1989. *Signs of the Spirit.* Grand Rapids, MI:Zondervan.

Stevens, Paul. 1985. *Liberating the Laity*. Downers Grove, IL:InterVarsity Press.

Stott, John R. W. 1970. *Christ the Controversialist.* London:Tyndale Press.

Stowell, Joseph. 1995. *Eternity*. Chicago, IL: Moody.

Tang, Edmond. 2005. "'Yellers' and Healers: Pentecostalism and the Study of Grassroots Christianity in China." In *Asian and Pentecostal: The Charismatic Face of Christianity in Asia.* Allan Anderson and Edmond Tang, eds.Oxford:Regnum Books International.

Walsh, Brian J. and J. Richard Middleton. 1983. *The Transforming Vision: Shaping a Christian Worldview.* Downers Grove, IL:InterVarsity Press.

Warren, Rick. 1995. *The Purpose Driven Church.* Grand Rapids, MI:Zondervan.

Wesley, Luke. 2004. "Is the Chinese Church Predominantly Pentecostal?" *Asian Journal of Pentecostal Studies* 7.2 (July 2004):225-254.

White, John. 1979. *The Golden Cow*. Downers Grove, IL:InterVarsity Press.

Yeo, Khiok-khng. 1991. "The Meaning and Usage of the Theology of 'Rest' (*katapauausis* and *sabbatismos*) in Hebrews 3:7-4:13'" *Asia Journal of Theology*. 5.1(1991):2-33.

Zdero, Rad. 2004. *The Global House-Church Movement*. Pasadena, CA:William Carey Library.

Chapter 3

Adeney, Frances S. 2003. *Christian Women in Indonesia: A Narrative Study of Gender and Religion.* Syracuse, NY:Syracuse University Press.

________. 2007. "Contextualizing Universal Values." *International Bulletin of Missionary Research.* Vol. 31(1).

________. 2005. "Factors in the Rise of Women Leaders in the Sulawesi Protestant Churches." In *Een vakkracht in het Koninkrijk Kerk-en zendings historische opstellen.* Chr. G. F. de Jong, ed. Netherlands:UITGEVERIJ GROEN-HEERENVEEN.

Anderson, Benedict O. 1990 *Language and Power in Indonesia.* Cornell, NY:Cornell University Press.

Bell, Catherine. 1997. *Ritual: Perspectives and Dimensions.* NY:Oxford University Press.

Bellah, Robert N. 1970. *Beyond Belief: Essays on Religion in a Post-Traditional World.* NY:Harper & Row.

Berg, Temma F. 1989. *Engendering the Word.* DeKalb, IL:University of Illinois Press.

Berger, Peter. 1969. *The Sacred Canopy: Elements of a Sociological Theory.* Garden City, NY:Doubleday & Co.

Bourdieu, Pierre. 1991. *Language and Symbolic Power.* Gino Raymond and Matthew Adamson, trans. Cambridge MA:Harvard University Press.

Christian Broadcasting News August 29, 2006. The 700 Club with Pat Robertson.

Deegalle, Mahinda. 2006. *Popularizing Buddhism: Preaching as Performance in Sri Lanka.* Albany, NY:State University of New York Press.

Gadamer, Hans Georg. 1975. *Truth and Method.* NY:Seabury Press.

Geertz, Clifford. 1973. *The Interpretation of Cultures.* NY:HarperCollins.

Habermas, Juergen. 1979. *Communication and the Evolution of Society.* Thomas McCarthy, trans. Boston, MA:Beacon Press.

Kuipers, Joel. 1998. *Language, Identity, and Marginality in Indonesia: The Changing Nature of Ritual Speech on the Island of Sumba.* Cambridge, MA:Cambridge University Press.

LeBacqz, Karen. 1986. "The Power of Definition." Lecture given at Graduate Theological Union Women's Retreat, May 15.

Moreau, Scott. "Contextualization that is Comprehensive." *Missiology,* 34(3):333.

Mejudhon, Nantachai. 2003. *Meekness Evangelism,* doctoral dissertation. Stanley School of World Mission, Asbury Theological Seminary, Wilmore, KY.

Porterfield, Amanda. 1998. *The Power of Religion: A Comparative Introduction*. NY:Oxford University Press.

Rappaport, Roy A. 1999. *Ritual and Religion in the Making of Humanity*. Cambridge, England:Cambridge University Press.

Redmond, Mont. 1998. *Wondering into Thai Culture*. Bangkok:Redmondian Insight Enterprises, Inc.

Turner, Victor. 1977. *The Ritual Process: Structure and Anti-Structure*. Ithaca, NY:Cornell University Press.

Chapter 4

Abu-Lughod, Lila. 1986. *Veiled Sentiments: Honor and Poetry in Bedouin Society*. Berkeley, CA:University of California Press.

Adeney, Miriam. 1980. *Filipino Narrative: A Model for Ethnic Identity Balancing Pakikisama and Protest* (dissertation). Ann Arbor, MI.

________. 1985. "Teaching Missionaries Through Stories: The Anthropological Analysis of Indigenous Literature as an Aspect of a Cross-Cultural Orientation Program." In *Missionaries, Anthropologists, and Cultural Change*. Darrell Whiteman, ed. Pp. 347-413. Williamsburg, VA:Department of Anthropology, College of William and Mary.

Bowen, John. 1995. "The Forms Culture Takes: A State-of-the-Field Essay on the Anthropology of Southeast Asia," *The Journal of Asian Studies*. 54(4)1047-1078.

Brandon, James. 1967. *Theatre in Southeast Asia.*_Cambridge, MA: Harvard University Press.

Butterfield, Herbert. 1957. *Christianity and History.*_London:Fontana Books.

Coward, Harold. 1988. *Sacred Word and Sacred Text.*_Maryknoll, NY:Orbis Publishers.

Cragg, Kenneth. 1975. *The House of Islam.*_Encino, CA:Dickenson Publishing Company, Inc.

Dominey, Mark. 2005 "Abortion and *Mizuku* Rites in Japan." In *Sharing Jesus Holistically with the Buddhist World*. David Lim and Steve Spaulding, eds. Pp. 291-321. Pasadena, CA:William Carey Library.

Geertz, Clifford. 1964. "Ideology as a Cultural System." In *Ideology and Discontent*. David Apter, ed. New York:The Free Press.

________. 1966. “Religion as a Cultural System,” In *Anthropological Approaches to the Study of Religion (*American Sociological Association Monograph No.3). Michael Banton, ed. Pp. 1-46. London:Tavistock Publications.

________. 1973. *The Interpretation of Culture*. New York:Basic Books.

Goudeau, Eugene. 1980. *Toward an Indigenous Hymnody* (thesis). Memphis, TN:Harding Graduate School of Religion.

Guruge, Ananda W.P. 1975. *Buddhism: The Religion and Its Culture.* Madras, India:M. Seshachalam & Co.

Hansen, Anne. “The Image of an Orphan: Cambodian Narrative Sites for Buddhist Ethical Reflection,” *The Journal of Asian Studies*, August 2003 62(3)811-834..

Hovey, Kevin. 1983. *A Manual for Cross-Cultural Christians with Special Emphasis on Papua New Guinea*, thesis. Pasadena, CA: Fuller Theological Seminary.

Jethani, Skye. 2006. “Recapturing Imagination.” *Leadership*. Fall.

Klem, Herbert. 1982. *Oral Communication of the Scripture: Insights from African Oral Art*. Pasadena, CA:William Carey Library.

Lebra, Takie Sugiyama. 1976. *Japanese Patterns of Behavior.* Honolulu:University of Hawaii Press.

Mejudhon, Ubolwan. 2005. “The Ritual of Reconciliation of Thai Culture.” In *Sharing Jesus Holistically with the Buddhist World.* David Lim and Steve Spaulding, eds. Pp. 249-289. Pasadena CA:William Carey Library.

Nida, Eugene. 1952. *God’s Word in Man’s Language.* New York:Harper and Row.

Paterson, Katherine. 1988. *Gates of Excellence: On Reading and Writing Books for Children*. E.P. Dutton.

Peacock, James. 1968. *Rites of Modernization: Symbolic and Social Aspects of Indonesian Proletarian Drama.* Chicago, IL:University of Chicago Press.

Pramoj, Kukrit. 1966. “The Hell Which Heaven Forgot.” *Practical Anthropology* May-June 13(3)129-139.

Primrose, Robert. 1976. *Discipling Nonliterates* (unpublished manuscript). Nairobi:Daystar Communications Centre.

Rice, Delbert. 1971. “Developing an Indigenous Hymnody.” *Practical Anthropology*. 18(1971)97-113.

Søgaard, Viggo. 1975. *Everything You Need to Know for a Cassette Ministry*. Minneapolis, MN:Bethany Publishers.

Spiro, Melford. 1982. *Buddhism and Society:A Great Tradition and Its Burmese Vicissitudes.*_Berkeley, CA:University of California Press.

Spurgeon, Catherine. 1935. *Shakespeare's Imagery, and What It Tells Us*. New York:Macmillan.

Statler, Oliver. 1985. "Pilgrims' Path in Buddhist Japan. " In *Great Religions of the World.* Merle Severy, ed. Washington D.C.: National Geographic Society.

Tamanoi, Mariko Asano. 1991. "Songs as Weapons:The Culture and History of *Komori* in Modern Japan." *The Journal of Asian Studies*. 50(4)793-817.

Trankell, Ing-Britt. 2003. "Songs of Our Spirits:Possession and Historical Imagination among the Cham in Cambodia." *Ethnicity.* Feb.

Tsering, Marku. 2005 "Islands in the Sky: Tibetan Buddhism and the Gospel." In *Sharing Jesus Effectively in the Buddhist World.* David Lim, Steve Spaulding, and Paul De Neui, eds. Pp. 243-261. Pasadena, CA:William Carey Library.

Ukosakul, Chaiyun.1993. *A Turn From the Wheel to the Cross: Crucial Considerations for Discipling New Thai Christians*, thesis. Vancouver, British Columbia: Regent College.

Vander Werff, Lyle. 1989. "The Names of Christ in Worship." In *Muslims and Christians on the Emmaus Road.* J. Dudley Woodberry, ed. Pp.174-194. Monrovia, CA:World Vision Resources.

Vansina, Jan. 1985. *Oral Tradition as History.*_Madison, WI:University of Wisconsin Press.

Wang, Thomas. 1986. Unpublished lecture. Annual Chinese Conference. Vancouver, British Columbia:Regent College.

Weber, H.R. 1957. *Communication of the Gospel to Illiterates*. London:SCM Press Ltd.

Chapter 5

Adeney, Frances and Terry Muck. 2008. *Encountering the World Religions*. Grand Rapids, MI: Baker.

Adherents. www.adherents.com.

Barrett, David, et. al. 2003. *World Christian Trends*. Pasadena, CA:William Carey Library.

Bowers, Russell H., ed. 1999. *Folk Buddhism in Southeast Asia.* Tacoma, WA:World Vision.

Castells, Manuel. 2003. *The Power of Identity*, 2nd ed. Oxford:Blackwell.

De Neui, Paul. 2003. "Contextualizing With Thai Folk Buddhists." *Sharing Jesus in the Buddhist World*, David Lim and Steve Spaulding, ed. Pp. Pasadena, CA:William Carey Library.

Gombrich, Richard and Gananath Obeyesekere. 1988. *Buddhism Transformed: Religious Change in Sri Lanka*. Princeton, NJ:Princeton University.

Harris, Elizabeth. 2006. *Theravada Buddhism and the British Encounter.* London:Routledge.

Heim, Maria. 2004. *Theories of the Gift in South Asia.* London:Routledge.

Jayanta, Bhatta. 2005. *Much Ado About Religion.* Scaba Dezso, tr. New York:New York University.

Mauss, Marcell. [1954] 2006. *The Gift: The Form and Reason for Exchange in Archaic Societies*. London:Routledge.

Mejudhon, Nantachai. 1998. *Meekness: A New Approach to Christian Witness to the Thai People*. Dissertation, Asbury Theological Seminary.

Mejudhon, Ubolwan. 1998. *The Way of Meekness: Being Christian and Thai in the Thai Way*. Dissertation, Asbury Theological Seminary.

Mother Theresa. 2007. *Come Be My Light*. New York:Doubleday.

Neill, Stephen. 1964. *A History of Christian Missions*. Middlesex, UK:Penguin.

Ong, Walter. 2002. *Orality and Literacy*, 2nd ed. London:Routledge.

Rynkiewich, Michael. April 2007. "Corporate Metaphors and Strategic Thinking: The 10/40 Window in the American Evangelical Worldview." *Missiology: An International Review* 35(2)217-241.

Wood, David and Jose Medina, ed. 2005. *Truth: Engagement Across Philosophical Traditions*. Oxford:Blackwell.

Chapter 6

Abraham, Sam. 2006. *Simply Tell the Story*. Unpublished manuscript.

Boomershine, Thomas E. 1988. *Story Journey: An Invitation to the Gospel as Storytelling*. Nashville, TN:Abingdon Press.

Curtis, Brent and John Elderedge. 1997. *The Sacred Romance: Drawing Closer to the Heart of God*. Nashville, TN:Thomas Nelson Publishers.

Dowman, Keith and Sonam Paljor, trans. 2000. *The Divine Madman: The Sublime Life and Songs of Drukpa Kunley*. Varanasi and Kathmandu:Pilgrims Publishing.

Forest, Heather. 1996. *Wisdom Tales from Around the World*. Little Rock, AR:August House Publishers.

Hesselgrave, David J. 1994. *Scripture and Strategy: The Use of the Bible in Postmodern Church and Mission*. Pasadena, CA:William Carey Library.

Kraft, Charles H. 1981. *Christianity in Culture*. Maryknoll, NY:Orbis Books.

Kraft, Charles H. 2002. *Worldview for Christian Witness*. Unpublished Manuscript.

Lovejoy, Grant, ed.. 2005. *Making Disciples of Oral Learners*. Richmond, VA:ION/LCWE.

Mayers, Marvin K. 1974. *Christianity Confronts Culture: A Strategy for Crosscultural Evangelism*. Grand Rapids, MI:Zondervan Publishing House.

McKinney, Carol V. 2000. "Globetrotting." In *Sandals: A Field Guide to Cultural Research*. Dallas, TX:SIL International.

Peterson, Eugene H. 1999. *Stories of Jesus: From The Message, a Contemporary Rendering of the Bible*. Colorado Springs, CO:NavPress.

Peterson, Eugene H. 2003. *The Message*. Colorado Springs, CO:NavPress.

Reagan, Timothy. 2000. *Non-Western Educational Traditions* (2nd ed.). Mahwah, NJ:Lawrence Erlbaum Associates, Inc., Publishers.

Steffen, Tom A. 1996. *Reconnecting God's Story to Ministry: Crosscultural Storytelling at Home and Abroad*. La Habra, CA:Center for Organizational and Ministry Development.

Thinley, Dorji. 2005. *The Boneless Tongue*. Phuntsholing, Bhutan:KMT Publishers.

Walker, Andrew. 1996. *Telling the Story: Gospel, Mission and Culture*. London:SPCK.

Weber, H. R. N.d. *The Communication of the Gospel to Illiterates*. London:SCM Press Ltd.

Wright, N. T. 1992. *The New Testament and the People of God.* Minneapolis, MN:Fortress Press.

Yolen, Jane, ed. 1999. *Gray Heroes: Elder Tales from Around the World.* New York:Penguin Books.

Chapter 7

Ariyaratna, Sunil. 1987. *A Survey of Sinhala Christian Hymns in Sri Lanka.* Colombo:Samayawardene.

Buhler, G., trans. 1866. *Laws of Manu*, Sacred Books of the East, Vol. XXV, Oxford.

Davy, John. 1983. *An account of the interior of Ceylon and of its inhabitants with Travels in that Island.* Dehiwela:Tisara, (First published 1821).

Dewaraja, L.S.. 1981. *The Position of Women in Buddhism.* The Wheel Publication No. 280, Kandy:Buddhist Publication Society.

Dhammananda, K.Sri. 2000. *The Buddhist Way,* Kualalumpur.

Kariyawasam, A.G.S. 1995. *Buddhist Ceremonies and Rituals of Sri Lanka.* The Wheel Publication. No. 402/404, Kandy:Buddhist Publication Society.

Kariyawasam, Tissa. 2001. *Mahasohon Samayam Vimarshanaya.* Colombo:Godage.

King, Sallie B. and Christopher S Queen. 1996. *Engaged Buddhism: Buddhist Liberation Movements in Asia.* New York:Sunny Press

Knox, Robert. 1981. *An Historical Religion of Ceylon.* Dehiwela:Tisara. First published in 1691

Law, Bimala Churn, 1936. *The Buddhist Conception of Spirit.* London:Luzac and Co.

Narada, Thero. 1988. *The Buddha and His Teachings.* Kualalumpur: Buddhist Missionary Society.

Obeyesekere, Gananath. 1988. *Buddhism Transformed: Religious Change in Sri Lanka.* Delhi:Motilal Banarsidas

Pannasara and Wimaladhamma, ed. 1831. *Attanagaluvamsa.* Colombo.

Pannatisssa, Balummahara. 1992. *Cartitra varitra Cakraya.* Colombo:Samayavaradana.

Percival, Robert. 1975. *An Account of the island of Ceylon, 1803.* Dehiwela: Tisara.

Pieris, Edmund and Achilles Meersman, trans.. 1972. *Chapters on the Introduction of Christianity to Ceylon, taken from the Conquista*

Spiritual do Oriente, by Friar Paulo da Trindade. Colombo:Catholic Press.

Quere, M. 1995. *Christianity in Sri Lanka under the Portuguese Padroado, 1587-1658*. Colombo:Catholic Press.

Sannasgala, P.B. 1964. *Sinhala Sahitya Vamsaya*. Colombo:Lakehouse.

Udita, Hittetiye Sri Vimalakirti. 1989. *Bharatiya Dhama Sastra saha sinhala Sirit*. Colombo:Gunasena

Vajira, Sister and Francis Story. 1998. *Last Days of the Buddha: The Maha-parinibbana Sutta* (Revised edition). Translated from the Pali. Kandy:Buddhist Publication Society.

Wijesuriya, S, A.J. Gynawardena and P. Gananathapillai. 1995. *Sri Lanka Traditional Life Style.* Kotte:Participatory Development Forum.

Young, Richard Fox. 1995. "The Carpenter-Preta: An Eighteenth-Century Sinhala-Buddhist Folktale about Jesus." In *Asian Folklore Studies*. Vol. 54(1)49-68.

Chapter 8

Bowman, Jim. 2003. "Communicating Christ through Oral Tradition: A Training Model for Grass Roots Church Planters" in *International Journal of Frontier Missions*_20 (Spring)25-27.

Falley, Gerald. 1987. "Communicating Christ Cross-Culturally", a senior-level undergraduate course taught at North Central University, Minneapolis, MN.

Holy Bible, New International Version. 1983. International Bible Society.

International Orality Network. 2005. *Making Disciples of Oral Learners.* Lausanne Committee for World Evangelization Publication.

Kelber, Werner H. 1983. *The Oral and the Written Gospel*. Philadelphia, PA:Fortress Press.

Koy Sarun. 2006. Dec. 6th Personal Interview on the Pros and Cons of Oral Approaches.

Pinthammarak, Bee. 2006. Dec. 6th Personal Interview Bible Storying in Ratanakiri Province, Cambodia.

Rosenbloom, Jackie. 2004. UNESCO/UNDP Report on Literacy in Cambodia.

Sok Leng. 2005. Dec. 6th Personal Interview on the Pros and Cons of Oral Approaches, Kandal Province, Cambodia.

Steffen, Tom A. 1996. *Reconnecting God's Story to Ministry: Cross-cultural Storytelling at Home and Abroad.* La Habra, CA:Center for Organizational & Ministry Development

The Strategy Network. 2005. *The Task Literate Communicators of the Gospel Face among Oral Communicators.* www.newwway.org/strategy_network/Default.htm.

Wan, Lena. 2004. Dec. 8th Personal Interview on Oral Learners, Phnom Penh, Cambodia.

Yeth Ye. 2006. Dec. 6th Personal Interview on the Pros and Cons of Oral Approaches, Prey Veng Province, Cambodia.

Chapter 9

Bowers, Russell H. Jr. 2003. *Folk Buddhism in Southeast Asia.* Phnom Penh:Training of Timothys.

Burk, Todd and De Anne. 1989. *Anointed For Burial: Cambodia's Like a Might Wind.* Frontline Communications.

CAMA Services. 1993. *Cambodian Hymnal.* Phnom Penh.

Chandler, David.1996. *A History of Cambodia, 2nd ed.* Chiang Mai, Thailand:Silkworm Books.

Chou Ta-Kuan. 1992. *The Customs of Cambodia: An Account of Chou Ta-Kuan's visit to Cambodia late 13th Century.* Bangkok:Siam Society.

Cormack, Don. 1997. *Killing Fields Living Fields.* Crowborough, UK:OMF Int./MARC.

Council of Khmer Customs. 2001. "Collections of Khmer Folk Stories." In *Folk Stories and Traditions of Cambodia: Traditions,* Vol. 9 (Khmer) Phnom Penh:CKCBI.

De Neui, Paul H. 2001. *Voices From Asia: Communicating Contextualization Through Story.* Fuller Theological Seminary. Unpublished manuscript.

Fount of Wisdom. 2004. *Commentary on the Book of Ephesians,* (Khmer). *The Bridge Bible Commentary,* Vol 4 . Phnom Penh:Fount of Wisdom Publishing House.

Encarta. 2006. *Cambodia General and Political.* Encyclopedia CD rom.

Himm, Sokreaksa S. and Jan Greenough. 2003. *The Tears of My Soul.* Oxford:Monarch.

Hun, Sarin. 2004. *Khmer Orchestra,* (Khmer). In *Khmer Classical Music in Cambodia.* Phnom Penh: Ministry of Culture and Fine Arts.

Lockerbie, Jean. 1976 *When Blood Flows the Heart Grows Soft.* Wheaton, IL:Tyndale.

Mam, Barnabas. 2006. *Buddhism: An Overview.* Unpublished manuscript.

________. 2006. "Testimonies: Songs of the Survivors." Haggai Institute.

www.AFCIworld.org/Cambodia. Accessed 7 Dec. 2006.

Mills, Laurence. 1999. *Buddhism Explained.* Chiang Mai, Thailand:Silkworm Books.

Nov Nhek. 1958, second ed. *Funeral services: Khmer Costumes and traditions*, (Khmer). Phnom Penh.

Pin, Chab, Pich Sal and Ly Thiem Teng. 1964. *Khmer Folk Dance,* (Khmer). Phnom Penh:Buddhist Institute.

Pin, Chab. 1965. *The Protocol of Wedding* (Khmer). Phnom Penh: Seng Nguon Huot.

Ponchaud, Francois. 1990. *The Cathedral of the Rice Paddy: 450 Years' History of the Church in Cambodia.* Paris:Librarie Arthgeme Fayard.

Sloggett, Brenda. 2005. *Jewels of Cambodia.* Bletchley, UK:Authentic.

Smith, Alex G. 2001. *Buddhism Through Christian Eyes.* Littleton, CO:OMF International.

Sovy, Ly. 2001. "The Tradition of Old Khmer Weddings." In *Weddings From the 19th to Early 20th Century, Vols 1 and 2* (Khmer). Phnom Penh:UNESCO.

Chapter 10

Baily, John. 2005. "So Near, So Far: Kabul's Music in Exile." *Ethnomusicology Forum 14/2 Music and Identity in Central Asia*: 213-233.

Collinge, Ian. 1993. "The Dra-nyen – An Emblem of Tibetan Culture." *Chime* No. 6:22-33.

Corbitt, J. Nathan. 1988. *The Sound of the Harvest: Music's Mission in Church and Culture*. Grand Rapids, Michigan:Baker Books.

Diehl, Keila. 2002. *Echoes from Dharamsala, Music in the life of a Tibetan Refugee Community.* Berkeley and Los Angeles, CA:University of California Press.

Duncan, Marion H. 1961. *Love Songs and Proverbs of Tibet.* London:The Mitre Press.

Ellingson, Ter. 1979. "'DON RTA DBYANGS GSUM: Tibetan Chant and Melodic Categories." *Asian Music* Vol X-2 Tibet Issue:112-156.

Fortunato, Frank. 1999. "Two church plants trace back to a concert of indigenous music." *Global Worship Report Vol 2, no. 4*: Global Worship Report website: http://www.worship-arts-network.com/GWR-2-4-Nov99.html.

Fortunato, Frank, Paul Neeley, and Linda Neeley. 2002. Mongolia 2004, "Giving Artistic Expressions Back to the Creator As Worship." website:http://heartsounds.org/mongolia %202004.htm.

Gcod Pa Don Grub and Sangs Rgyas Rin Chen (*Jöpa Dondrub and Sangye Rinchen*). n.d.a. (*A Lotus Bouquet Of The Oral Literature Of Do Mé*). Qinghai. *Chinese People's Art And Culture Research Institute, Qinghai Branch Association*):681-746.

International Council of Ethnodoxologists. www.worldofworship.org.

Lomax, Alan. 1968. *Folk Song and Culture*. New Brunswick, NJ:Transaction Books.

Marini, Elio. 2004. *The History of the Bell of Lhasa*. Project Orazio oraziodellapenna.com/eng_campana_storia.htm.

Merriam, Alan P. 1964. *The Anthropology of Music*. Chicago, IL:Northwestern University Press.

Mini-Consultation on Reaching Buddhists. 1980. *Christian Witness to Buddhists, Lausanne Occasional Papers, No.15 Thailand Report.* Wheaton, IL:Lausanne Committee for World Evangelization.

Mejudhon, Nantachai. 2005. *Meekness: A New Approach of Doing Missions in Thailand.* Chiang Mai, Thailand, January. Lecture.

No Author Details. 1995. Döyang Pü Shi "Offer A Praise Song" A Collection of 100 Tibetan Hymns, Psalms and Spiritual Songs. No publication details.

Oswald, John. 2001. *A New Song Rising In Tibetan Hearts, Tibetan Christian Worship in the Early 21st Century*. Informal printing tbwcentral@psmail.net.

Smith, Bruce. 2002. *Update*. Personal communication.

Sørensen, Per K. 1990. *Divinity Secularized, An Enquiry Into The Nature And Form Of The Songs Ascribed To The Sixth Dalai Lama.* Wiener Studien Zur Tibetologie Und Buddhismuskunde Heft 25. Arbeitskreis Für Tibetische Und Buddhistische Studien Universität Wien, Vienna, Austria.

INDEX

C

D

E

F

G

H

I

J

K

L

M

N

O

Q

R

S

U

V

W

Y

Z